This book could change your life. Really. As week-by-week Anne Le Tissier helps us to dive deeply into God's life-giving words in Scripture, God will meet us and change us to be more like Jesus. Without reservation I recommend that you accept her gentle invitation, backed up by her embodied example, to dwell in God's word. From a hesitant star-giver, five stars.

Amy Boucher Pye, author of 7 Ways to Pray

For those of us – and I suspect it is a majority – who read the Bible diligently, then close it and carry on with our day as normal, *Dwell* is a true gift. By dwelling on just one or two verses a week, Anne Le Tissier invites us to allow Scripture to speak to the very depths of our souls, changing and challenging our decisions as we go about our days. Do not be mistaken that this is a superficial approach, however: Anne squeezes insight after insight out of such short passages, via personal testimony, cross-referencing, questions, reflections and her own pertinent commentary. Right from page one I was deeply moved by Anne's words, which seemed to cut right to the heart of my own situation, and reignited my passion for delving into the Bible to see what it has to say to me at this moment. A rich resource which offers a fresh way of reading Scripture. Hugely welcome.

Lucy Rycroft, founder of The Hope-Filled Family

Truth be told, with the pace of life often set to maximum speed, we are more likely to 'dash' than to 'dwell'. That is why I am grateful for Anne's book, designed to accompany us through a year. *Dwell* is a sacred space for readers to linger in God's Word. And in the chaos of the world in which we live, it has never been needed more.

Cathy Madavan, author, speaker and broadcaster

It is a precious gift to be able to dwell deeply in Scripture. It enables us to behold God more profoundly and very slowly and gently helps us to become more Christlike. Through the pages of *Dwell* author Anne Le Tissier accompanies you on a journey of deeper reflection. This is a wonderfully enriching resource that will bless your soul.

Lynn Green, General Secretary of the Baptist Union of Great Britain

For a busy journalist this felt like a weighty tome to pick up. How does a media professional expected to be at the forefront of breaking news, ever have time to slow down?

Fortunately, and unlike many other books of this genre, *Dwell* is not about putting down anything, it's about including God in everything. A truly enlightening read.

Tola Doll Fisher, editor and creative director of Premier Woman Alive

I have known Anne's work for a number of years and always appreciate her insights and the practical application she draws from biblical texts. In this book she shows us how to let God's Word nourish us and minister to us. Lingering over the verse in the chapter 'But God' and following Anne's suggestions was both affirming and empowering in a week when I was feeling anxious. I am sure these studies will delight both those looking to refresh their Bible study and those looking for a guide to help them begin. I warmly recommend it.

Jackie Harris, editor of Day by Day with God
Bible studies for women (published by BRF Ministries)

What a beautiful book! I was thrilled to be offered the chance to read through *Dwell* and really appreciated the way that Anne encourages us as readers to really slow down, digest and live with small portions of Scripture, allowing them the time and space to speak to us in a deep way. Anne gently guides us through the process with her insightful daily reflections. Spending a whole week with a short phrase or passage is quite a unique approach to Bible reading in our otherwise fast and frenetic world and, as such, felt like a breath of fresh air. *Dwell* would make a wonderful gift – I truly benefited from the short time I had with this book so I know a year would be such a blessing.

Claire Musters, author, speaker, editor and
host of the Woman Alive book club

In *Dwell*, Anne encourages us to do just that: to dwell on single verses of the Word of God, to mull them over during our week, and to reflect on the truth of the Scripture as well as the application it has in our daily lives. Anne leads us to consider multiple facets of each verse day-by-day which allows the truth to shape our lives, for us to be spiritually encouraged and challenged, and to reflect on the verse throughout our day. *Dwell* is an accessible devotional designed for anyone who needs to learn to take time out of their busy life to reflect on God's word for them – and don't we all need that these days.

Robin Stephens, Chair of ICCC UK & Ireland,
CEO of Psephos Biomedica and AoG minister

Anne has successfully decanted into this remarkable book the decades of her experience of walking with God. Her insight, wisdom and helpful self-revealing have created a tool for us that will open many treasures as the year unfolds. If you long to dwell more intimately with God through his Word, this book will serve you well. If you struggle to hold onto more than just a fragment of Scripture due to pain or suffering of any kind, the format here is kind and reassuring. I recommend it warmly.

Revd Dr Eric Gaudion, pastor and author

This is a book for the soul. I love the room it gives to soak in truth and allow the words to permeate your consciousness. It's life-giving.

Jane Kirby, author of Say Goodbye to Anxiety *and editor of Truth magazine*

I love this invitation from Anne to dwell daily in short phrases from the Bible. It is doable but deep. As someone who is passionate about 'dwellbeing', this great tool will be something I enjoy engaging with as I practise dwelling in God's presence more and more. A refreshing way to engage with God's Word and one that anyone could manage.

Ruth Rice, author and founder of Renew Wellbeing

When I was first asked to share my thoughts on Anne Le Tissier's book, *Dwell*, I instantly had a sense of excitement and anticipation. The word alone led my heart to hope for a resource that would inspire intimacy with Jesus and in reading the subtitle, '*Inviting God's Word to make a home in our lives, one verse at a time*', I imagined myself sitting with him at the kitchen table and chatting before the day got busy. The thought of 'home' makes me yearn for a safe place where I can relax and be wholly me, embraced, treasured, and loved. The earthly 'home' isn't always like this, but I do find it in God's Word. I grew up memorising Bible verses for Sunday school and these often came to mind when, years later, I needed something to anchor me in stormy seas. In recent years, the emphasis of my Bible reading has been in journeying through the whole Bible, but I've always enjoyed doing this at my own pace. I never considered meditating on one verse or passage for an entire week though. Anne's devotional does not disappoint and has inspired me to linger. Rather than rush through a Bible reading and quickly into the day, *Dwell* invites us to remain with, chew on and meditate on a verse or passage from the Bible throughout the day and into the whole week. With relatable illustrations, thoughtful questions, practical suggestions, and beautiful prayers, we lean in close to the heart of God and find our rest.

Ruth O'Reilly-Smith, broadcaster and author of
God Speaks – 40 Letters from the Father's Heart

Note from author: Due to the nature of this devotional, it is designed to be read slowly over the course of a year. Endorsers either read the full content faster than intended, or read a portion of the book over a shorter time.

dwell

Inviting God's Word
to make a home in our lives,
one verse at a time

ANNE LE TISSIER

A

Authentic

First published 2024 by Authentic Media Limited,
PO Box 6326, Bletchley, Milton Keynes, MK1 9GG.
authenticmedia.co.uk

British Library Cataloguing in Publication Data
A catalogue record for this book is available from the British Library.
ISBN: 978-1-78893-272-1
978-1-78893-273-8 (e-book)

Cover design by Jennifer Burrell, Fresh Vision Designs
Printed and bound in China

DEDICATION

For Neil
with whom my life – both at work and at rest –
is so intricately and beautifully entwined.
I'm daily grateful for the precious gift of who you are –
to me
and to so many others.

CONTENTS

INTRODUCTION

The whole Bible was given to us by inspiration from God and is useful to teach us what is true and to make us realize what is wrong in our lives; it straightens us out and helps us do what is right. It is God's way of making us well prepared at every point, fully equipped to do good to everyone . . . God has transmitted his very substance into every Scripture, for it is God-breathed. It will empower you by its instruction and correction, giving you the strength to take the right direction and lead you deeper into the path of godliness. Then you will be God's servant, fully mature and perfectly prepared to fulfill any assignment God gives you.

2 Timothy 3:16–17, TLB, TPT

29 October 1991

The early flight to London Heathrow Airport, departed from Guernsey as scheduled on that cool but bright autumn morning. Buckled up in my window seat after weeks of farewells to family and friends, I pressed my forehead against the glass for one last glimpse of my island home encircled by clear aqua sea – watching as it faded from view beneath the ascending plane.

My hands caressed a new pocket Bible resting on my lap, its fake leather cover still stiff. I had bought it especially for this extended trip; travels that would take me through Hong Kong, Australia, New Zealand, Singapore, India and America, and enable my participation in a six month 'Discipleship Training School' with Youth With a Mission (YWAM).[1] I'm not sure if it was my own idea or the prompting of the Holy Spirit, but I'd decided to read only my Bible for the entire time I was away (and so I did, aside of three obligatory reading books set by YWAM).

The engines settled back from their take off roar and I was served complimentary tea. Opening my Bible to Psalms, I turned to chapter 139:

> Where can I go from your Spirit? Where can I flee from your presence? . . . If I rise on the wings of the dawn, if I settle on the far side of the sea, even there your hand will guide me, your right hand will hold me fast.

Ps. 139:7,9–10

The words were comforting in the moment at hand, but little did I realise how they'd continue to shape and sustain me in my subsequent travels. I declared in faith that God's hand would 'guide' me when I frequently lost my bearings in unfamiliar streets, and as I prayed for his direction for my future. I leaned into the promise that his hand would 'hold me fast' when the airline lost my luggage for three weeks, and when my already thin frame was ravaged by sickness and diarrhoea; a familiar problem for Westerners visiting India at the time. These and other Scriptures never failed me as I believed them, not just in my head, but with an intentional trust and yielded response. And the key to my experiencing their transforming power was by remaining in a verse or short passage for at least one week; to give time, space and a receptive soul for God to work its life-giving power in and through me. And so, as Paul taught the Colossians, I began to learn how to let God's words *dwell in me richly.*[2]

To *dwell* is to remain conscious of and responsive to Scripture, not just while reading the Bible but throughout our day. It's our welcome to God's words to make a home in our life; to abide in our thinking and permeate our being, inviting him to transform our choices, responses, priorities, perspective, behaviour . . . and more. To dwell '*richly*' is to ensure God's words have full, thorough and abundant effect in and through our life; shaping, influencing, guiding, empowering and nurturing an awareness of his presence at all times.

I still have that pocket Bible, it's cover now soft and slightly torn, with underlining, miniature scribble and colour-coded highlights spanning its pages. Different verses have breathed life to my soul for different reasons and seasons, guiding me through marriage, motherhood, relationships, work and ministry. There were words that highlighted my eating disorder, and those that upheld me through ill health, financial concerns, my brother's alcoholism and his subsequent death. There were verses infusing deep comfort when God called me to leave Guernsey and family again, to settle in England permanently. Words that have challenged me to accept God's calling to teach and preach, despite my natural fears and timidity. Living words that have empowered my thinking and praying, inspired insights and alleviated anxiety. And of course, God's words still convict, refine and remould my fallen self, little by ever so little into the likeness of Christ. They continue to anchor me in truth, infuse wisdom, strengthen resistance to temptation, steady fitful emotions, fine-tune dreams with kingdom priorities and captivate my heart increasingly with God. And they can do the same for you too. But first, we need to *Dwell*; to remain and be at home in God's Word as it makes its home in us.

Who this book is for

You've been a Christian believer for years but feel flat from your Bible reading, and long for deeper connection with God. You're new to the faith and not yet conversant with God through Scripture; overwhelmed by the size of the text or struggling to find any relevance that connects with your daily reality. Or else, like me, you love and long to hear from God in fresh ways, to meet with him in his Word in the ups and downs of life.

For most readers, *Dwell* is intended as a companion to regular, lengthier Bible-reading, but some of you will be in seasons where you struggle to read for long, if at all – you are parents with babies and toddlers, for example, or struggling with health issues. *Dwell* offers you a bridge from a place of sporadic or no Scripture reading to reflecting and responding to at least one verse each week.

Whichever description best fits your situation, *Dwell* is for you. For each of these reader scenarios shares the same heart; for your Bible reading to move beyond informing the mind, to permeating your life and releasing its promised power.

Dwell will keep you connected with God; rooting your life in truth that will deepen your relationship, nourish your growth and transform your responses as you invite his words to saturate your whole being. When we read Scripture with prayerful receptivity, God's words come alive *to* us as his Spirit breathes life to them in our hearts, minds and souls. God's words come alive *in* us as we assimilate their truth and formative influence. And God's words come alive *through* us as we participate in their story, submit to their teachings and actively respond to their guidance and transforming effect.

HOW TO USE THIS BOOK

I'm still walking the journey of learning to dwell in God's Word and let it dwell in me, so I'm delighted that you're joining me. Together, we will focus on just one verse, sometimes a few verses, or for the purpose of Ignatian contemplation, a short passage. And we'll dwell with this nugget of Scripture for an entire week.

Dwelling for a week slows down our reading and prayerful response. It gives time and space in our hurried routines for God to breathe life to his words, so in turn, they become 'flesh' in and through us. A week provides a 'spacious place' (Ps. 18:19) in our hearts, minds and souls, to process, participate in and be shaped by what we read.

On the first day of each week, you're encouraged to mull on the verse with fewer prompts and questions from me, discerning what God might reveal to you before reading the next six days. Some weeks offer more guidelines than others, using ancient, modern or my own practices to inspire your meditation and response. You can read *Dwell* from start to finish, or use the Index of Weekly Scriptures (see page 375) to immerse yourself in a verse that's pertinent to you that week. But whichever way you choose to read this book, remember to keep dwelling with the verse(s) right through your day.

Focused reflection on a verse, both in devoted times of prayer and in whatever you face through the day, sustains an open heart and mind to God as he forms his truth within you. It gives time for his Spirit to enliven his words to your soul; inspiring insights, guiding choices, shaping responses, moulding perspective and nourishing your whole being. Through this practice you will be hiding God's words in your heart without any conscious attempt to memorise them. Even when you can't recall chapter or verse, God's truth will continue to nurture, shape and inform you, long after the week has passed. You'll feel stronger in spirit, reassured in heart and be clearer in your thinking, as you respond to life with truths applied – even when the path gets bumpy. You'll also find yourself praying God's words; appropriating his truths to strengthen and enrich both yourself and those you pray for.

It helps to record how God speaks or begins to work through your reflective response, in a journal or notetaking app. Later, you can refer back to it and remember how God made a home for his Word in your heart. But to re-emphasise what I've said above, do consider how you can hold each week's Scripture in mind through the day. I use a week-to-view diary with my verse(s) written out in green ink, standing out from my red and blue deadlines and appointments. What do you often turn to in the day? If it's your phone, make the verse your background 'wallpaper'. If it's your laptop, use the verse as a screen saver. If it's a mirror, desk, dashboard, or windowsill above the kitchen sink, pop the verse on a sticky note for the week. Be creative, just keep those verses prominent to remind you that God wants to bring them to life through your everyday roles and routines; through your relationships, choices and responsibilities – and of course, your worship.

In summary:

- Take a week to mull on each verse or short passage – even longer if that's helpful.
- Find ways to keep the verse in mind throughout your day.
- Record or journal what God reveals to you.
- Read through the book chronologically, or use the Index of Weekly Scriptures to choose appropriate themes each week.

God describes his written words as living, active and life-giving. You've now read how I began to experience this but it's available to anyone. Whoever anchors themselves in his words through prayerful reflection and proactive response, will gain wisdom, guidance and hope, will know peace, assurance and encouragement, and will flourish in life; in prayer and pursuing his kingdom. As you follow the suggestions in this book on how to dwell in God's Word and let it dwell in you, these promises can become a reality for you too.

My prayer, while writing this book, has been for 'wheat words' to nourish your whole being, as you dwell, absorb and respond to the life-giving truths of God's Word. And I continue to pray that, for both the happier and more difficult days that you face.

DAY 1

'Don't look back' Genesis 19:17

I'd returned to Guernsey to provide post-op care for my mum. It was 'home' until I was 27, so I quickly slipped back into island life. But driving past old haunts, gazing at clear blue seas and relishing a daily walk in familiar places, my heart began to hanker for what I'd left behind.

Many years earlier, God had clearly called my husband to train for church ministry in England. I'd happily sold our home and waved goodbye, eager to pursue his will. But as I began comparing my current life to what could have been if we hadn't left, resentment and frustration took root. *If only we had stayed. Just think where I would live now. Imagine how I'd have succeeded if . . . How I miss being near my mum.*

One afternoon, at the end of a favourite clifftop walk, I looked back over my shoulder for a final glimpse of the beauty tugging my heart, when some words struck my conscience: *Stop looking back at where you have been and concentrate on where you are going.* My attention was caught; stunned by the words so clearly conveyed to my soul.

I'll continue the story tomorrow, but for now, consider how you're feeling about life. Do you identify with any sense of grief, disgruntlement or even anger over what was but is no more? Be honest with God who cares for you deeply. Express your emotions freely.

Rest in God's love and understanding as you dwell with this verse, now and throughout your day.

DAY 2

'Don't look back' Genesis 19:17

My story continues:

Prayerfully mulling on the Spirit-inspired words, a Scripture came to mind: 'Remember Lot's wife!' (Luke 17:32) – prompting me to reread her story.[1] Angelic messengers warned Abraham's nephew, Lot, of Sodom's imminent destruction. Its grievous, heinous wickedness could no longer be tolerated. 'Flee for your lives!' they said. 'Don't look back, and don't stop anywhere in the plain … or you will be swept away!' (Gen. 19:17). But despite God's warning, Lot's wife stopped to look back while her family raced ahead, and a violent deluge of burning sulphur enveloped her and her home.

We aren't told why she looked back. Perhaps she yearned for her home and possessions, the wealth of her husband's flocks, for her friends or her daughters' fiancées. But the Holy Spirit convicted me of the choice I now had to make: stop looking back or, spiritually speaking, become a lifeless pillar of salt.

Where do your thoughts often wonder to? What does your heart yearn for? Do you believe in God's love, purpose and presence for you *today*?

God doesn't condemn you for looking back:

- Reflect on what you can learn from your past.
- Give thanks for its good gifts.
- Identify anything you need to process that undermines peace today.

God doesn't condemn but he does care if you get stuck in the past. He warns of risks and implications which we'll look at tomorrow.

Dwell with the words, 'Don't look back' through your day. Hear the gentle, loving, urging voice of God's Spirit to your soul.

DAY 3

'Don't look back' Genesis 19:17

Jesus said, 'No one who puts a hand to the plough and looks back is fit for service in the kingdom of God' (Luke 9:62). We don't lose our salvation by looking back but it may distract our experience of an abundant life in Christ and restrict us from fulfilling our God-given potential *today*.

The familiar plough Jesus pictured included a shaft attached to the yoke of two oxen, dipping down between them with a blade at the end that just touched the soil, before rising back up to the farmer standing behind. Goading the oxen forward, the farmer leant his weight on the shaft to push the blade into the ground. But if he looked back, his weight would rise off the shaft. Instead of ploughing deep, life-giving furrows for seed, the blade would barely scratch the surface.

To plough straight furrows and make best use of the land, it was also essential to focus on a single point ahead. If he looked back, both he and the oxen would make a right mess of the ground!

Reflect on this image of the plough.

Jesus wants your life to bear 'much fruit' (John 15:5), so consider:

- Has looking back distracted you from God's presence, purpose and anointing for today?
- Is looking back undermining your potential God-given effectiveness and productivity?

Talk with God about whatever comes to mind.

Dwell with this verse through your day. There is *no* condemnation. God just wants to help you experience his best for your life, today.

DAY 4

'Don't look back' Genesis 19:17

I'm mindful of readers who hurt for something lost to their past. A job, an identity, a home or relationship, health . . . etc. God cares about your feelings. Allow time to grieve and process.[2] He is your comforter; he brings healing and wholeness to your wellbeing. But also know that God still has a life to fulfil you today.

For the rest of the week, we'll consider different things that tempt us to look back, and how that may undermine our today. Our first question asks, is comparing your past with your present, fuelling discontent or disgruntlement? If so, who or what were you relying on for contentment? God gently invites you to *Stop looking back at that source . . . and concentrate on his goodness today.* Life may have changed but God is still with you. Paul suffered rejection, hunger, whipping, stoning, imprisonment, shipwreck and a 'weakness' (2 Cor. 12:9); possibly a limiting health condition. And yet, he'd learned the secret of being content in *all* these circumstances[3] through his relationship with Jesus.

Focus on God with you now; the beauty, comfort and power of his presence and promises. Receive all he wants to be for you, and all he wants to inspire you with for the future. Keeping a gratitude journal can also help you focus and receive.[4]

Dwell with this verse through your day. There is *no* condemnation. God just wants to help you experience his best for your life, today.

DAY 5

'Don't look back' Genesis 19:17

Some readers may feel discouraged or disillusioned by a shattered dream or unanswered prayer. With love and gentleness, the Holy Spirit whispers to your heart, *Stop looking at the source of your disappointment . . . and concentrate on how God wants to equip you and work through you, today.*

Letting go can be painful. Moses' mother had to give up, not only her dream shared by all Hebrew women, of having many sons, but also, a son she'd given birth to.[5] I picture her by the Nile, barely able to let go of the little basket hiding her baby in the reeds. Such heart-wrenching pain. But as she let go, God did something amazing with her broken dream.[6]

Are you clinging on to an unfulfilled dream or unanswered prayer? Perhaps you still need to persevere in prayer as you wait for its fulfilment. But if you sense God's gentle conviction that it's time to let go, be honest about your pain with him now. Ask him to envision you with his ongoing purposes, and open your heart to all he wants to work through your life. I can't promise how God will respond, but I do know he wants to fulfil you as he walks with you today, 'for it is God who works in you to will and to act in order to fulfil his good purpose' (Phil. 2:13).

Dwell with this verse through your day. There is *no* condemnation. God just wants to help you experience his best for your life, today.

DAY 6

'Don't look back' Genesis 19:17

Occasionally, God has challenged me for slipping into a stagnant mindset, a set routine or way of doing something; when I've stopped pursuing God's ongoing growth of my gifts, or have given up on a promise yet to be fulfilled.

We can't be constantly changing what we do; we need to dig deep with roles and responsibilities for the long haul to see them to completion, especially when obstacles make that harder for us. But if you sense you're stuck in past ways of being and doing, *stop looking back at the way you've always done it, ask God if he wants to do a new thing, and if so, concentrate on adopting this new way of working, thinking, prioritising your time and resources or putting your belief into action . . .*

A well-known quote says, 'If you always do what you always did, you will always get what you always got.' Are you asking or expecting God to do something new in your life while you keep on doing what's now well past its season, or which hasn't worked previously? If you don't like the results you're seeing today, is it time to stop looking back and repeating what you've been doing in all your yesterdays? Is it time to take the step of trying something new?

Reflect on these thoughts and talk with God about them.

Dwell with this verse through your day. There is *no* condemnation. God just wants to help you experience his best for your life, today.

DAY 7

'Don't look back' Genesis 19:17

We can also lose momentum when we've one foot stuck in an ungodly habit, holding us back from moving forward into the fullness of life in Christ. Or perhaps we're unable to forgive a past hurt, or forgive ourselves for a past mistake. We keep looking back, shackling ourselves with bitterness and anger or with fear, doubts and shame. There are many other reasons why we sometimes need to stop looking back and concentrate on where we are going. Perhaps today's examples, however, might prompt you to talk and pray with a trusted Christian friend. Someone whose love and wisdom may help you embrace God's truth and find release to keep pressing onwards.

Reflect on what God has been saying to *you* this week. Thank him for his grace and understanding. Praise him for all that he still wants for you to be and to do. And place your hand in his; trusting his presence, provision and guidance as you move on from the past.

Let's pray: Lord, envision my heart with the life you want me to live today. Let me know your hand in mine, gently leading me onwards. I no longer want my spiritual life to be crippled by the past. Today, I choose to trust in your presence and kingdom calling, to help me pursue all that you still want me to be and to do.

Dwell with this verse through your day. There is *no* condemnation. God just wants to help you experience his best for your life, today.

DAY 1

'Our Father' Matthew 6:9b

I wasn't brought up to know Jesus, but throughout my school life I attended regular 'Assembly'. All ages gathered to sing songs, hear notices, listen to a talk and say the 'Lord's Prayer'. I write, *say* because that's how it felt. I *said* it so often it was quickly committed to memory and rattled off by rote. The words tripped off my tongue without ever engaging my heart; my thoughts focused on the friend beside me, my next class, or on the contents of my lunchbox. I've since grown to cherish Jesus' prayer, and it's a wonderful place to dwell for a week.

It's good to pray this prayer corporately, as written. But as it's Jesus' pattern of prayer, we can also rephrase and pray it for ourselves, for others, or as we intercede for world issues.

Drink deep of these precious words, given to help you to pray. Take one line at a time, pausing before moving on; open to how the Holy Spirit may lead you in prayer:

> Our Father in heaven,
> hallowed be your name,
> your kingdom come,
> your will be done,
> on earth as it is in heaven.
> Give us today our daily bread.
> And forgive us our debts,
> as we also have forgiven our debtors.
> And lead us not into temptation
> but deliver us from the evil one.
>
> *Matt. 6:9–13*[1]

Dwell with this prayer through your day. Could you set an alarm to pray it again at another time, rephrasing it for a personal situation, for someone else or a national issue?

DAY 2

'Our Father' Matthew 6:9b

Pray Jesus' prayer from Day 1, before we dwell with 'Our Father in heaven . . .'

What exquisite intimacy Jesus encourages us to enjoy in prayer. As you pray, remember the fatherly care of the one who 'knows what you need' (Matt. 6:8). He adores and delights in you. He's developing you to be more like him. He provides, supports and protects you in ways you may never realise. He knew you as you were formed in the womb; he's your source of physical and spiritual life. He's a Father you can trust; a Father you've no need to fear – even if you've wandered away from him. A Father who wants the very best for you. A Father who is calling you to come close, and keep close.

'. . . hallowed be your name . . .'

We draw near to God as 'Father' . . . then pause to 'hallow' who he is; to esteem and honour his holy presence. We pray for God to be revered in the world, but recognise we're part of the answer to that prayer.

As you pray these words, you're committing to seeking to reflect your Father's image; to adopting his lifestyle and ways so that others will know you're his child.

Dwell with these words through your day. Could you set an alarm to pray it again at another time, rephrasing it for a personal situation, for someone else or a national issue?

DAY 3

'Our Father' Matthew 6:9b

Pray Jesus' prayer from Day 1, dwelling with 'your kingdom come, your will be done, on earth as it is in heaven'.

We pray Jesus' prayer to seek the final consummation of God's kingdom. But we also use this pattern of prayer to pray for its progressive establishment today; in our own lives and in the world. We've adored God as Father and now we surrender ourselves to his will. Praying *your* kingdom . . . *your* will . . . on earth (in my life) stops us dictating to God what we want and creates space to hear what *he* wants. It guards against me-centred prayers with a God-centred focus, where we align our wills with his as we pray for ourselves, for others and for his world.

Pray this phrase slowly, meditatively – repeating your request as often as your heart needs. Be open to how God may speak to you; to convict or guide you into praying, reflecting and pursuing more of his kingdom, and less of 'yours'.

You might also find it helpful to adapt Paul's prayer: 'Father God, please fill me with the knowledge of your will through all the wisdom and understanding of the Holy Spirit within me' (Col. 1:9). Believe that God will give you what you ask for in faith; now and ongoing.[2]

Dwell with these words through your day. Could you set an alarm to pray it again at another time, rephrasing it for a personal situation, for someone else or a national issue?

DAY 4

'Our Father' Matthew 6:9b

Pray Jesus' prayer from Day 1, dwelling with 'Give us today our daily bread'.

When Jesus prayed for 'bread' he asked for 'needs', not wants or extras. God provides enough for 'today'. We see this worked out in Exodus where he provided sufficient 'manna and quail' each day as his people traipsed through the desert. If they tried to hoard more for 'tomorrow' it went mouldy![3] It's also a promise that follows our praying and pursuing, 'Your kingdom come'. As we seek first for his kingdom to rule and guide our lives, he promises to provide what we need.[4]

If you've no felt needs, pray for those who do, and how you might be part of the answer by sharing what you have. Or perhaps you have no felt needs today but are worried for 'tomorrow's'; your job is uncertain, your pension is small, your health is failing . . . As mentioned above, Jesus promised that as you seek his kingdom purpose in your life, he *will* provide what you need. With that in mind, keep praying this phrase in faith.

But some of you *are* in need. God doesn't break his promises. Trust him to provide, even though it may not come in the way you'd like or expect. Trust 'Our Father' who loves and cares for you.

Dwell with these words through your day. Could you set an alarm to pray it again at another time, rephrasing it for a personal situation, for someone else or a national issue?

DAY 5

'Our Father' Matthew 6:9b

Pray Jesus' prayer from Day 1, dwelling with 'And forgive us our debts'.

'Debts' are 'sins'; the ways we live out of sync with God. Jesus' pattern of prayer includes daily confession to restore broken union with him.[5] I always find myself convicted of something to confess. That said, I'll often ask God to convict me of things I've missed too. I don't search for unconfessed sin, but praying psalms 19:12–13 or 139:23–24 can give breadth to Jesus' pattern of prayer and space to discern God's voice.

God's loving discipline is for your absolute good; for your relationship with him and others, your inner wellbeing, your spiritual growth, your character and more. Pray Jesus' words now to restore intimacy with 'Our Father'.

' . . . as we also have forgiven our debtors.'

It's a truth Jesus taught on other occasions too.[6] We must first forgive others to restore intimacy with God. I know how hard that is when we've been hurt. But choosing to forgive others prayerfully, as well as in words and action, i.e., living out forgiveness, affirms God's forgiveness to us. It also helps release anger or bitterness, infusing us with his peace. Is there someone you need to forgive today, in prayer – and/or in person? As you do, open your heart to draw close again to 'Our Father'.

Dwell with these words through your day. Could you set an alarm to pray it again at another time, rephrasing it for a personal situation, for someone else or a national issue?

DAY 6

'Our Father' Matthew 6:9b

Pray Jesus' prayer from Day 1, dwelling with 'lead us not into temptation . . .'
Or, if you find it more helpful, 'don't let us yield to temptation' (Matthew
6:13, NLT).

We may be tempted to ignore God's ways by our own sinful desires, by others
luring us into ungodly words or behaviour and by our spiritual enemy. Consequently, this prayer has been described as 'a plea for God to protect us from
the evil that is both within and without'.[7] When we give in to temptation, we
uphold the enemy's character and purposes. But when we oppose temptation in
the opposite spirit (kindness instead of hostility, self-control instead of greed,
etc.) we honour and continue to establish God's kingdom through our lives.
God doesn't tempt us,[8] but Jesus knows we're more vulnerable to temptation
in some areas than others. Praying this prayer keeps us mindful of yielding to
God's righteousness.

But then we also continue in prayer, asking our Father to 'deliver us from the
evil one'. Our enemy, the devil or Satan, is at work in many ways. Whether we're
oblivious to his activity, aware of a subtle oppression or discerning a persistent
force set against us, we can ask for God's protection and deliverance.

Take a moment now to reflect on and adapt these prayers for yourself or for
others.

Dwell with these words through your day. Could you set an alarm to pray it
again at another time, rephrasing it for a personal situation, for someone
else or a national issue?

DAY 7

'Our Father' Matthew 6:9b

Pray Jesus' prayer from Day 1.

Depending on your Christian experience or church tradition, you may be familiar with an additional sentence that glorifies God to conclude Jesus' prayer, but which doesn't appear in your Bible: 'For yours is the kingdom, the power and the glory for ever. Amen.' It was traditional to end Jewish prayers with some form of praise. Whether these words date to the time of Jesus, we can't be sure,[9] but the form we now use is based on 1 Chronicles 29:11–12, which we'll use in prayer below.

But before we do, take time to mull on how God has inspired or challenged you from your dwelling with Jesus' prayer. As you keep praying it and responding to God, he will continue to transform you; and in turn, as you live out this prayer it may influence those around you.

Let's pray, praising our Father, together: 'Yours, LORD, is the greatness and the power and the glory and the majesty and the splendour, for everything in heaven and earth is yours. Yours, LORD, is the kingdom; you are exalted as head over all. Wealth and honour come from you; you are the ruler of all things. In your hands are strength and power to exalt and give strength to all.'

Dwell with this prayer through your day. Could you set an alarm to pray it again at another time, rephrasing it for a personal situation, for someone else or a national issue?

DAY 1

'Some trust in chariots and some in horses, but we trust in the name of the LORD our God.' Psalm 20:7

'But' is a short, nondescript word, don't you think? A word, while at school, that I wasn't allowed to use to begin a sentence. But – times have changed! That said, we do need to be careful where we place the 'but'. Our natural inclination is to focus on what comes after it rather than on what came before, and what we focus on will shape our thoughts, attitudes, responses and behaviour. Where we place 'but' can therefore have a powerful effect on our faith in God.

If we say, 'I believe in God's promise to provide *but* I'm worried about my future security,' our thoughts and feelings will focus on the 'worry'. But, if we say, in line with God's Word,[1] 'I am concerned about my future financial security *but* I believe in God's promise to provide all I need as I immerse myself in his ways,' our mind, will and emotions are assured by our faith in God. Try that with a subject you're concerned about, switching who you believe God is to before the *but*, then afterward. Notice how differently you feel and the shift in your faith response.

Playback your conversations or thought patterns from the past few days. Where are you placing *but*? Does it change depending on what you're talking or thinking about?

Dwell with this verse through your day, asking God to start speaking to your heart through its words and emphases.

DAY 2

'Some trust in chariots and some in horses, but we trust in the
name of the LORD our God.' Psalm 20:7

'Chariots and horses' were a formidable force in ancient battle, so many armies relied on them. We can all be tempted to rely on secondary things for security too, but David reminds us where to place the important *but*.[2] When the wrong thing appears after *but* it can undermine our confidence in God, steal his peace from our hearts, confuse our thinking, twist or even misrepresent his truth and in turn, hamper the flow of his blessings in and through us. So, let's join David in making 'the name of the LORD' the object of our trust.

Our belief in God can risk slipping into an intellectual exercise when we merely know about him and study to understand or memorise his Word. But to *trust* God is a personal challenge to place our full confidence in him. It is to intentionally rely on the wonderful attributes of his nature, power and promises.

Prayerfully reflect on God's love, mercy, compassion, knowledge, counsel, wisdom, faithfulness, provision, protection . . . whatever comes to mind as you focus on his presence. It will build your trusting dependence on him and reassure your mind and heart.

Insert a pertinent characteristic or promise where the verse reads [name] and keep dwelling on it through your day. Be open to God's whispers to your heart as you build your trust in him.

DAY 3

'Some trust in chariots and some in horses, but we trust in the name of the LORD our God.' Psalm 20:7

When David felt threatened and abandoned by friends, he poured out his feelings to God.

> I am in distress; my eyes grow weak with sorrow, my soul and body with grief. My life is consumed by anguish and my years by groaning; my strength fails because of my affliction, and my bones grow weak . . . I am forgotten as though I were dead; I have become like broken pottery.
>
> *Ps. 31:9–10,12*

David encourages us to pour out our fears, concerns, pain and uncertainties to God too. The stuff of life that comes before the *but* is real; it's unhealthy and unwise to deny our feelings and pretend that everything's OK. But we release those feelings in partnership with what comes after the *but*: '*But* I trust in you, LORD; I say, "You are my God." My times are in your hands' (Ps. 31:14–15). As David acknowledged his feelings then focused on God, he gained peace and strength which overflowed in faith-filled prayer and praise.[3]

Be honest about your feelings. Recognise what is rooted in truth, but also what may be based on assumptions, misunderstandings or lies. Then reflect on specific characteristics or promises of God that will reassure you.

Dwell with this verse through your day, proclaiming it for your own circumstances. For example: some rely on the love and approval of others, *but* I trust in God's favour and steadfast love.

DAY 4

'Some trust in chariots and some in horses, but we trust in the name of the LORD our God.' Psalm 20:7

King Saul and his men trembled with fear as a veteran Philistine warrior pounded the opposite hilltop, bawling obscenities at them. Young David watched the formidable giant too, *but* he knew where to place his focus, declaring where his confidence lay: 'You come against me with sword and spear and javelin,' he yelled, running towards Goliath armed with a sling. '*But* I come against you in the name of the LORD Almighty . . . This day the LORD will deliver you into my hands . . .' (1 Sam. 17:45–46). And despite the massive odds against David, that's exactly what God did.[4]

David didn't downplay Goliath's strength and proficiency *but* he focused on God's greater power. 'Giants' still bawl their threats, potentially disturbing our peace and undermining our faith. Who or what might be your 'Goliath'? A setback, problem or difficulty? A challenging, criticising or demanding relationship? A giant sense of worthlessness, anxiety, insecurity?

Reflect on aspects of God's nature or promises that reassure your heart and mind for your specific situation. Ask for the 'sword' of a Spirit-breathed Scripture to proclaim, to dispel any fear or uncertainty. Whether or not your giant topples literally, as you focus on who God is you'll know peace, wisdom and authority to stand and overcome any lies, doubts and fears.

Dwell with this verse through your day, proclaiming it for your own circumstances: some rely on themselves *but* I trust in the power of God with me.

DAY 5

'Some trust in chariots and some in horses, but we trust in the name of the Lord our God.' Psalm 20:7

When powerful, marauding Midianites plundered Israel's harvests, God sent a messenger to Gideon as he attempted to hide his wheat out of sight in a winepress: 'The Lord is with you, mighty warrior' (Judg. 6:12).

What an uplifting and faith-building announcement; God was still very present, and had called and empowered Gideon to lead Israel against their enemy. But Gideon didn't focus on the truth, he focused on his circumstances: '. . . *but* if the Lord is with us, why has all this happened to us? Where are all his wonders that our ancestors told us about . . . now the Lord has abandoned us and given us into the hand of Midian' (Judg. 6:13, emphasis mine).

Hard times can undermine our faith in God's presence and his loving care. *But* although we're not shielded from problems, we can know God with us in the ensuing pain and difficulty. So, if you're burdened with worry and fear, focus on his presence in faith. God *is* with you. Believe in his promise to never leave you,[5] and trust in his unseen presence no matter what you see or feel.[6]

Dwell with this verse through your day, proclaiming it for your own circumstances:
Some rely on comfort, ease and the resolution of problems to believe in God with them, *but* I believe in God's unseen presence. I open my heart to his sustaining strength, provision and wisdom *in* these circumstances.

DAY 6

'Some trust in chariots and some in horses, but we trust in the name of the LORD our God.' Psalm 20:7

God's messenger repeated his reassuring call to Gideon. This time, however, Gideon rejected the truth with his felt inadequacy: '. . . *but* how can I save Israel? My clan is the weakest in Manasseh, and I am the least in my family' (Judg. 6:14–15, emphasis mine). Thankfully God was patient and with his third affirmation, Gideon shifted the '*but*' in his thinking and response.

Perhaps you're feeling insufficient or unworthy for God's calling too. God has clearly revealed how he's leading you through Scripture or a prophetic word, *but* your focus and therefore your fears remain on your incapability.

If you believe in God's leading but your sense of inadequacy holds you back, remember Jesus' words, 'apart from me you can do nothing' (John 15:5). It doesn't matter how capable you feel, if this is God's purpose for you then you're assured he will equip, empower and provide for you.

Make today the day you say 'yes' to being available for God to use. Commit yourself to working conscientiously on what he's asked you to do. And steep yourself in prayerful dependence for God's wisdom, provision, creativity and whatever gifting you need.

Dwell with this verse through your day, proclaiming it for your own circumstances:
some rely on their own capabilities and resources, *but* I trust in the call and therefore the equipping of God, and step forward into his purposes.

DAY 7

'Some trust in chariots and some in horses, but we trust in the
name of the LORD our God.' Psalm 20:7

Scripture has other examples of people who placed the right thing after the *but*, and of people who didn't. When we tackle life's challenges using our own understanding or capabilities, they can easily get the better of us. But when we see them in the light of God's love, power and promises, it puts everything back in perspective. It empowers us to live and think God's way instead of battling and losing to negative thoughts. It encourages us to face life in God's strength rather than in our own, with the resources and blessings he offers.

David spent years nurturing his knowledge of God in the Bethlehem hills. His trust and reverence for God honed the right perspective. I hope *Dwell* helps you with this too. Determine today to be a person who acknowledges their feelings and circumstances *but* trusts in all God is and has promised. Talk with God about this now.

Let me pray for you by adapting David's words:[7]

May the Lord answer you when you are in distress; may his nature and promises protect you. May his presence help and support you as you align your life to his. May he give you the desire of your heart and make all your plans succeed. May you shout for joy in your God-given victory and lift your heart to him.

Dwell with this verse for one last day, adapting it for your circumstances.

DAY 1

'But the tax collector stood at a distance. He would not even look
up to heaven, but beat his breast and said,
"God, have mercy on me, a sinner."' Luke 18:13

A friend[1] shared a poignant story during a church service one Sunday. Earlier that morning, he'd been walking his dog, but while cleaning up some poo, his finger inadvertently touched it. He even showed us which one! Back home, he'd washed his hands thoroughly with soap and water, then sanitised them. But he still felt dirty. The point being that we can't wash ourselves clean; only God can. But the story captured my attention for a different reason. We can believe in God's forgiveness but still feel foul, smelly, grotty and even untouchable to God, because we can't forgive ourselves.

Our dwelling place introduces a forlorn man, standing at a distance from God's presence in the temple.[2] Deeply ashamed, he couldn't look up to heaven. He felt utterly unworthy and kept beating his chest in anguish and self-reproach.[3] In fact, 'a' sinner is more accurately translated as 'the' sinner. He believed he was the very worst of all. And yet his desperate prayer for mercy was answered (v. 14).

Do you relate to his despair, struggling to forgive yourself for something you've said, done, or failed to do? God doesn't want you chained up in shame and blame any longer. Alternatively, do you know someone else who is struggling whom you can be praying for this week?

Dwell with this man's heartfelt prayer, now and through your day.

DAY 2

'But the tax collector stood at a distance. He would not even look up to heaven, but beat his breast and said, "God, have mercy on me, a sinner."' Luke 18:13

There are many reasons why you might struggle to forgive yourself. You're consumed with shame. You've marred your reputation with family, friends or colleagues. You deeply regret hurting someone through what you've said or done; or regret hurting yourself through self-destructive behaviour. You've made an unwise decision or have allowed someone else to pressure you into making it. You've failed to keep your job or to work at your marriage. You've let your children or friends down.

To help you forgive yourself be specific about your remorse. Name it out loud or write it down. Don't let the enemy drown you in unspecified condemnation. Then consider: 'have I asked for God's forgiveness for this already?' If not, ask him now. If yes, then believe for God's forgiveness.

Jesus gave his life to release you from guilt, shame and condemnation. God's forgiveness in Christ is available to you the moment you sincerely confess your offence.[4] The tax collector 'stood at a distance'. Self-condemnation will keep you from drawing close to God too; it may even drive you further away from him. So, make today the day you determine to believe in God's Word that promises his acceptance of your heartfelt confession, and let his loving mercy flood your soul.

Dwell with this reassurance now and through your day, as you pray the tax collector's heartfelt prayer.

DAY 3

'But the tax collector stood at a distance. He would not even look up to heaven, but beat his breast and said, "God, have mercy on me, a sinner."' Luke 18:13

You can also be struggling to forgive yourself when, in fact, there is nothing to forgive. For example, someone is refusing to forgive you, even though you've sincerely and repeatedly asked, and have offered practical gestures to prove your desire for reconciliation. If you've only asked once, then ask again; with a visit, a phone call, an invitation to coffee, a text or handwritten message. But if repeated requests have been blocked, it may be time to step back. You can't excuse yourself with a token 'ought-to' apology, like little children sometimes give! But neither can you take responsibility for their choice not to forgive. Provided your apology was sincere, then it's time to call a halt on their unforgiveness holding you back from self-forgiveness. God is your judge – not them. If you've received his forgiveness and you've reached out to them as a peacemaker but they've rejected it, then let it be. At least, until you discern opportunities to ask again.

Alternatively, you feel you've let yourself down in achieving a standard you believe yourself capable of. But don't confuse disappointment with sin. If you've confessed any lack of effort, receive forgiveness. But consider what you've learned and be released to seek further resources or training to move forward.

Dwell with this reassurance now and through your day, as you pray the tax collector's heartfelt prayer.

DAY 4

'But the tax collector stood at a distance. He would not even look
up to heaven, but beat his breast and said,
"God, have mercy on me, a sinner."' Luke 18:13

If you're struggling to forgive yourself, it's time to stifle the negative voice of
your inner critic. It's time to press 'stop' on any auto-repeat message that reminds you how you've failed and how awful you must be. It's time to listen to
God's truth and let it fill your heart and mind. Not just once but repeatedly
until it reroutes your thought patterns.

God forgives you (see Day 2). God doesn't forgive based on your worthiness.
His forgiveness is based on his mercy; the only thing the tax collector felt able
to ask for.

Reflect on these truths, prayerfully receiving them for yourself:

- He does not treat us as our sins deserve or repay us according to our in-
  iquities. For as high as the heavens are above the earth, so great is his love
  for those who fear him . . .

  Ps. 103:10–11

- The Lord our God is merciful and forgiving, even though we have rebelled
  against him . . . We do not make requests of you because we are righteous,
  but because of your great mercy.

  Dan. 9:9,18b

Which aspects of God's nature (unconditional love, unwavering faithfulness,
etc.) and promises ('I will never leave you', for example), do you need to recall,
to silence your inner critic and reroute your thoughts?

Dwell with this reassurance now and through your day, as you pray the tax
collector's heartfelt prayer.

DAY 5

'But the tax collector stood at a distance. He would not even look up to heaven, but beat his breast and said, "God, have mercy on me, a sinner."' Luke 18:13

You may struggle with self-forgiveness if you're not being completely honest with God, with others, or with yourself, for our hearts easily deceive us. You can ask forgiveness of God or someone else, yet remain unsettled because your subconscious knows what's still buried; something the Holy Spirit is gently convicting you of. Something you're not permitting to surface. Something that allows you to pursue what you want or protects your reputation. Something it's now time to recognise, confess and let go.

God will highlight the issue preventing your self-forgiveness if you ask him to, and his Word offers the perfect prayer to help unzip your soul: 'Search me, God, and know my heart; test me and know my anxious thoughts. See if there is any offensive way in me, and lead me in the way everlasting' (Ps. 139:23–24). Pray these words now with a humble, open heart. Then give space for the Holy Spirit to reveal whatever he needs to.

You may not discern anything at all. Great! At least you know that's not the reason for your lack of self-forgiveness. But if you're convicted about covering things up, false intentions, self-righteousness or anything else, be honest in prayer. Invite God's mercy to flood your soul and instruct you, going forward.

Dwell with this reassurance now and through your day, as you pray the tax collector's heartfelt prayer.

DAY 6

'But the tax collector stood at a distance. He would not even look
up to heaven, but beat his breast and said,
"God, have mercy on me, a sinner."' Luke 18:13

I chose the wrong subjects to study at O level. A number of factors influenced that decision, but ultimately, it was my choice. When I later recognised my blunder and how different my subsequent A levels and career should have been, I had to take responsibility and stop blaming others for my decision. But for many years I struggled to forgive myself, until I realised, I was limiting my experience of God's love by festering in regret. Self-forgiveness is vital for inner healing, releasing destructive anger or sorrow as well as guilt and shame.

Your mistake may be more serious, but start by acknowledging your responsibility and release anyone you've been blaming. Ask for and receive God's forgiveness. Then reflect on what you can *learn* from your mistake to shape good choices in future. And remember, no one is perfect. We all make mistakes. The key is not allowing them to hold you back from receiving God's promised fulness of life.

- Rest in God's immeasurable love and forgiveness. Let that put a smile on your heart and lips.
- Pray and be open to God's response: 'Lead me along your chosen paths, Lord, and help me to make right choices, so that your glorious presence will be made known through my life.'[5]

Dwell with this reassurance now and through your day, as you pray the tax collector's heartfelt prayer.

DAY 7

'But the tax collector stood at a distance. He would not even look up to heaven, but beat his breast and said, "God, have mercy on me, a sinner."' Luke 18:13

As I mentioned on Day 1, if you're *not* struggling with self-forgiveness, I trust these reflections will help you to help others. When a child hurts itself despite our warnings 'not' to touch the hot water, play with the scissors, etc. we don't say, 'it's your fault' then dismiss them. We stay with them, comfort them, and help them understand what they can learn. Similarly, when someone gets themselves into a scrape, is hurting from the consequences and unable to forgive themselves, God draws us to their side to sit with them in their pain without judgement, and to support them in how to move forward.

If, however, you've identified personally with this week's dwelling place, I trust you are now moving on. But if you're still struggling, please do talk and pray these things through with someone you trust.

Let's pray together: Loving God, like the forlorn tax collector, I confess, 'I am a sinner'. I have no excuse but have every need of your mercy. I draw close to you now, through Jesus. I ask your forgiveness, and your help to turn away from how I've let you down. Thank you for your love. I receive your mercy and I give it to myself too. Amen.

Dwell with this reassurance now and through your day, as you pray the tax collector's heartfelt prayer.

DAY 1

'Quiet! Be still!' Mark 4:39

Jesus spoke these words after a violent storm erupted on the Sea of Galilee.[1] Picture the scene:

The disciples battle to keep their boat afloat as Jesus sleeps on a cushion in the rear. Feel the swell, then the wind-whipped waves, crashing overhead, sapping strength as they heave on dragging oars. Water sloshes across the lurching deck, threatening to swamp it. Hear frightened shouts waking Jesus, then his confident command taking authority: 'Quiet! Be still!'

Storms come in many guises. Whether it manifests as racing thoughts, emotional turmoil, a challenging situation or all three, picture Jesus with you.

Jesus is in your 'boat'. He is with you in your storm.

Hear his authority in these three simple but powerful words.

How does this make you feel?

How does it inspire or challenge you?

Is God revealing anything new about himself, about you, about your relationship with and response to him?

Keep this image and the command, 'Quiet! Be still!' in your mind and heart through your day. Mull on it, pray it, proclaim it. Remain attentive to how its truth and implications shape your faith, emotions and perspective.

DAY 2

'Quiet! Be still!' Mark 4:39

Repeating this command isn't a practice of mind over matter. Declaring this command reflects your wholehearted belief in God's promises for every situation you face; for strength, provision and guidance, for example. It prompts you to dwell on God's presence, character and word, instead of the nature of your storm. And in turn, it invites his promised peace[2] to settle the turmoil invading your soul.

Choose a place today where you may enact outwardly what you want to experience inwardly; a place that encourages physically what you want to experience spiritually, i.e. God's promise of peace and composure. Some of you may sit with eyes closed in a familiar chair at home, or gaze out of a window across gardens, carparks, rooftops or roads, nursing your favourite brew. Others may be able to venture outside; to absorb the countryside's soul-enriching beauty, to stand on a bridge to watch river water flowing through your town, or to lean up against an eye-catching tree in your city park, gazing skywards through its branches.

Wherever you choose to encounter his peace, focus on one or two characteristics of God that counter your inner storm, then adopt Jesus' words for yourself; acknowledging his presence and power. And remember: just as Jesus was in the boat with the disciples, he is with you now. Dwell with that awareness.

Continue as per Day 1, to hold this verse in your mind and heart both now, and throughout your day.

DAY 3

'Quiet! Be still!' Mark 4:39

A familiar stormy condition that batters the soul is a busy mind. It blows up out of difficult situations, from excessive daily tension, or when you've simply got too much on your to-do list.

It's a turmoil of thoughts running riot by day, distracting you from being fully present in the moment at hand. And it's the fear and confusion disrupting quality sleep. In fact, the questions, concerns and related emotions of this storm steal peace and contentment and exhaust body and soul. But the words Jesus used to calm the storm, swamping the disciples' boat, are powerful in defence: 'Quiet! Be still!'

Identify specific thoughts that thunder relentlessly through your mind:

If they're prompting you with something you can and need to deal with, then do it today. It will deflate their power to cause you further stress.

If your thoughts are reminding you of a task yet to be done, make a note or, if possible, diarise it. Name the reason why you can't do it immediately to diffuse the tension.

If your thoughts are simply unnecessary, irrational or irrelevant debris provoked by a turmoil of fear or confusion, acknowledge them for what they are, focus on what you believe about God and command them with faith and authority: 'Quiet! Be still!'

Thank God, in faith, for his presence with you. Dwell with this reality; it will calm and clarify your thoughts.

Continue as per Day 1, to hold this verse in your mind and heart both now, and throughout your day.

DAY 4

'Quiet! Be still!' Mark 4:39

Troubled emotions can also be intrinsic to the storms in our soul. Identify specifically what may be troubling you today – anxiety, worry, doubt, fear, shame, confusion, hurt, negativity, etc. Then reflect on aspects of God's nature and promises which refute these stormy emotions. For example, God's promised peace where you feel troubled; his forgiveness where you feel hurt; his grace where you feel condemnation; the assurance of your life in him where you feel unsettled; confidence in God's power and purpose where you feel afraid.

God's power, peace, presence, etc. are *already* yours to encounter through your life in Christ and his Spirit dwelling within you. Name each aspect of God's character or specific promise that you need to receive in fuller measure, then invite these truths to step forward from the front door of your thinking, to make their home in your heart.

Declaring this command requires a wholehearted belief that your emotional storm isn't rooted in God, willed by God or condoned by God. As you declare to your inner turbulence, 'Quiet! Be still!', you open your heart to God's calming presence.

Even if you can't feel his presence, give thanks, in faith, that God is with you right now – his power to calm and permeate peace to your soul.

Continue as per Day 1, to hold this verse in your mind and heart both now, and throughout your day.

DAY 5

'Quiet! Be still!' Mark 4:39

Circumstances trigger life's storms. What situations are battering your mind, body and soul? Acknowledge to God how they make you feel. He loves and cares for you, and longs for you to draw close to him in prayer, whatever situation you face. Pray about these circumstances as your heart and the Holy Spirit leads you, asking for his insight and perspective, that will quieten and still your fears and concerns.

You can also take authority over the storm by praying truth prophetically over the issue, that 'in all things God works for the good of those who love him, who have been called according to his purpose' (Rom. 8:28). Declare God's promises into each situation, trusting yourself and the outcome into his hands. For example, you might declare God's promise to provide for what you need,[3] his offer of balance in life where you feel overwhelmed,[4] his presence with you to sustain, guide or intervene in ongoing problems.[5] As you do, you will know the effect of Jesus' command: 'Quiet! Be still!'

Know in your heart as well as your head, that God is with you, even if you can't feel or perceive him in the fallout of the storm.

Continue as per Day 1, to hold this verse in your mind and heart both now, and throughout your day.

DAY 6

'Quiet! Be still!' Mark 4:39

Picture yourself in the boat as you did on Day 1: see Jesus stand up and take authority. Open your soul to his power and truth. Dwell with his ensuing peace and reassurance.

At some point in your day, repeat the suggestion from Day 2, finding a place to be still in your home or outside in the way that works best for you and your situation. And as you do, take authority over your personal storm.

Take command over disrupting thoughts and emotions by declaring:

a) Confidence in who God is (loving, faithful, merciful, etc.);
b) Confidence in who you are in God (adopted, beloved, valued, empowered, etc.);
c) Confidence in God's Word (name specific truths and promises applicable to your storm).

This isn't something to be rushed. Even if you've only five minutes, focus your heart and soul on who God is and what he has promised.

Take authority over your circumstances in prayer, declaring truths about God's character and purposes into the situation, trusting the outcome to him and being open to any steps he may guide you to take.

God is with you; believe in his presence. Take a long and loving look at who you know him to be. Open your heart to his qualities infusing your soul in this moment.

Continue as per Day 1, to hold this verse in your mind and heart both now, and throughout your day.

DAY 7

'Quiet! Be still!' Mark 4:39

How has God been working his peace and reassurance into your mind, body and soul this week? Even if your circumstances haven't changed, be mindful of how God is changing your response to them. Thank God for the power of his presence with you now and at all times.

As we conclude, you might like to pray this prayer, which I've adapted from Psalm 46:

God, you are my safe place; my impenetrable refuge and sustaining strength.

You are my ever-present support, always waiting to help when I face trouble.

Therefore, I will not be afraid though the storm bellows around me, though my feet feel tremors beneath me, though problems mount up against me and securities crash around me.

God, you are my true source of life, your streams of living water refresh and revive me.

I long to dwell and remain in your Presence, for there I can stand strong; battered perhaps, but unmoved.

You, O Lord, are my stronghold. Though problems roar and missiles assail, you are with me, your Presence is a shield around me.

You, O Lord, are Sovereign over my life. My times are in your hands. The whole world is in your hands.

I will quieten my soul before you. I will still my thoughts. I will bring to mind who I know you to be.

And I will exalt you.

Amen.

Continue as per Day 1, to hold this verse in your mind and heart both now, and throughout your day.

DAY 1

'May these words of my mouth and this meditation of my heart
be pleasing in your sight, LORD, my Rock and my Redeemer.'
Psalm 19:14

I was driving to church through beautiful countryside, which usually inspired gratitude and praise. But my thoughts were consumed with a deep hurt, distracting my attention from God's healing presence; a distraction undermining my inner peace, and also my productivity at work; a distraction that could sow bitterness which in turn, might birth angry, critical and self-righteous words. Such is the potential power of what we ruminate on. Sensing God's gentle conviction, I was prompted with my next dwelling-place: David's prayer concluding Psalm 19.[1]

We'll have space this week to reflect on what influences our hearts and therefore our words, but today, let's follow the ancient steps of Lectio Divina[2] to help us dwell with Psalm 19:14.

Still your thoughts and focus on God with you. Ask him to speak with you through his Word.

Read the verse a few times. Slowly. Reflect on a word that especially resonates, or on something else God brings to mind. Pray through your response. What have you been inspired with or learned, and how might you put it into practise?

Dwell with David's prayer through your day, let it prompt you to set your thoughts on God to shape your thinking, perspective and responses; in your working and resting, in the busyness and mundane, and when you speak to, message or listen to others.

DAY 2

'May these words of my mouth and this meditation of my heart
be pleasing in your sight, LORD, my Rock and my Redeemer.'
Psalm 19:14

Many years ago, I began highlighting verses about the mouth, tongue or words. The regular splashes of blue in my Bible constantly remind me that words are important to God. Words can build up or tear down, encourage or dishearten, heal or wound. Dwelling with David's prayer reminds us to speak words that are *pleasing* to God, inspiring speech that reflects his character. Words that are tolerant not judgemental, thankful not grumpy, pleasant not bitter, patient not irritable, kind not hurtful, complimentary not fault-finding.

If you tend to rush your words or written messages, slow down. Slowing your speed of talking, even a little, gives pause for your mouth to remain in tune with the nature and will of the Holy Spirit; prompting, guiding or convicting you about what to say, and how; words that are true, helpful, encouraging, kind, understanding . . . and 'full of grace' (Col. 4:6).

Take a few moments to pray another of David's prayers that asks for God's help with words:

'Set a guard over my mouth, LORD; keep watch over the door of my lips' (Ps. 141:3).

Perhaps you'd like to start highlighting such verses in your Bible too?

Dwell with David's prayer through your day, let it prompt you to set your thoughts on God to shape your thinking, perspective and responses; in your working and resting, in the busyness and mundane, and when you speak to, message or listen to others.

DAY 3

'May these words of my mouth and this meditation of my heart
be mindful be pleasing in your sight, LORD, my Rock and my Redeemer.'
Psalm 19:14

In Psalm 19, David ponders the glory of God revealed through creation (vv. 1–6) and contemplates the power of his Word to nurture a godly life (vv. 7–13). As you meditate and think deeply on God, and fill your mind, will and emotions with his power and creativity, on the beauty of his character, truth, wisdom and guidance, the transformation he works in you will influence your words.[3] For our words are the overflow of our hearts.[4] Some would even say that they're a barometer of our spirituality.[5]

Look out of a window. Be mindful of God with you as you reflect on all he's created; the expanse of an ever-changing sky, a magnificent or humble tree, a countryside scene, a planted pot, or the fortitude of a weed breaking through tarmac. Fill your mind, soul and emotions with how you perceive God's brushstrokes, and respond in prayerful praise.

What aspect of God's nature or promise in his Word might you meditate on today? Respond with praise, self-examination or confession as the Holy Spirit guides you.

Dwell with David's prayer through your day, let it prompt you to set your thoughts on God to shape your thinking, perspective and responses; in your working and resting, in the busyness and mundane, and when you speak to, message or listen to others.

DAY 4

'May these words of my mouth and this meditation of my heart
be pleasing in your sight, LORD, my Rock and my Redeemer.'
Psalm 19:14

The subject of 'mindfulness' often appears in my online feed; the importance of focusing our attention and response on the present moment. It certainly helps us honour God with conscientious work and attentive listening to others, for example. But dwelling with David's prayer enriches this further. It helps maintain our awareness of and response to God's constant presence. It encourages us to seek to love and honour him in all we say and do, in every activity and relationship. It guards against drifting into negative, critical, selfish, anxious thoughts that may influence our responses.

Consider the past twenty-four hours. How did your thoughts, motives and words reflect God's love, grace, truth, kindness, etc.? How were they inspired by faith in all God is and does?

Were there many minutes – or hours – when negative, anxious or deflating and undermining thoughts consumed your mind, will, emotions and perhaps, in turn, your words? Relive those scenes again with David's prayer in your heart and on your lips. How might David's desire to love, please and honour God have influenced your own thinking and responses? Give time for God to encourage and inspire you.

Dwell with David's prayer through your day, let it prompt you to set your thoughts on God to shape your thinking, perspective and responses; in your working and resting, in the busyness and mundane, and when you speak to, message or listen to others.

DAY 5

'May these words of my mouth and this meditation of my heart
be pleasing in your sight, LORD, my Rock and my Redeemer.'
Psalm 19:14

Every so often, my husband shares something about me with others that he values, whether that's something about who I am or what I do. His loving, appreciative affirmation embarrasses me a little, but naturally warms, delights and encourages my heart as well. I hope every reader can relate to this; from a partner, relative, colleague or friend. Yes, God warns against seeking praise from others,[6] but I share how I've felt to help us understand how our words and meditations can be 'pleasing' to God.

When you pray David's prayer, you're not looking to *appease* God with words of confession and a repentant heart. Nor are you seeking to *earn* his favour. You're praying that your loving appreciation and response to all that he is and does would bring him delight and fill his heart with joy. It's about speaking and thinking in ways that show God how much he is loved and appreciated.

How does this idea of delighting God inspire you?

Take a few moments to adore him in heartfelt worship, but also use opportunities today to share your love and appreciation of who he is with others.

Dwell with David's prayer through your day, let it prompt you to set your thoughts on God to shape your thinking, perspective and responses; in your working and resting, in the busyness and mundane, and when you speak to, message or listen to others.

DAY 6

'May these words of my mouth and this meditation of my heart
be pleasing in your sight, LORD, my Rock and my Redeemer.'
Psalm 19:14

Although I was familiar with David's prayer, it was only in writing it out for my dwelling place one week that I was struck by the capital 'R's' for 'Rock' and 'Redeemer'. It prompted my meditation on these significant names for God, to respond and encounter him afresh in these roles. So, that's my encouragement to you today.

God, your Rock, is solid, i.e. dependable. You can take refuge in his unfailing strength and support as you open your heart to his presence. God is your true source of security.

God, your Redeemer, is your deliverer. He cares for and protects you. He frees you from guilt as you confess your sin and liberates you from enemy lies.

Meditate on – fill your mind and soul – with these truths and implications.

Pray Psalm 18:1–2, to affirm who God is to you, to infuse comfort and assurance, and inspire your own words of trust and praise: 'I love you, LORD, my strength. [You are] my rock, my fortress and my deliverer; [you are] my rock, in whom I take refuge, my shield and the horn of my salvation, my stronghold.'

Dwell with David's prayer through your day, let it prompt you to set your thoughts on God to shape your thinking, perspective and responses; in your working and resting, in the busyness and mundane, and when you speak to, message or listen to others.

DAY 7

'May these words of my mouth and this meditation of my heart
be pleasing in your sight, LORD, my Rock and my Redeemer.'
Psalm 19:14

As we conclude this week, consider the truth of Psalm 23:6: 'Surely your goodness and love will follow me all the days of my life . . .' Sometimes we allow ourselves to be so distracted or consumed by problems or negative thoughts that we focus on what we *haven't* got, rather than what we have. And one thing that's ever-present is God's goodness and love.

So, name, and if possible, write down, aspects of God's goodness to you. For example, his unconditional love, his gift of eternal life, his forgiveness and faithfulness; your loved ones or other relationships, your home, wardrobe, food on the table, your job, income, opportunities to use your gifts and experiences, your health, or medication to aid symptoms . . .

Meditate on God's goodness to you today. How does that transform any discontented thoughts, and inspire your prayerful response?

Let's pray: Lord of life, I choose to set my mind and heart on you; ever-present, ever-faithful, loving God of my life. 'May my spoken words and unspoken thoughts be pleasing even to you, O Lord my Rock and my Redeemer' (Ps. 19:14, TLB). Amen.

Dwell with David's prayer through your day, let it prompt you to set your thoughts on God to shape your thinking, perspective and responses; in your working and resting, in the busyness and mundane, and when you speak to, message or listen to others.

DAY 1

'Love is patient, love is kind. It does not envy, it does not boast, it is not proud. It does not dishonour others, it is not self-seeking, it is not easily angered, it keeps no record of wrongs. Love does not delight in evil but rejoices with the truth. It always protects, always trusts, always hopes, always perseveres.' 1 Corinthians 13:4–7

'What is Love?' the eighties' pop-singer Howard Jones asked my teenage self. Love received and felt can mean so much. It can be fickle or consistent, shallow or deep, demanding or self-giving, controlling or serving. But *God's* love, described in our dwelling place, is pure, unfailing, infinite in width, length, height and depth; unconditional, undeserving, protective, compassionate and . . . gosh, what an endless list it would be to describe God's amazing love!

Scripture uses different words for love to differentiate between a) passionate desire or feelings for someone, b) affection and care, or c) a choice to love someone, no matter our desires or feelings for them or how they respond. It's this third word for love, *agapé*, that's used in our dwelling place.

How have you been let down by love? Do you ever feel reticent to love?

How have you been encouraged, comforted, valued, supported, cared for, known, built up by love?

Has your experience of love influenced how you understand, receive or reciprocate God's love, positively or negatively?

God wants to hear your heart.

Dwell on this passage through your day, keeping the words close to hand, as always, to embed them in your heart.

DAY 2

'Love is patient, love is kind. It does not envy, it does not boast, it is not proud. It does not dishonour others, it is not self-seeking, it is not easily angered, it keeps no record of wrongs. Love does not delight in evil but rejoices with the truth. It always protects, always trusts, always hopes, always perseveres.' 1 Corinthians 13:4–7

Still your heart, and pray: 'Father, how great is your love that you've lavished on me, your child. Your cherished, treasured, adored child, is who and what I am.'[1]

Pause momentarily to rest in his love.

'God is love' (1 John 4:8). God isn't just loving; love is the very essence of his being. The ultimate demonstration of his love was revealed in Jesus, and his boundless unconditional love reaches out to you.

Read through our verses, taking note of each description that reveals how God loves you.

How does it make you feel to know God loves you in each of these ways?

How does it encourage or surprise you?

Do you find it easy to accept and receive his love? If not, could you say why?

What other insights is God giving you? Talk with him about these things.

God longs for you to believe, experience and be filled with his love at the core of your being. His love heals, calms, inspires, builds up, refines, and wants the very best of his life for you.

Dwell on this passage throughout your day, and enjoy his loving attention.

DAY 3

'Love is patient, love is kind. It does not envy, it does not boast, it is not proud. It does not dishonour others, it is not self-seeking, it is not easily angered, it keeps no record of wrongs. Love does not delight in evil but rejoices with the truth. It always protects, always trusts, always hopes, always perseveres.' 1 Corinthians 13:4–7

Still your heart, and pray: 'Father, how great is your love that you've lavished on me, your child. Your cherished, treasured, adored child, is who and what I am.'

Pause momentarily to rest in his love.

Read our verses – slowly. Read with expectancy that God wants to meet with you through his Word. Remember, God longs for you to believe, experience and be filled with his love at the core of your being.

Which word or phrase stands out to you, resonating with greater depth than the others?

Focus on this word or phrase. What do you understand it to mean? How does it make you feel:

- About God?
- About yourself?
- About God's love for someone else?

What insights is God giving you? Do they suggest some kind of response? Talk with him now about them.

If no particular word or phrase stands out, continue to dwell on these verses. Invite the depth and breadth of God's love to nurture healing, assurance and peace to your soul.

Dwell on these verses throughout your day, and receive his love in ever greater measure.

DAY 4

'Love is patient, love is kind. It does not envy, it does not boast,
it is not proud.' 1 Corinthians 13:4

Still your heart, and pray: 'Father, how great is your love that you've lavished on me, your child. Your cherished, treasured, adored child, is who and what I am.'

Pause momentarily to rest in his love.

God asks us to love others as he loves us.[2]

- Does **patience** come naturally to you? When do you struggle? Does it depend on your current mood, someone's character and personality, the nature of your relationship with them, or do you simply find it easier to be patient about some things more than others?
- If '**kind**' is the word you're drawn to, insert 'kindness/kind' for 'patience/patient' in the previous question.
- Are you **envious** of anyone? How does that affect your relationship with them, how you react or respond to them and how you talk about them to others?
- Few would recognise themselves being **boastful**, but give time for God to search your heart and to speak, if he has need.
- How does **pride** influence how you think about, talk with or relate to others?

Reflect on the word that most resonates, and confess any conviction. How are you inspired to love someone/others in this way? Talk with God about it.

God longs for you to encounter his love at the core of your being so you may love others as he loves you. Dwell with the truth of this verse through your day.

DAY 5

'[Love] does not dishonour others, it is not self-seeking, it is not easily angered, it keeps no record of wrongs.'
1 Corinthians 13:5

Still your heart, and pray: 'Father, how great is your love that you've lavished on me, your child. Your cherished, treasured, adored child, is who and what I am.'

Pause momentarily to rest in his love.

Once again, God asks us to love others as he loves us.

- To **dishonour** someone is to show a lack of respect, to be discourteous, tactless, blunt or without grace. Is there any conviction of a specific occasion you dishonoured someone, or a growing ungodly character trait?
- **Self-seeking** promotes rights over responsibilities. It insists on getting its own way. It is inconsiderate of others in its pursuit of self-satisfaction. It loves oneself before God or anyone else.
- Love is not **easily angered**. You may feel irritated, exasperated or provoked at times, but love diffuses an angry reaction.
- There's **no record keeping of wrongs**; no holding something against someone or nursing a sense of injury. Rather, love makes allowances for others and chooses to let go of the wrong.

Give time for God to search your heart. Reflect on the word that most resonates and confess any conviction. How are you inspired to love someone/others in this way? Talk with God about it.

God longs for you to encounter his love at the core of your being so you may love others as he loves you. Dwell with the truth of this verse through your day.

DAY 6

*'Love does not delight in evil but rejoices with the truth.
It always protects, always trusts, always hopes,
always perseveres.' 1 Corinthians 13:6–7*

Still your heart, and pray: 'Father, how great is your love that you've lavished on me, your child. Your cherished, treasured, adored child, is who and what I am.'

Pause momentarily to rest in his love.

Remember: God asks us to love others as he loves us.

- **Does not delight in evil** reveals a flaw in human nature that takes pleasure in others' misfortunes; especially those you envy, who irritate you or have hurt you. Rather, love **rejoices with the truth**; it delights in seeing others transformed in response to God's love.
- Love **protects** reputations by seeking to make amends in private or enduring insults and disappointments in its desire for them to encounter God's love.[3]
- Love **trusts** by looking for the best in others without being deceived by false pretences. It **hopes** for the good in everyone; confident of God's promises to anyone seeking to yield to his ways.
- Love **perseveres**. It remains steadfast, even when faced with unpleasant reactions or behaviour. It isn't resigned to passive acceptance but continually acts with intention to love.

Reflect on the word that most resonates and confess any conviction. How are you inspired to love someone/others in this way? Talk with God about it.

God longs for you to encounter his love at the core of your being so you may love others as he loves you. Dwell with the truth of these verses through your day.

DAY 7

'Love is patient, love is kind. It does not envy, it does not boast, it is not proud. It does not dishonour others, it is not self-seeking, it is not easily angered, it keeps no record of wrongs. Love does not delight in evil but rejoices with the truth. It always protects, always trusts, always hopes, always perseveres.' 1 Corinthians 13:4–7

Still your heart, and pray: 'Father, how great is your love that you've lavished on me, your child. Your cherished, treasured, adored child, is who and what I am.'

Pause momentarily to rest in his love.

Read through these verses again. Read with expectancy that God still wants to meet with you in fresh ways through his Word.

How has God reassured or encouraged you this week?

In what ways has our dwelling place refined, inspired and shaped your responses or influenced your words and conduct?

Is there a particular word or phrase God is prompting you to keep dwelling on to let its transforming work continue, in and through your life?

Let's pray: Father God, thank you for reassuring me this week of your unconditional, faithful and sacrificial love for me. Help me to root myself ever deeper into this truth. And thank you, for so gently and graciously teaching me how to love others – especially those I find difficult. I name and pray for them now . . .

Rest in the loving reassurance from God's Word to you today. Let it flood your heart, soul and mind, and ease any tension in your body.

DAY 1

'I am the LORD your God; consecrate yourselves and
be holy, because I am holy.' Leviticus 11:44a

Although I'm unique, my genetic make-up reveals my family likeness in a number of ways. I've inherited my father's large front teeth and petite frame, for example; my mother's quick-tanning skin and unfortunately, her bulbous, arthritic big toes! Scripture also speaks of being transformed into our Lord's likeness; the family likeness of being children of our holy Father.[1] We are loved and created by a holy God. We are made holy through our life in Jesus. We are called to be holy; to share and reflect our Father's holy likeness.

Holiness is the core theme of Leviticus. It was to infuse every area of Israel's life. To 'be holy' is to be entirely devoted to God's presence and purposes. It's to be increasingly saturated with our Father's nature as we yield to his ways and reflect his holiness to the world.

'Lord, what do you desire from me?'

That's the question we're dwelling with this week. So often we ask God for things outside of ourselves, but seeking to be transformed increasingly into his likeness prompts us to ask him what he desires in and from us. And his answer begins: 'Be holy . . . '

Prayerfully mull on that question and answer, asking God to speak to you about it during the week.

Dwell with this verse throughout your day, being mindful of how it makes you feel, think and respond.

DAY 2

'I am the LORD your God; consecrate yourselves and
be holy, because I am holy.' Leviticus 11:44a

'Holy God, what do you desire from me?'

'Be holy, [Anne], because I, the LORD your God, am holy' (Lev. 19:1).

God is holy. His perfect purity and goodness invite our response, not just in words or songs of praise and adoration, but through how we seek to live. God made us holy through Jesus,[2] but we continue to grow in holiness as we cooperate with the ongoing sanctifying work of the Holy Spirit; working out what he has worked within.[3] This is who we are: chosen to be God's holy people and to live his holy life.[4] I admit, these facts in themselves may fail to enthuse a response. But when we take time to gaze on the beauty of God's holiness, revealed in all he is and all he has done, we can't help but be inspired.

'Holy, holy, holy is the LORD Almighty; the whole earth is full of his glory' (Isa. 6:3).

'"Holy, holy, holy is the Lord God Almighty," who was, and is, and is to come' (Rev. 4:8).

Use these declarations to help you worship God today.

Pray them slowly and with thought. Pause between phrases. What does holiness look like to you? How are you stirred to pray? And how are you inspired to be holy?

You might also like to worship God's holiness in song.[5]

Dwell with this verse throughout your day, reflecting on how it continues to shape and inform your response.

DAY 3

'I am the LORD your God; consecrate yourselves and be holy, because I am holy.' Leviticus 11:44a

'Holy God, what do you desire from me?'

'Consecrate yourself and be holy.'

Taking time each day to appreciate and worship the beauty of God's holiness inspires us to *consecrate* ourselves to him; to choose to let God's holiness shape and mould us. To consecrate ourselves is devoting ourselves to love, serve and worship him through all we are, do and say.

Does anything hold you back from dedicating yourself fully to your holy Father, or make you afraid to do so? Perhaps you have habits, pleasures or goals you feel you'd have to give up. You may be afraid it would affect a relationship adversely. As you're honest with God, you may find some of your worries are unwarranted. But if there are things you need to change or abandon, be reassured that God knows and truly desires the best of his life for you.

Immerse yourself in God's loving presence as you consider his command to consecration. Ask him to envision you with his holiness, with the holy, eternal life that you'll enjoy forever and which has already begun in you. As you drink in his beauty, you'll be inspired to live the life of eternity – God's holy life – today. This is who and what you are living for. God *is* your life.

Dwell with this verse throughout your day, reflecting on how it continues to shape and inform your response.

DAY 4

'I am the LORD your God; consecrate yourselves and be holy, because I am holy.' Leviticus 11:44a

'Holy God, what do you desire from me?'

> As obedient children, do not conform to the evil desires you had when you lived in ignorance. But just as he who called you is holy, so be holy in all you do; for it is written: 'Be holy, because I am holy.'
>
> *1 Pet. 1:14–16*

We grow in holiness as we remain close to our Father in prayerful response to his convictions and as we conform to his Word. God's commands help us to be holy. It's as we obey them and put them into practise that we grow in holiness.[6] Of course, we'll slip up! But God disciplines our open hearts, not just to reprimand, but 'that we may share in his holiness' (Heb. 12:10). God's discipline really is for our good.

Holiness is to permeate every aspect of life. Work. Rest. Relationships. Eating and drinking. Speaking and behaving, etc. Thank God for his loving presence with you, then ask him to highlight anything in your life that undermines his holy nature and ways. If you have a tendency to yield to God in some things but not others, be honest about it. How would your life be different if holiness was your benchmark for everything?

Dwell with this verse throughout your day, reflecting on how it continues to shape and inform your response.

DAY 5

'I am the LORD your God; consecrate yourselves and be holy, because I am holy.' Leviticus 11:44a

'Holy God, what do you desire from me?'

' . . . do not grieve the Holy Spirit' (Eph. 4:30); 'live by my Holy Spirit'.[7]

Living a *holy* life goes hand-in-hand with being empowered by God's *Holy* Spirit. In the Bible, fire is often symbolic of the power of God's presence. The fire of God's presence meeting with Moses through a burning bush and leading the Israelites through the desert at night. The tongues of fire resting on believers at Pentecost, equipping them with Spirit-empowered life. But there's another symbol for the Holy Spirit too. After Jesus was baptised, the Holy Spirit was seen to descend and settle on him in the form of a dove. Doves are sensitive, flitting away if even slightly disturbed; unlike pigeons in crowded towns, milling among clumping feet. The Spirit was at home with and empowered Jesus' yielded, holy life.[8] Likewise, God urges us to respect the holy nature of his Spirit so we too can know his power.[9]

Compromise. Excuses. Self-justification. Unintentional error. Wilful disobedience. Self-focused goals. Ouch! Perhaps some of these resonate with your habits, attitudes, words or behaviour. But no matter how you may sense you've grieved the Holy Spirit, you're warmly urged to bring your sincere confession. To gaze once again on the beauty of your Father's holiness. To be inspired by his love and grace, going forward.

Dwell with this verse throughout your day, reflecting on how it continues to shape and inform your response.

DAY 6

'I am the LORD your God; consecrate yourselves and be holy, because I am holy.' Leviticus 11:44a

'Holy God, what do you desire from me?'

'Make every effort to … be holy; without holiness no one will see the Lord' (Heb. 12:14).

I was looking forward to sharing dinner with friends, but although I may have appeared to be a nice enough person, I was later convicted of my unattractive ego and self. My heart was more often motivated by me than by God.

It's pleasant to meet nice people, but without holiness we lack the conviction of God's presence. If we're amiable and kind-mannered, many may like us, but holiness goes further and deeper. Holiness stands for God's divine nature and intentions for life. As we seek to be holy, our values may not always be acceptable to others, but we will reflect who God is.

I've been challenged to prayerfully consider some questions which I share with you here.

When have I appeared to be nice but have:

- Compromised truth?
- Conceded to principles or beliefs that are lower than God's standard?
- Nurtured negativity?
- Subtly (or overtly) shifted the blame onto someone else?
- Subtly (or overtly) shamed or put someone down?
- Turned a blind eye to injustice?
- Spoken or acted hypocritically or deceptively?
- Turned the focus of attention onto me?

No one is perfect! Just pray through your response as you feel led. Your Father loves to help you grow into his likeness.

Dwell with this verse throughout your day, reflecting on how it continues to shape and inform your response.

DAY 7

'I am the LORD your God; consecrate yourselves and
be holy, because I am holy.' Leviticus 11:44a

'Holy Father, what do you desire from my habits, attitudes, time, resources, finance, Sabbath, work, relationships, roles at church, use of your spiritual gifts, hobbies, social interaction, raising my family . . . ?'

What else might you add to that list to encompass the entirety of life?

His answer? [insert your name] 'Be holy'.

The consecration of objects, buildings or individuals for God's service can be accompanied by a special ceremony to mark the occasion. Perhaps this is something you'd like to do in response to what God's been growing in you this week. It can be formal or informal, alone or with a close friend. Its purpose is to simply affirm your decision to dedicate yourself again to God's holiness. A memorable and meaningful prompt for you to seek to remain committed to growing into God's holy likeness.

Prayerfully consider if, how and when you might like to dedicate yourself afresh to God.

Let's pray: Holy God, I hear your Father's loving call to be holy. I choose to commit myself to keeping in step with your holy nature, obeying your holy commands and opening my heart to your holy purpose to bring your love and life to this broken world. I know I'll never be perfect, but thank you for helping me grow increasingly into your holy likeness.

Dwell with this verse throughout your day, reflecting on how it continues to shape and inform your response.

DAY 1

'Be joyful in hope, patient in affliction, faithful in prayer.' Romans 12:12

Some readers will be facing tough challenges. You are on my heart as I pray these words onto the page, trusting God will use them to help, support and encourage you. Others may be anxious for what may await in the future, afraid of how you'd cope. Again, I trust this week will help you dismiss your fears, as you strengthen your resilience to problems through your life in Christ.

Resilience is the ability to cope and recover from setbacks, shock, difficulty, stress or any kind of hardship. While some may adopt unhealthy coping strategies, fall into despair or try to hide from the issue, pretending it didn't exist, resilient people are able to face the issue, remain calm and handle the situation with measured thought and response. There are character traits and skills we can learn to become more resilient, but it's a Christ-like quality too. And our dwelling place this week offers strategies to strengthen resilience to life's challenges based on the person of Jesus and the power and promises of God.

Whatever problems you're facing today and whatever you fear may happen in future, talk through your sadness, worries or disappointments with God.

Now thank him in faith for his promise to be with you, to help you overcome or endure the troubles of this world.

Dwell with these words from Paul through your day; they'll begin to infuse God's promised wellbeing to your heart, mind and soul.

DAY 2

'Be joyful in hope.' Romans 12:12

When facing hardship, it's natural to hope it will be over as soon as possible; resolution achieved, health restored, relationships healed. Our definition of hope in English, however, means the outcome we want is possible, but not guaranteed. Hope can therefore fluctuate between expectancy and doubt; a definition we need to be wary of when reading of hope in the Bible.

The Greek word translated *hope*, here and elsewhere, conveys absolute certainty. It doesn't refer to what may or may not happen; it's a confident expectation that something *will* happen because it's promised by God, based on his character and/or fulfilling his divine purpose. God is faithful, so when we put our hope in who he is, what he says and what he does, we can confidently expect it to happen, even if we don't know how or when. This is essential when we face life's difficulties and desperate tragedies.

What are you hoping for specifically in this season of hardship? Consider what you can be assured of from God's nature, power or promises to help you face, endure or overcome your problem.[1] Pray about it, seek God's insight on it, and as you proclaim it in faith, let the truth fill you with peace and assurance. If it would help, do talk with someone to discern promises in context that you can hold on to.

Dwell with all you can hope for in God through the rest of your day.

DAY 3

'Be joyful in hope.' Romans 12:12

Joy may be accompanied by feelings of happiness, but not always (reflect more on this in Week 18). Our hearts break for lost loved ones. We grieve relationship splits, redundancy or a poor health diagnosis. But joy is more than an emotion; it doesn't depend on circumstances, it's the deep-rooted experience of God's goodness with and within us. Joy is the 'fruit' of God's indwelling Spirit (Gal. 5:22), nurtured as we shift our focus away from our problem and onto God's infinite goodness. So, when Paul says, *be* joyful, he's saying, be intentional with your dependence on and belief for God's nature, power and promises, rather than allowing your difficulties to overwhelm or undermine your feelings, faith and perspective. Even in felt sorrow, as we lean into God's presence, we know the inward joy of his steadying, sustaining, calm poise and well-being.

You can't fake this kind of well-being; this inward joy of God. It grows as you put your hope in his faithfulness to who he is and what he has promised. It grows as you nurture your relationship with him.

Use what time you have to focus on God's presence with you. If you've a Scripture that you're finding helpful, allow God to minister it to your soul. Let the knowledge of his love and promises settle your heart and still your racing thoughts before you move on with your day.

Dwell with the hope you have in God and on his nature and promises that infuse your soul with joy.

DAY 4

'Be . . . patient in affliction.' Romans 12:12

It's natural to want an affliction resolved as soon as possible. But we endure with fortitude and serenity in the unwavering strength and peace we have from our hope in God.

Being joyful in hope nurtures patience in affliction. When we're confident in God's goodness and promises, we're encouraged to wait for him.[2] Instead of becoming fretful we are secure in who he is. But *patience* also implies that we remain constant in responding to challenges with grace, forgiveness, kindness, goodness etc., without letting hurt or fear control our reactions.

I was once publicly slandered. It was a deeply upsetting experience. A few days later while I was ironing, God's Spirit prompted a word to my heart: 'no weapon forged against you will prevail'. Not being familiar with the text I wasn't even sure it was in my Bible, but found the full promise in Isaiah 54:17. I was worshipping and pleading in tears when this nugget dropped into my being, but the peace and, in turn, the patience it inspired was phenomenal.

What is God saying to you from his Word about your situation? Thank him for it. Pray it and proclaim it. Your hope in its assurance will nurture both joy and patience as you wait for its fulfilment.

How does your problem challenge you to remain constant to God's character in your responses?

Dwell with your specific hope from God; it will settle your soul to wait patiently for how and when he'll respond.

DAY 5

'Be . . . faithful in prayer.' Romans 12:12

The word for be *faithful* is translated from the Greek meaning 'be devoted to'. I prefer the latter as it's imbued with the essence of developing relationship with God rather than completing a task of prayer we're obliged to do. To be *faithful in prayer* is to consistently devote ourselves to God's presence, no matter our circumstances.

It's in prayer that we're more aware of God's power infusing our being; we find release, peace and perspective as we offload our troubles and listen for his response. It's through prayer that we lean dependently on God's grace, wisdom and provision, and gain his strength to endure trouble. Prayer is communication but so much more; it's our connection to our spiritual power source. Jesus was afflicted with exile, jealousy, misunderstanding, threats to his life, ridicule, homelessness, false accusations, physical abuse and torture. But Jesus remained resilient because he was regularly in prayer.[3]

Are you praying? If not, be inspired to know it's God's precious gift, to help you be more aware of him through your day as you pray.

Are you praying but only telling God your problems and what you want him to do? Take time to listen for his response to your difficulties. But also take time to thank him for other things in your life; and to worship. It takes your mind off your problem and onto God's goodness, with and for you.

Dwell with this encouragement to receive God's help through prayer to endure this difficult season.

DAY 6

'Be . . . faithful in prayer' Romans 12:12

Growing resilience in prayer is best nurtured when we're not facing difficulty, so when hardship strikes, it's already an intrinsic part of life; it's already an ingrained response to be with God, to trust in him and receive what we need that we may know joy in hope and patience in affliction. But we devote ourselves to prayer in more ways than one.

To be faithful, i.e. devoted to God in prayer is, among other things:

- To love, delight in, thank and worship God; not just with others in church but also when you're alone.
- To pray for specific burdens God has put on your heart for individuals or local/national/global situations.
- To pray as the Holy Spirit leads you . . .[4]
- To listen to him and rest in his love.
- To pray for those who are hostile to you.
- To pray for church and country leaders.
- To pray the prayer Jesus taught his disciples.[5]
- To pray for other believers.
- To pray for the unsaved.
- To pray for someone who may have no one else praying for them but you.

Don't let this list of prayer needs burden you. The first four points are key. Be open to how God inspires *you* to devote yourself to prayer.

Dwell with the prayer God has nudged you with today, and how you can develop prayer to be an intrinsic part of your being.

DAY 7

'Be joyful in hope, patient in affliction, faithful in prayer.' Romans 12:12

Paul had written at length to the church in Rome covering many aspects of weighty doctrine and theology, but from chapter 12, he began to unpack its practical application.[6] Jesus Christ isn't just a name to be known, or the Son of God to be believed in. He's to be Lord of every area of life; including our seasons of difficulty.

Reflect on how God has been encouraging you this week to grow your resilience through the joy of knowing assured hope in him which nurtures patience in difficulty and is strengthened through devoted prayer. How will you adopt these things, going forward?

Prayerfully reflect on these Scriptures. Thank God for their promise of resilience as you trust in and depend on him for any difficulties you may face in the future:

- [Those who are committed to God] will have no fear of bad news; their hearts are steadfast, trusting in the LORD. (Ps. 112:7)
- Have no fear of sudden disaster or of the ruin that overtakes the wicked, for the LORD will be at your side and will keep your foot from being snared. (Prov. 3:25–26)

Let's pray: Loving, Almighty God, thank you for your promise to support, strengthen, guide and provide for me in life's problems. Your presence, your love and your Word to my soul are the assurance I need.

Continue to dwell with Paul's words through your day and let them infuse God's promised wellbeing to your heart, mind and soul.

DAY 1

'I have set before you life and death, blessings and curses.
Now choose life . . . For the LORD is your life.'
Deuteronomy 30:19–20

'We had been together for three-and-a-half years. Even I could hear the wedding bells close friends anticipated, and I would have willingly married him but for one thing. A niggle. An unsettled heart.

'I had come to faith and been baptised, but had lapsed in my commitment by the time he appeared in my life. Doting, loving, kind – he couldn't have been more different to my previous partner.

'When I later recommitted my heart to Jesus, I prayed and waited for my man to accept him too. He listened to my beliefs and came to a few Christian events. But Jesus wasn't for him . . . In my heart, I knew I couldn't marry a man who did not share my faith, even though I knew of some women who appeared to be happily married to non-Christians. Consequently, I had to make a choice: would I fully commit to the God who called me to love him with *all* my heart, or to someone who couldn't decide if God even existed?'[1]

I made the right choice, though sadly have made others I regret. But God continues to hold out his life and its inherent blessing. Whatever choices you've made, right or wrong, God loves you, is for you, and is here this week to inspire your choice for the blessings of his life, going forward.

Dwell with God's Word for you through your day.

DAY 2

'I have set before you life and death, blessings and curses.
Now choose life . . . For the LORD is your life.'
Deuteronomy 30:19–20

What does *life* bring to mind? Your physicality, relationships, jobs, roles and/or activities, perhaps. These certainly constitute biological life, but God also offers us *his* life; the same energised and abundant life of his divine nature that we see lived out in Jesus. God's life makes our physical, relational and active life in the world, rich, full and productive, just as he created it to be.[2]

Divine life isn't earned,[3] but while its inherent blessings are imparted into our spirit when we are saved, we experience them in increasing measure as we *choose* his life; as we yield to his inner promptings and teachings. It's our devoted response that increases the flow of his life-enriching blessings in and through us.

Deuteronomy is Moses' farewell message.[4] Unlike the straightforward laws and historical records of Leviticus and Numbers, Deuteronomy carries the warmth of Moses' heart. The future of God's people was theirs to choose but his love pervades the message to *choose life*. Choose *blessing*. Obedience isn't about trying to appease or earn favour from a stern, aloof, over-demanding divine authority. It's a response to God's loving invitation to live the intimate and abundant life he intended.

Reread Moses' words. Hear the tender urging of his tone, resonating with God's unreserved, unrelenting, immeasurable love for you.

Dwell with God's offer to help steer life-giving choices through your day.

DAY 3

'I have set before you life and death, blessings and curses.
Now choose life . . . For the LORD is your life.'
Deuteronomy 30:19–20

We choose life as we love God. We love God as we 'listen' to him and 'hold fast' (Deut. 30:20) to him. And we learn how to love, listen and hold fast to God from his living Word.

'Take to heart all the words I have solemnly declared to you this day,' Moses concluded. 'They are not just idle words for you – they are your life' (Deut. 32:46–47). We listen to God through prayerful reading of his Word, letting it inform our thinking, perspective and the way we live. And we hold fast to God as we live out his life-giving Word; as we devote ourselves to delighting, affirming and honouring him.

How has God's Word proven to be life-giving for you?

Daily, he offers his life-giving words to nourish and grow our relationship with him and to transform us into his likeness. As we read Scripture, we 'hear' his voice; it's one of the fundamental ways we can listen to him. Isn't that awesome? Inspiring too, I hope! Where might you turn in your Bible to listen to and learn how to love him today?

Is there someone you can share God's life-giving Word with who can't afford a Bible, or an organisation you can support that donates it, or translates it into languages of people who've yet to hear it?[5]

Dwell with God's offer to help steer life-giving choices through your day.

DAY 4

'I have set before you life and death, blessings and curses.
Now choose life . . . For the LORD is your life.'
Deuteronomy 30:19–20

If we firmly believe that choosing God's life with its inherent blessings of peace, contentment, enabling, wisdom, etc. is the best decision to make, you'd think it would be easy. A cinch, a breeze! In fact, why wouldn't we when God's life is our very best thing?[6] But knowing and believing something is or isn't good for us doesn't mean we do or don't do it. (I know coffee cake with lashings of buttercream icing isn't good for me, but . . . !) Appetites and emotions are powerful forces undermining our desire to choose God's life, but we can learn to pause. To take a breath.

> Stand at the crossroads and look;
> ask for the ancient paths, ask where the good way is, and walk in it,
> and you will find rest for your souls.
>
> *Jer. 6:16*

Identify the different roads you could choose and where they lead. Will your choice lead to guilt, shame, disharmony, hurt, pride, self-effort, stinginess . . . etc? Will it promote good health? Will it convey God's love and encouragement to others?

In the heat of the moment, take a deep breath to hold back a reactive choice. Consider your options as you remind yourself to *choose life*, and in turn, rest for your soul.

Practise this by picturing yourself in a scenario where you've struggled to make the right choice previously.

Dwell with God's offer to steer life-giving choices through your day.

DAY 5

*'I have set before you life and death, blessings and curses.
Now choose life . . . For the LORD is your life.'*
Deuteronomy 30:19–20

Deep down, I really do want to choose God's life. I'm sure you do too. Yet so often I slip up. Perhaps you can relate. Other things wheedle their way into our thoughts and feelings, influencing our decision-making process. A choice to boost, protect or justify our reputation, for example, rather than affirm someone else; especially someone we envy or who's hurt us.

We will never be perfect, but following on from yesterday, it helps to write down the false, fickle, fleeting or fallible reward of a choice, and compare it to God's blessing if we choose his life instead; a visual reminder that's etched into our being through the physicality of writing. Prayerfully consider, and if possible, write down, the habits or temptations you repeatedly choose instead of God's way of life. What might God's life, flourishing in and through you, look like instead if you chose his way?

I'm fallible. I guess you are too. I'm a long way from God's perfect life, but he meets us where we're at, picks us up when we've slipped, and re-energises our desire by his constant loving encouragement to *choose life*. 'Choose life [insert your name]', 'take hold of the life that is truly life . . . ' (1 Tim. 6:19). Choose between immersing yourself in a deeper encounter of God's life or remain paddling in the shallows.

Dwell with God's offer to help steer life-giving choices through your day.

DAY 6

'I have set before you life and death, blessings and curses.
Now choose life . . . For the LORD is your life.'
Deuteronomy 30:19–20

You may have been dwelling this week with a pit in your stomach; afraid that your wrong choice last month, last year, or a long time ago has estranged you from God's favour. Not so. God knew his people wouldn't always choose his way and would reap the consequences. God is just; as he is faithful to his promises, he is faithful to his judgements. But God also promised that if they turned back to him, he would show them compassion; he would gather them again to himself and restore his blessings.[7]

You can't undo past choices, but you can choose to live differently from now on. Your story isn't over, you've new chapters to write. God promises to forgive the sincere, repentant soul. Receive his forgiveness. Believe for his blessings of peace, purpose and provision for all he has envisioned for you. Be mindful of God's presence with you. Pour out any unconfessed regret or your struggles to forgive yourself.

Speak out the words: 'I choose life; your life. I choose blessing; your promised blessing. I choose you, loving Father.' Now rest with him quietly in the stillness of your time of prayer, and, as you continue with your day. Rest in his immense love and life for you.

Dwell with God's offer to help steer life-giving choices through your day.

DAY 7

'I have set before you life and death, blessings and curses.
Now choose life . . . For the LORD is your life.'
Deuteronomy 30:19–20

We might not be able to control what happens *to* us, but we can control our choice in how we react or respond. Sometimes we'll make right choices; sometimes, wilfully or unwittingly, we won't. But choices are important because they determine who we're becoming, and therefore, our future.

As our week draws to a close, bring to mind or turn to the story of Zacchaeus (Luke 19:1–10). Here's a man who made lots of bad choices but Jesus called out to him, spent time with him and forgave him. Being in Jesus' presence transformed his outlook and Zacchaeus chose a very different life from that day on. Jesus invites you to do that too.

Imagine yourself in the story. As it begins, how are you feeling about your past or current choices? What do you hope for in or from Jesus? What do you talk with Jesus about in the privacy of your home? How does Jesus make you feel? How are you inspired to make new life-giving choices from now on? Talk with God about these things.

Let's pray: Thank you, loving Father, that your relentless love and goodness pursue me, even when I turn my back on your ways. I do desire your promised life. Envision and inspire me with how Jesus lived as I seek to choose *life* today.

Dwell with God's offer to help steer life-giving choices through your day.

DAY 1

'One thing I ask from the LORD, this only do I seek: that
I may dwell in the house of the LORD all the days of my life,
to gaze on the beauty of the LORD and to seek him in his temple.'
Psalm 27:4

What are your deepest desires? Your persistent longings? What do you really want? Be honest with yourself and with God, as it will help you discern his voice this week. Whether your longings relate to work, home, faith, relationships, or anything else, jot them all down.

Now take a look at your list. How would you prioritise your desires, even if it's just a top three? What wins the number one spot? What's your *one thing*?

David wrote Psalm 27.[1] Born into obscurity as the youngest of ten, he became a skilled shepherd, slinger, poet, harpist and warrior of war. After more than six years as a fugitive he then became king of a kingdom that God promised would last forever, fulfilled in the eternal throne of Christ. David wasn't perfect, with lying, adultery and murder among his faults. But his deep longing is a precious place to dwell with this week.

Read his prayer again – slowly. Let the rich imagery of his words paint a picture of the man, whose most important biography was described by God himself, as 'a man after my own heart' (1 Sam. 13:14; see also Acts 13:22).

Dwell with David's prayer through the rest of your day; steep yourself in his deepest desire and what God, in turn, may reveal to you.

DAY 2

'One thing I ask from the LORD, this only do I seek: that
I may dwell in the house of the LORD all the days of my life,
to gaze on the beauty of the LORD and to seek him in his temple.'
Psalm 27:4

One thing . . . this only . . .

Have you ever wondered why? Why did David yearn for God's presence? Why was his deepest desire and singleness of purpose to dwell with God 'all the days of [his] life'?

David a) believed in God's close care he lacked nothing,[2] b) knew God as the very best thing in his life,[3] c) believed God was his source of life, in whose presence, he could feast and drink deep of his blessings,[4] d) knew God as his refuge, shelter and safe place.[5] Of course, David experienced happiness in others ways too, but e) he knew that abundant, unending fullness of joy was only found with God.[6] David's deep yet practical, meaningful understanding of God explains why God's presence was the one thing he yearned for. Reading through that explanation I can't help but think it's so natural we should long for God too.

Reflect on each of these points that describe David's understanding of God.

How do these truths inspire your own longing to be more present to God's presence too?

Dwell with David's prayer through the rest of your day; steep yourself in his deepest desire and what God, in turn, may reveal to you.

DAY 3

*'One thing I ask from the LORD, this only do I seek: that
I may dwell in the house of the LORD all the days of my life,
to gaze on the beauty of the LORD and to seek him in his temple.'*
Psalm 27:4

. . . dwell . . .

To dwell is to remain with, settle into and be at home with – God's presence. The heart of this book! Mull on this idea for a few moments to warm your heart's yearning for God too.

The house of the Lord was, for David, the tabernacle. But David was also one of few Old Testament characters anointed with God's Spirit;[7] his personal experience of God's presence nurtured his thirst for heightened awareness of it. But perhaps you find yourself dwelling on anything but God. Me too. On a problem or worrying concern. On which choice to make, on critical remarks or looming exams and deadlines. On a loved one, a job opportunity, holiday plans – or what's for dinner! Many things can consume our attention. But David's longing to be at home with and preoccupied with God's presence encourages us to heighten our awareness of God's presence too. Dwelling on Scripture helps, as does keeping up prayerful conversation and a listening ear through the day.

Dwell with David's prayer through the rest of your day; steep yourself in his deepest desire and what God, in turn, may reveal to you.

DAY 4

*'One thing I ask from the LORD, this only do I seek: that
I may dwell in the house of the LORD all the days of my life,
to gaze on the beauty of the LORD and to seek him in his temple.'
Psalm 27:4*

. . . all the days of my life . . .

Whether I'm struggling to clarify my thoughts on the page, feeling tense about pressing deadlines, nervously standing to preach, cleaning the house, caught up in traffic, buying in food, playing with my grandchildren or relaxing with friends . . . I love how this prayer shifts my focus onto God with me – and in turn, my response to his presence.

God doesn't come and go. He is permanently present by his Spirit.[8] But perhaps you find it easier to focus on him in times of personal prayer, Bible reading, or when gathered for corporate worship. Perhaps you seek his presence more when needing wisdom and inspiration to teach, lead, counsel or pray with a group or individual. Or maybe you're more inclined to seek him when you're struggling with a problem. Either way, as you immerse yourself in David's understanding of God (see Day 2), it will inspire your own longing for his presence, 'all the days of [your] life' – every moment of your day. And remember, praying this prayer through your day will heighten your ongoing awareness of God too.

Dwell with David's prayer through the rest of your day; steep yourself in his deepest desire and what God, in turn, may reveal to you.

DAY 5

'One thing I ask from the LORD, this only do I seek: that
I may dwell in the house of the LORD all the days of my life,
to gaze on the beauty of the LORD and to seek him in his temple.'
Psalm 27:4

. . . to gaze . . .

I love this word for the way it speaks of love, warmth and appreciation. To gaze is so much more than a glance. A gaze focuses our attention on what we love and admire.

. . . on the beauty of the LORD . . .

David delighted to gaze with his eye of faith on the beauty of God's character, to wonder at his holiness, righteousness and justice, and marvel on the magnificence and loveliness of all he is. Introspection or self-pity feeds doubt, anxiety, fear or negativity. But gazing on God through the moments of our day calls forth a response. It steadies emotions and slows racing thoughts as heart and mind appreciate who God is: the reassurance of his peace easing tension and stress; his grace diffusing our hurt or angry reactions; his wisdom enhancing our response, so that in turn, our life reflects his beauty – the beauty of a soul content in God.

Give time to gaze on God in worship, but also in snatched moments through your day. To ponder, praise and be nurtured by the beauty of his ways.

Dwell with David's prayer through the rest of your day; steep yourself in his deepest desire and what God, in turn, may reveal to you.

DAY 6

'One thing I ask from the LORD, this only do I seek: that
I may dwell in the house of the LORD all the days of my life,
to gaze on the beauty of the LORD and to seek him in his temple.'
Psalm 27:4

. . . this only do I seek . . . to seek him . . .

David's longing for God's presence wasn't purely for himself; it was to seek God's will and purpose. David was intentional in seeking to determine what it was; he didn't passively assume it or rely on his own understanding.

To seek God's face – his countenance – is to seek to discern where his attention is focused, and in turn, his intentions. David treasured God's purposes more than his own goals or other people's expectations, for David knew God's purpose was his very best thing to pursue.

To desire intimate communion with God involves discerning how his story is unfolding so we can join in and walk in step with him. It's our heart's devoted response to who he is. Worship isn't just adoring God in words but offering ourselves as disciples to discern and fulfil his purposes.[9]

What is it that you seek: more *from* God or more *of* God? Or both?

Take time to talk with God about how your heart is being prompted, but also pause to simply be; and enjoy his love for *you*.

Dwell with David's prayer through the rest of your day; steep yourself in his deepest desire and what God, in turn, may reveal to you.

DAY 7

'One thing I ask from the LORD, this only do I seek: that
I may dwell in the house of the LORD all the days of my life,
to gaze on the beauty of the LORD and to seek him in his temple.'
Psalm 27:4

Recall your list from Day 1. What shapes your decisions, or inspires you to keep pressing forward for its fulfilment? What do you passionately pray for? Some or all of your answers will be good and God-given dreams. Thank him now for how he's envisioned and equipped you to be and to do. But see your answers in the light of your one good thing as you linger in prayerful awareness of God's presence.

God made you to *know him*: You may not always feel his presence but he *is* with you. He loves and delights in you. He is for you.

God made you to be *known by him*: You are accepted. Forgiven. Loved. Valued. Treasured. Gifted. Understood. Appreciated. Receive these truths deep into your being.

God created you to *reflect* his love and your love for him to others, in whatever your hands find to do.

Let's pray: Thank you, Father God, for your unfailing love for me. Thank you, Jesus, for restoring me into relationship with God. Thank you, Holy Spirit, for imparting God's divine life in and through me. There is no thing I long for more.

Dwell with David's prayer through the rest of your day; steep yourself in his deepest desire and what God, in turn, may reveal to you.

DAY 1

'Rabboni!' John 20:16b

Easter Sunday fills many hearts and mouths with joy and vibrant praise that Jesus is alive; a celebration we can, in theory, enjoy every day. Sometimes, however, our experience may feel more in tune with the opening scene of the first Easter morning; one of sorrow and confusion. Jesus is alive today, but do I know it?

This week, we're going to dwell with Mary outside the empty tomb. Familiarise yourself with John 20:1–18. Read it slowly. Picture the scene. What do you see, hear and feel? Ask God to help you discern how he wants to reveal himself afresh to you through it.

Imagine the early morning light, the circular stone, the dark tomb, the stained linen cloths. What else can you see?

Hear the birds, footsteps, your own sobbing. What else do you hear?

Picture Mary as the scene progresses, hear Jesus call out her name, feel her changing emotions as you read.

Read the story twice if you're able, letting the scene fill your heart and mind.

In what ways does it resonate?

The word *Rabboni* means: 'My Master' or 'My Teacher'.

What do the implications of those words say to you personally? How do they inspire or challenge you? Is God revealing anything new about himself, about you, about your relationship with and response to him?

Dwell on this word in your mind and heart through your day. Mull on it, pray it, proclaim it. Remain open and responsive to how its truth and implications may shape your feelings and perspective.

DAY 2

'Rabboni!' John 20:16b

I was brought up in a non-believing home. When I received Jesus into my life in my teens, my atheist father ripped apart my foundling faith with his considered arguments. Consequently, doubts about my beliefs often hounded me; doubts which at times cooled my heart towards God and created a felt distance from him. I've also been blind to his presence when I've been side-tracked by the world's pleasures instead of pursuing God's spiritual blessings. I've let mounting problems blinker my perspective on life while neglecting his comforting presence. And at times, I've let my personal dreams distract me from yielding to his lead.

Picture yourself again outside the empty tomb. Be aware of and take note of your feelings.

Do you feel abandoned in your doubts, loss, loneliness or confusion?

Are you distracted from the reality of God's presence by the tangible world you inhabit?

What is your uppermost heart's desire?

What's the source or motivation of the dreams you pursue?

Now turn your attention onto Jesus with you. Hear him say your name with loving affection.

Hear him say it again . . . Does that change your feelings or perspective in any way? Accept and embrace his presence in faith; let him enrich your soul.

Dwell on this word in your mind and heart through your day. Mull on it, pray it, proclaim it. Remain open and responsive to how its truth and implications may shape your feelings and perspective.

DAY 3

'Rabboni!' John 20:16b

I've mentioned elsewhere how my brother struggled with alcohol addiction for more than twenty years, within which there were 'dry' periods and seasons of drunken stupor. There were times when he was content in pursuing his passions, but others when this gifted, fun-filled man we so loved was overcome by alcoholism. And tragically, aged 43, the years of abuse took their toll.

We often knew the comfort of Christ's presence, but sometimes, the devastating reality hit hard; a pain-wrecked reality that many of you can no doubt describe in countless ways. A felt reality that can numb our awareness of Jesus with us.

Picture yourself once again outside the empty tomb. Be aware of and take note of your feelings.

Mary was unable to recognise Jesus through her tears. Focused on her felt reality, she'd turned her back on him, preoccupied with the cold, empty slab where she'd previously known him to be. What might be your 'cold empty slab', blinding you to his presence; consuming your thoughts and feelings? Jesus wants to reveal himself to you. Be still, and know him with you in faith, even though you may not 'see' or 'feel' him. Jesus *is* alive. Jesus *is* with you. Let this reality reignite faith in his living presence as you focus your whole being on what is truly true.

Dwell on this word in your mind and heart through your day. Mull on it, pray it, proclaim it. Remain open and responsive to how its truth and implications may shape your feelings and perspective.

DAY 4

'Rabboni!' John 20:16b

Whether faith in or awareness of God has been undermined by doubts, pleasures or problems, it has been during these seasons that God's presence has felt far from me, rather than being at home in my heart. When my faith has been restricted to head belief instead of infusing my daily experience.

Reflecting on this passage, however, revives my passionate response, reconnecting my head belief with my heart and soul. It can even bring me to tears on my knees, as I reaffirm that Jesus – truly alive – is with me and for me. As you dwell with the image of Jesus raised from the dead, it will reassure you of his presence too.

Picture yourself again outside the empty tomb. Be aware of and take note of your feelings, then turn your attention onto Jesus with you.

Rabboni! My Master. My Teacher.

When Mary recognised Jesus, she exclaimed, 'Rabboni!', rich with the depth of feeling one has when reunited with someone who means so much to us.

Which word, name or description of Jesus, comes to mind as you're reminded that Jesus is with you right now, in this moment? Say it silently. Whisper it. Repeat it as often as the overflow of your heart delights to do. But also speak out your reassurance of his presence, to encourage yourself in God's truth.

Dwell on this word in your mind and heart through your day. Mull on it, pray it, proclaim it. Remain open and responsive to how its truth and implications may shape your feelings and perspective.

DAY 5

'Rabboni!' John 20:16b

In the days following his resurrection, Jesus wasn't always immediately recognised. When turning around to see a man standing behind her, Mary thought he was the gardener.[1] When Jesus joined two of his followers walking the road to Emmaus, they didn't realise who it was until much later when he broke bread in their home.[2] And when seven disciples went fishing and a man stood on the shore, the disciples didn't initially realise it was Jesus.[3] Distraught in her despair, immersed in their discussion, and distracted by their old way of life, neither Mary nor the disciples immediately recognised the answer to their grief, confusion and insecurity, standing right there with them.

Picture yourself once again outside the empty tomb but with Jesus beside you. Be aware of and take note of your feelings.

Have you been depending on God to do something, reveal something, or provide something with, as yet, no discernible response? Perhaps Jesus is speaking or revealing his answer to you, but in an unexpected way. Be honest and open in prayer about your feelings and thoughts, as you reach out again for the living Lord Jesus with you. Still your soul as you open your heart to how God may speak or reveal himself to you.

Respond with worship as your heart leads.

Dwell on this word in your mind and heart through your day. Mull on it, pray it, proclaim it. Remain open and responsive to how its truth and implications may shape your feelings and perspective.

DAY 6

'Rabboni!' John 20:16b

When Mary saw and believed that the man standing before her was Jesus, alive having been dead, she evidently ran to embrace him, for Jesus said, 'Do not hold on to me' (John 20:17a). Quite naturally, Mary didn't want to lose him again, but Jesus had to reveal himself to others then ascend to God in heaven so that his presence with her would remain permanently through the coming of the Holy Spirit. Embrace this truth that is yours today: You will never lose Jesus. He is with you always through God's indwelling Spirit.

Picture yourself once again outside the empty tomb but with Jesus beside you. Be aware of and take note of your feelings.

Rest in his presence. Relish this moment of intimate reunion. Don't rush away to your next task.

Keep yourself turned towards him and not away from him. Enjoy being in the living presence of Jesus Christ.

Love and be loved through simple companionship. Enjoy silence or speak out your worship.

In whatever way you feel drawn or inspired, relish his presence with you.

If it helps, you might like to listen to or sing along to the song, 'To Be in Your Presence' by Noel Richards.[4]

Dwell on this word in your mind and heart through your day. Mull on it, pray it, proclaim it. Remain open and responsive to how its truth and implications may shape your feelings and perspective.

DAY 7

'Rabboni!' John 20:16b

Read the story again as you did on Day 1: John 20:1–18. Read it slowly. Picture the scene. What do you see, hear or feel? Has your response changed in any way, compared to your initial reflections? Remind yourself how God has been speaking or revealing himself to you this week.

How could you maintain your revived awareness of the risen Jesus, alive and present with you, from now on? It's time to allow any thoughts or good intentions to shape your inner being and outward actions. Consider the following questions to encourage the faith, excitement and gratitude aroused this week, and the yielding and rededication inspired.

How might Jesus alive with you:

- Change your perspective on work, goals, feelings or problems? Write it out so you can easily refer back to it.
- Influence your use of time and resources? Make a note of the steps you now need to take.
- Mould your responses to others? Write these down too as a future reminder.

Join me now in prayer: Lord Jesus, thank you for revealing your presence afresh to my soul this week, filling my heart and mind with the truth of your resurrected life. I choose to open the eyes of my heart daily, to know you are with me always, no matter how I feel or what I'm doing. Amen.

Dwell on this word in your mind and heart through your day. Mull on it, pray it, proclaim it. Remain open and responsive to how its truth and implications may shape your feelings and perspective.

DAY 1

'They could find no corruption in him, because he was trustworthy and neither corrupt nor negligent.' Daniel 6:4b

Babylon. The great nation that humbled Israel, hauling thousands of captives into exile, had itself been conquered by the Persians. Darius, the new ruler of this part of the vast Persian empire, pinpointed his first priority: overhaul Babylon's governance by appointing 120 rulers with three overseers; one of whom was the exiled Israelite, Daniel. Daniel so excelled at his job that Darius planned to set him as chief administrator over the kingdom. You guessed it, the others fumed behind closed curtains. Nursing their deflated egos, they searched for a charge to bring against the young man but were unable to, 'because he was trustworthy and neither corrupt nor negligent' (Dan. 6:1–4). Daniel was a role model of godly integrity.

I researched many definitions of integrity but this verse provides the best of descriptions:

Trustworthy: People could depend on Daniel to do what he'd said he would do. He was truthful and reliable.

Not corrupt: Daniel lived a good, decent, principled life. He was authentic both in public and in private, honest and sincere in his dealings with others. There was no hypocrisy or duplicity about him.

Not negligent: In all aspects of life, work and worship, Daniel was conscientious; not careless, half-hearted, flippant, apathetic or disinterested.

Dwell with these ideas and images of integrity through your day, being open to how God's Spirit may begin to speak to your heart.

DAY 2

'They could find no corruption in him, because he was trustworthy and neither corrupt nor negligent.' Daniel 6:4b

Integrity is valued and admired; a character trait we hope for in others and perhaps, even expect. Integrity is also intrinsic to becoming more like Jesus, who himself was acknowledged and admired as a man of integrity, even by those who were hostile to him.[1]

Integrity ensures we remain true to God's nature in private as well as in public. Integrity is beneficial. It guides and nurtures good, upright, decent, godly living. It invites God's help and blessing.[2] And integrity grows confidence. Instead of worrying that our shortcomings will be exposed, or damage ourselves or others, integrity nurtures peace and assurance in who we are and what we do. But integrity, like all Christ-like characteristics, isn't a given.

How, in any of these situations, have you recently compromised your integrity:

- In private;
- With someone you love, trust and/or a good friend;
- At work;
- Among people who don't yet know Jesus personally;
- In social or interest groups;
- Among believers;
- . . . ?

How did compromising your integrity make you feel in the moment, or afterward?

What were the potential consequences to yourself, to someone else and to God's honour?

Are there certain people or situations with whom or in which you find it harder to uphold your integrity than others?

Talk with God about anything that comes to mind and listen for any response.

Dwell with this verse through your day to strengthen your resolve to be a person of godly integrity.

DAY 3

'They could find no corruption in him, because he was trustworthy and neither corrupt nor negligent.' Daniel 6:4b

Daniel was a teenager when King Nebuchadnezzar ransacked Jerusalem, exiled him to Babylon and chose him to be specially educated to serve his captor.[3] When King Darius reigned, however, Daniel was elderly, having served Babylon's king for roughly sixty-five years. And yet, his opponents failed to dredge up any charge against him.[4]

A key to his unstinting integrity is found in chapter one where Daniel 'resolved not to defile himself' (Dan. 1:8). Initially, he chose not to share the king's food, perhaps to protect himself from eating 'unclean' meat.[5] But there's another key reason. Sharing the king's meal signified allegiance to him. Daniel's decision proved his resolve to remain loyal to God. But Daniel was no more perfect than you or I. For his integrity to remain intact all those years, suggests he kept renewing his resolve throughout his life.

Bring to mind one thing that threatens your integrity; a particular temptation to compromise God's ways. Just for today, resolve to yourself and to God that you won't give in to it. Tomorrow, make that resolve again. And the next day . . .

If you resolve to *never* give into it again, the likelihood is you will; it can be self-defeating. But *today* is possible. So, make that resolve – for today. Then prayerfully recommit your resolve, day-by-day, going forward.

Dwell with this verse through your day to strengthen your resolve to be a person of godly integrity.

DAY 4

'They could find no corruption in him, because he was trustworthy and neither corrupt nor negligent.' Daniel 6:4b

Daniel prioritised focused prayer and thanksgiving three times a day, every day.[6] Prayer keeps us mindful of God's holy presence, it humbles our ego and inspires loving submission. Giving thanks to God strengthens our appreciation of and dependency on him. Prayer deepens our relationship through adoration, conversation and the flow of God's blessings, wisdom and fortitude. Regular prayer helped maintain Daniel's integrity and it will strengthen our resolve too.

Even if time is limited, the principle of Daniel's daily habit remains useful. We can pause, momentarily, three times a day, to focus on God, thank him for something, then repeat our resolve to remain true to his presence. When temptation comes to compromise or abandon God's nature and ways, our regular prayerful connection with him *will* strengthen our resolve to stay true.

Here's some ideas on how to adopt this practice:

- When you wake before getting out of bed, and on your commute to and from work.
- While feeding your baby.
- By setting an alarm for three different times in the day.
- As part of your prayer of thanks before breakfast, lunch and dinner.
- When you put on the kettle to brew a cuppa or wait at a vending machine.
- What other three times in your routines would dovetail with this practice of pausing to pray?

Dwell with this verse through your day to strengthen your resolve to be a person of godly integrity.

DAY 5

'They could find no corruption in him, because he was trustworthy and neither corrupt nor negligent.' Daniel 6:4b

Soon after Daniel's death, the Israelites were allowed to return home to rebuild God's temple in Jerusalem. Their initial work, however, stalled for a possible fourteen to twenty years;[7] partly in fear of enemy threats, but also through prioritising their own projects. Enter prophet Haggai, sent by God to arouse them from their lethargy. 'Give careful thought to your ways,' he repeated (Hag. 1:5,7) – i.e. consider in all honesty whether you've gained anything by seeking to please and protect yourself instead of being faithful to God. Look at what you've failed to produce, despite working so hard at doing your own thing.[8]

Our integrity will constantly be challenged in subtle or blatant ways, and God poses a challenging question through Haggai: Who am I *really* serving in the way I live, work and worship? Is my professed submission to God authentic through-and-through, or am I giving into fears of what people say and think, or pursuing my own agenda, reputation, comfort, satisfaction, praise . . . ?

Ask God to show you the true motives of your heart. This isn't an exercise to condemn, but to inspire authenticity, strengthen your integrity and to help you experience the blessing of living in step with God's ways (see Day 2).

Dwell with this verse through your day to strengthen your resolve to be a person of godly integrity.

DAY 6

'They could find no corruption in him, because he was trustworthy and neither corrupt nor negligent.' Daniel 6:4b

'Do as I say, not as I do!' says the parent warning their child not to copy their lapsed behaviour. What we say and the manner of our conduct *does* influence others, especially if they love, like or respect us.

As we uphold godly integrity, we reflect God's nature. True, we'll often fall short, but it's an ongoing process as we resolve to keep choosing his ways. We can say we believe in God, but it's how we live that affirms who he is and why we're convinced that our devoted response to him is the very best thing we can be and do.

Bring to mind all the people you relate or interact with:

- As a parent, child, sibling or spouse.
- As an employer, employee or colleague.
- As a friend and neighbour.
- When you're out and about at the bank, garage, dentist, doctor or shopping, etc.
- Those who serve you at home; those who deliver the post, refuse collectors, plumbers, etc.
- At the hairdresser, café, restaurant, sport event, party, pub, etc.
- At church events and gatherings.
- On your social media platforms.
- While walking the dog or out for a run.
- Who else comes to mind?

Pray for those on your heart today. Pray for yourself too, that as you yield to God's ways, the Holy Spirit would open their hearts to his presence.

Dwell with this verse through your day to strengthen your resolve to be a person of godly integrity.

DAY 7

'They could find no corruption in him, because he was trustworthy and neither corrupt nor negligent.' Daniel 6:4b

'For God's presence to be in attendance, it has to be genuine all the way to the core.'[9]

Genuine all the way to the core is a great image of integrity; being true to what we say we believe and being true to God's nature and ways.

> So don't lose a minute in building on what you've been given, complementing your basic faith with good character, spiritual understanding, alert discipline, passionate patience, reverent wonder, warm friendliness, and generous love, each dimension fitting into and developing the others. With these qualities active and growing in your lives, no grass will grow under your feet, no day will pass without its reward as you mature in your experience of our Master Jesus.
>
> *2 Pet. 1:5–8*, MSG

How does this passage further inspire you to adopt godly integrity, that you may 'mature in your experience' of Jesus?

Let's pray: Loving Father, what an awesome truth that your divine power has given me everything I need for a godly life of integrity. Thank you for revealing yourself to me and helping me to know your presence and goodness in prayer. Thank you for your promises that enable me to engage with your divine life.[10] I resolve to remain true to them that I may grow increasingly into the likeness of your Son, Jesus.

Dwell with this verse for one more day, to strengthen your resolve to be a person of godly integrity.

DAY 1

'Dear children, let us not love with words or speech but with actions and in truth.' 1 John 3:18

Bombay, 1992. Skinny, grubby children in ripped clothes grabbed our hands. By day they scavenged the streets for food and rifled through mountainous rubbish heaps. They drank dirty river water and slept huddled, if they were lucky, beneath shop porches or sheets of cardboard. Their bright white eyes and beautiful smiles were easy prey for prostitution pimps and slave-labour traffickers.

We never grew accustomed to the constant stream of beggars – young and old, tugging on sleeves for rupees – but the short time I spent on mission in India transformed my perspective on wealth and possessions forever. There are still certain shops that I'd struggle to enter; such was the impact of ministering among India's poorest of poor. And yet . . . Oh, how I wish I didn't have to write this – and yet, how easily I sit with the comparative wealth of my privileged life. I may not have as much as some, but I do have much more than so many; so much more than I need myself which I can therefore share with others.

John precedes our verse,[1] saying, 'If anyone has material possessions and sees a brother or sister in need but has no pity on them, how can the love of God be in that person?' (1 John 3:17). But God's loving, compassionate, all-seeing heart now beats in you and in me.

Dwell with this verse through your day as it sinks into your soul.

DAY 2

'Dear children, let us not love with words or speech but with actions and in truth.' 1 John 3:18

It was one of those rare occasions when my husband and I could go out for dinner while Fiona[2] babysat our daughter. I'm sure we enjoyed our evening, though I've no memory of it. What I *do* remember and will never forget is what happened when we returned.

Fiona appeared from the bathroom, her cheeks rosy and eyes unusually strained, carrying wet sheets. Evidently, after going to bed, our daughter had vomited. Everywhere! These were the days before mobile phones. Fiona had the restaurant number but wanted to bless us with the timeout she knew we needed, so cared for our daughter as attentively as we'd have; now fast asleep in fresh, dry sheets, her body at peace. Fiona so touched my heart with her care for my needy daughter that I share it thirty years later as a glimpse of how we delight God's fatherly heart when we care for his children who need our help.

Recall how you've felt when someone has helped your child, a loved one or cherished friend. Alternatively, place yourself in my story; feel my relief, reassurance and gratitude on knowing my little girl had received the loving help, comfort and care she needed. Sit with these feelings as they inform and inspire your response to God's fatherly heart for his needy children.

Dwell with how love in action is your natural response of knowing God's love for you.

DAY 3

'Dear children, let us not love with words or speech but with actions and in truth.' 1 John 3:18

Helping the needy demonstrates our love for God as we love others as ourselves.[3] Jesus said:

> I was hungry and you gave me something to eat, I was thirsty and you gave me something to drink, I was a stranger and you invited me in, I needed clothes and you clothed me, I was ill and you looked after me, I was in prison and you came to visit me ... whatever you did for one of the least of these brothers and sisters of mine, you did for me.
>
> *Matt. 25:35–36,40*

Some readers may have time or money to support organisations who help others in need. All of us, however, can seek to make a difference for one person. Then another. And another . . . Here's a few simple ideas:

Give one or two items into the foodbank each week, buy a drink or sandwich for someone living on the streets, prepare a meal for a family struggling financially.

Befriend and support an isolated neighbour or refugee living nearby.

Give clothing to reputable charities, or a sleeping bag, new underwear, hats and gloves to the homeless.

Volunteer as a visitor in hospital chaplaincy teams, collect groceries, prescriptions or make meals for someone too unwell to go out.

Be a pen pal for a prisoner[4] or volunteer to help at prisoner visiting times.

How else might God inspire your response to his heart as you dwell with love in action through your day?

DAY 4

'Dear children, let us not love with words or speech but with actions and in truth.' 1 John 3:18

When John the Baptist preached his message of repentance, he said, 'Anyone who has two shirts should share with the one who has none, and anyone who has food should do the same' (Luke 3:11). Repentance isn't merely a quiet private prayer; it's practically worked out as we align our lives to God's heart for the needy. No one, John suggested, could be content with too much while others struggle with too little.

We can't easily give away our excess food with a short shelf-life, but we can become more mindful in buying only what we need, releasing money, for example, to buy one or two weekly items for a food bank. We can check how many items of clothing we needlessly have, donating any excess to an individual or a charity, and decide from now on not to buy clothes that we don't actually *need*; releasing funds to help someone who can't afford the basics. The principle applies elsewhere. We need technology to engage with contemporary society, but let's be aware of what's merely added convenience, or sitting in a kitchen cupboard unused.

Prayerfully take a tour around your home, assessing what fills its walls, shelves, drawers, wardrobes and cupboards, remaining present to God's presence with you.

Talk with God about what stirs you. Listen for his response and let his love inspire you to action.

Dwell with how you can love God today as you practically love others in need.

DAY 5

'Dear children, let us not love with words or speech but with actions and in truth.' 1 John 3:18

Today we're going to seek to encounter God in his Word through the practice of Lectio Divina. Follow through the guidelines as you prayerfully reflect and respond to this selection of phrases taken from the parable of the good Samaritan.[5]

1. Slow your breathing, still your heart and mind and focus on God with you. Then pray: 'Lord, please meet with me through your teaching about how to be a good neighbour and speak your word into my life.'
2. Read through the parable, summarised below, or in full if you've time.

> He asked Jesus, 'Who is my neighbour?'
> Jesus said, 'A man was attacked by robbers. They stripped him of his clothes, beat him and went away, leaving him half-dead.
> A priest and a Levite passed by on the other side.
> But a Samaritan took pity on him.
> He bandaged his wounds and brought him to an inn and took care of him.
> Which of these was a neighbour?'
> 'The one who had mercy on him.'
> 'Go and do likewise.'

3. Read it again, slowly; chewing on each phrase, mindful of thoughts or feelings arising. What particularly stands out?
4. Talk with God about the word or phrase that's specifically resonates. Reflect on how you'll respond.
5. Rest in mindful awareness of God's presence.

Dwell with how God has met with you in his Word to inspire you in loving the needy in action.

DAY 6

'Dear children, let us not love with words or speech but with actions and in truth.' 1 John 3:18

Their home was a makeshift shack, constructed from sheets of metal leaning up against a stone wall. Welcoming our YWAM team, they squeezed us within, eager to learn more about Jesus. The father rattled off instructions to two sons. Moments later, they reappeared with small bottles of lemonade. They knew we'd be thirsty in India's heat; they also knew our Western tummies didn't cope with their water. Giving up their daily food allowance, they met our need. I learned more from them than they from me; imitating Christ's self-giving humility as they valued our needs above theirs.[6]

Paul taught we should give to others, not so we'd end up in need, but to pursue 'equality' (2 Cor. 8:13); a common principle in Scripture.[7] But there are times, as with my Indian hosts, when we temporarily forgo our need to help someone else's, and this is scriptural too. Such was the generous, self-giving, kindness of God on the Macedonian church, that despite their extreme poverty, they too gave generously to others.[8]

Reflect on these stories, not to condemn you into giving where you're unable, but to appreciate God's gracious, undeserved, self-giving love.

Still your heart and if you feel able, say 'yes' to being available when a time may come to forego a need in order to help someone else.

Dwell with this sacrificial theme of love in action, as you receive God's love in different ways through your day.

DAY 7

'Dear children, let us not love with words or speech but with actions and in truth.' 1 John 3:18

My early morning space of prayer alone with God includes confession of how I've been wrong in thought, word or action. But dwelling on God's heart for the needy reminds me not to become so blinkered with what I've done wrong that I ignore where I've failed to do what's right! To do nothing to help the needy when I have so much is one such gargantuan failure. One that God loves me into confessing, and inspires me to put right. For 'If anyone has material possessions and sees a brother or sister in need but has no pity on them, how can the love of God be in that person?' (1 John 3:17).

Looking back over the week, how has God prompted you with ways you can share with others out of what you have? What practical steps might you take to ensure this doesn't get left behind as our place of dwelling moves on? Talk with God about this.

And now, let's pray together: Father God, I yield my heart to yours. Open my eyes where I've been blind to the needs of others around me. Open my heart to feel your compassion and act on it. Open my mind to your creative ways that I can share what I have with those who haven't.

Dwell with this verse for one last day, as God further inspires you to love in action.

DAY 1

'What do you want me to do for you?' Mark 10:51

What an encouraging, comforting question to be asked by anyone, not least Jesus; one he asks of us this week as we immerse ourselves in the story of blind Bartimaeus, using the practice of 'Ignatian contemplation'.[1] Read slowly and prayerfully as the story unfolds. God wants to meet with you through it. Ask him to help you see, hear, touch, smell and, perhaps, taste the scene.

Leaving Jericho, Jesus and his disciples led an enthusiastic crowd; unhurried yet walking with purpose towards Jerusalem. Dust rose from jostling feet passing a line of beggars outside Jericho's gates.

> a . . . blind man, Bartimaeus . . . was sitting by the roadside begging. When he heard that it was Jesus of Nazareth, he began to shout, 'Jesus, Son of David, have mercy on me!' Many rebuked him and told him to be quiet, but he shouted all the more, 'Son of David, have mercy on me!'
> Jesus stopped and said, 'Call him.'
> So they called to the blind man, 'Cheer up! On your feet! He's calling you.' Throwing his cloak aside, he jumped to his feet and came to Jesus.
> 'What do you want me to do for you?' Jesus asked him.
> The blind man said, 'Rabbi, I want to see.'
> 'Go,' said Jesus, 'your faith has healed you.' Immediately he received his sight and followed Jesus along the road.
>
> *Mark 10:46–52*

Dwell in this story through your day, keeping an open heart to what God might show you.

DAY 2

'What do you want me to do for you?' Mark 10:51

Recall the details of the story as if you were Bartimaeus. Reread it if you're able; reading slowly as you picture the scene, anticipating God's desire to meet with you through his Word, while using your imagination to engage your senses.

Hear the murmuring crowd. Can you smell them? Taste the dust rising from their feet!

Someone says Jesus of Nazareth is here. Listen again for his name. How does that make you feel?

You may be blind physically but spiritually you know Jesus to be the Messiah. 'Jesus, Son of David, have mercy on me!' you shout (v. 47). But people push you roughly, telling you to shut up. Spittle flies in your face as someone hisses, 'Sssh!' But you keep shouting, 'Son of David, have mercy on me!' (v. 48). Your only hope lies in who Jesus is and what he can do.

Of all the things you could say to Jesus you're shouting for mercy. What prompts that plea? To be seen? To be heard? To be protected from the shoving crowd? To be forgiven? For your poverty? For your blindness?

What would *you* ask mercy for?

What would *you* be shouting to Jesus as he walks past?

What would *you* be feeling?

What/who, if anything, might you be 'blind' to?

Talk with God about these things.

Dwell in this story through your day, keeping an open heart to what God might show you.

DAY 3

'What do you want me to do for you?' Mark 10:51

Recall the details of the story, once again as Bartimaeus. Reread it if you're able; reading slowly as you picture the scene, anticipating God's desire to meet with you through his Word, while using your imagination to engage your senses.

'Call him [her]', Jesus is saying (v. 49).

Jesus has heard you. He has turned towards you.

The crowd stumble to a halt. The eyes that were blind to your presence now search for you. The gruff voices and rough hands that tried to stifle your presence are intrigued to see what Jesus will do. 'Cheer up! On your feet! He's calling you', they say (v. 49).

How do you feel as you're guided by the crowd towards Jesus? Can you feel their stares? Can you feel his tender gaze, fixed only on you?

You're standing before him now.

'What do you want me to do for you?' he asks (v. 51).

Hear the Spirit of love, joy, peace, patience, kindness and gentleness in his tone.

How does that make you feel?

Jesus is asking the same question to *you*, not just to Bartimaeus.

What is *your* answer?

What is your heart's longing?

This isn't the time to bring out your prayer list – this is your moment to ask Jesus for your deepest desire.

Talk with him about it.

Dwell in this story through your day, keeping an open heart to what God might show you.

DAY 4

'What do you want me to do for you?' Mark 10:51

Recall the details of the story, this time as someone in the crowd. Reread it if you're able; reading slowly as you picture the scene, anticipating God's desire to meet with you through his Word, while using your imagination to engage your senses.

Feel the pressing crowd jostling against you in a bid to get closer to Jesus. How does that make you feel inwardly? Can you relate to that in your own life?

Jesus is ahead of you, surrounded by his disciples; some of them burly fishermen. You glimpse his face occasionally but keep following with the crowd.

Do you want to be closer to him? Would you like to walk alongside him? Does being his disciple – his friend and close companion – appeal to you?

You hear a man shouting from the side of the road. Others are shouting back.

Do you stop and turn to look or press forward, not wishing to lose your space in the crowd?

The person ahead of you stops without warning. You bump into them. Someone behind crashes into you. You realise why, as you hear Jesus telling the crowd to call the man over from the roadside.

How does that make you feel? Do you wish Jesus was calling you? Do you long for Jesus' attention to be fixed on you?

Talk with God about these things.

Dwell in this story through your day, keeping an open heart to what God might show you.

DAY 5

'What do you want me to do for you?' Mark 10:51

Recall the details of the story, this time as one of Jesus' disciples. Reread it if you're able; reading slowly as you picture the scene, anticipating God's desire to meet with you through his Word, while using your imagination to engage your senses.

Jesus is heading for Jerusalem. Tensions are high.

Why is he so determined to go when he knows it will put his life in danger? Why is he going when he must know it might put your life in danger too?

The crowd leaving Jericho is large. How long will they follow? How long will it be before you can be alone with Jesus again? Surely, they won't go all the way to Jerusalem with you?

You're tired. Jesus must be so tired too. You need to protect him, but how, when he seems so happy to be surrounded by people?

If these examples of questions resonate as you imagine yourself in this scene, pause to reflect on your answers. If not, be open to other questions, feelings or revelations that the Holy Spirit may prompt to your heart as you walk alongside Jesus leading the crowd.

How are you feeling? What do *you* want? Are you afraid, worried, frustrated, convicted or filled with peace and joy?

Talk with God about these things.

Dwell in this story through your day, keeping an open heart to what God might show you.

DAY 6

'What do you want me to do for you?' Mark 10:51

See. Hear. Touch. Smell. Even taste the scene if you're able.

Where are you in the story today? On the roadside, begging? In the crowd following Jesus?

Among his disciples close to his side? On the city walls watching what's happening?

What happens in the story that especially resonates or speaks to your own feelings or situation? There are many ways we will each engage with God through this practice of Ignatian contemplation. Be free to remain with what is meaningful to you.

It was Bartimaeus's faith that prompted Jesus to heal him; and on being able to see, he started following Jesus too (v. 52). Look back over your week's journaling, or recall how God has been meeting with you through this story. Ask the Holy Spirit for further discernment to confirm what wasn't merely your own imagination; any key things he's revealed to you.

What has God revealed to you about Jesus? How does that reassure and deepen your faith?

What has God revealed to you about you? About your deepest longing. About your feelings and responses. About your belief?

How is God's story transforming your inward responses and building your faith?

How is God's story transforming your priorities or conduct?

Would it help to talk and pray with someone about your encounter with God?

Dwell in this story through your day. Keep talking and listening to God about all the things you've been thinking, feeling or discerning this week.

DAY 7

'What do you want me to do for you?' Mark 10:51

The first time I encountered God using Ignatian contemplation in this passage, I was drawn to Bartimaeus, especially when Jesus asked what he wanted from him. After prayerful reflection, I knew my answer: that Jesus would help me realise his promise of bearing 'much fruit' (John 15:5). Returning to this story a few years later, my answer was the same, but as I dwelt in the passage for a week, I unexpectedly found myself as someone in the crowd.

It caught me off guard. My half-heartedness towards the beggar as I pursued Jesus; yet, if I'd stopped to help him that's exactly where Jesus would be! My envy when hearing Jesus call his name when I yearned for him to see me. My desperate longing to be one of his disciples; his closest of friends. But as I confessed and talked with God about these things, I realised that I was the answer to that final desire. I could be one of his disciples too, enjoying his company as I lived in devoted relationship with him and served him by serving others.

Has God prompted you with some kind of active response this week? What three steps could you take to move on with that?

Let's pray: Loving Jesus, I see your warm gaze on me now, hearing me, seeing me and knowing my deepest desires. I choose to stay close as the week moves on.

Continue to dwell in this story for one last day.

DAY 1

'Wait for the LORD; be strong and take heart and wait for the LORD.'
Psalm 27:14

How good are you at waiting? Waiting in a traffic jam, in a long queue, for a reply to a text message? Do you remain upbeat, calm, full of God's grace, kindness and positivity, or do you find yourself grumbling, frustrated, distracted, tetchy? And how well do you cope when you're waiting on God for a response to a difficulty? Our natural response is to ask God to resolve it, and preferably as soon as possible. But sometimes we have to wait to discern his response. And waiting for the outcome of an upsetting, worrying or stressful situation isn't easy. If our wait is prolonged, it can affect how we feel about God's love, care, faithfulness and power. But David keeps our focus in the right place.

David wrote Psalm 27 when faced with malicious accusations and threats to his life. He longed for the sustaining help of God's presence, but unlike in some of his other psalms, he doesn't conclude with an outburst of thanks and praise for God's answer. David's difficult situation remained, but also, his confident expectation for God's deliverance.[1]

To wait, as David did, is to know peace and assurance from confidence in God's love, goodness and mercy for whatever you face.[2] Speak his affirmation to your soul today.

Dwell with David's faith-building words through your day, with an open heart to God who loves, supports and cares for you – always.

DAY 2

'Wait for the LORD; be strong and take heart and wait for the LORD.'
Psalm 27:14

Praying for something for a prolonged period without God seeming to respond can feel wearisome. Demoralising, even. Whether it's for a personal situation, a conflict or war, a brutal dictator or people suffering drought and famine, and nothing seems to change, it's natural to ask, 'What's the point of praying?' But the story of the persistent widow[3] reminds us that when we're praying to the beat of God's heart, we can persevere and not give up while waiting for his answer. You never know how God is working in the unseen realm that will one day break through into what you can see and hear.

Perseverance demonstrates passion; it's hard to keep praying if your heart isn't in it. God will give you strength to keep praying if it's something he's laid on your heart. And perseverance deepens trust which, in turn, strengthens faith.

Talk with God if you're feeling weary in prayer for a situation. Be honest with him about your doubts or demoralised soul. Be honest too about what distracts you from prayer and if your spiritual 'prayer muscles' feel weak. Ask him to help you overcome any lack in concentration and, step by step, to build your capacity to keep praying into all that you believe he's promised and purposed.

Dwell with David's faith-building words through your day with an open heart to God, who loves, supports and cares for you – always.

DAY 3

'Wait for the LORD; be strong and take heart and wait for the LORD.'
Psalm 27:14

Esther's story is no fairy-tale dream of an orphan rising to be queen. She was forced, as a teenager, to leave her home for the royal harem, and groomed in how to please the pagan king. But when her people, the Jews, were doomed for massacre, her cousin realised it was 'for such a time as this' (Esth. 4:14) that she'd endured what she had; finding herself in a place where God could use her to save them.

Esther encourages us to wait on God for strength, assurance, grace and wisdom when our circumstances are anything but easy; to believe that God 'works for the good' in everything (Rom. 8:28). If you're facing a situation that you didn't want or choose, be honest with God about your thoughts and feelings. Take as long as needed with this conversation. It can be hard to discern God's voice or receive the good things he has for you if your heart is hardened towards him.

When you're ready, you may like to open your hands, palms upward as a gesture that you trust in God's love for you, and that you want to hear him speak into your situation. Let him inspire and encourage you for yourself, and for others involved. Picture their faces and let God minister his grace to your soul.

Dwell with David's faith-building words through your day with an open heart to God, who loves, supports and cares for you – always.

DAY 4

'Wait for the LORD; be strong and take heart and wait for the LORD.'
Psalm 27:14

There have been times I've fallen to my knees or lain face down in prayer. Times when I've wept long, hard tears, crying out to God for relief or deliverance. But I've never known such anguish and earnestness in prayer as Jesus did in Gethsemane, where his sweat fell to the ground like blood. 'Father, if you are willing,' he prayed before being tortured and crucified, 'take this cup from me' (Luke 22:39–44). God didn't take 'the cup' from Jesus; he didn't answer his prayer as Jesus wanted, but he did send divine help to strengthen him.

Being honest with God helps release stress, fear or pent-up tension. As you open your heart to wait for him in your place of felt helplessness, God *will* strengthen you because God *cares* for you, and promises to equip and sustain you.

Allow any anxiety to flow from your heart, mind and soul, with tears, words, whispers, groans, or in silently being present to God's presence. Releasing it will create space in your inner being for a deeper awareness of God, and to receive his sustaining strength and comfort. But, if possible, don't rush away. Continue to be still with God, open to how he will minister to you through his Word and Spirit, in the way he knows is best.

Dwell with David's faith-building words through your day with an open heart to God, who loves, supports and cares for you – always.

DAY 5

'Wait for the LORD; be strong and take heart and wait for the LORD.'
Psalm 27:14

'. . . yet not my will, but yours be done' (Luke 22:42). Jesus was honest with God about his feelings, but he didn't run away from fulfilling God's will when God said 'no' to his prayer. He gave up his life in excruciating pain and shame that we may receive the gift of eternal life, and the blessings of Spirit-filled life today.

Gosh, that's so easy to write, but how might we surrender to something difficult in practice? We'll dwell on this today and tomorrow.

For today, reflect on Psalm 37:3–7a: 'Trust in the LORD and do good . . . delight in the LORD . . . Commit your way to the LORD . . . Be still before the LORD and wait patiently for him'.

Chew on these words and how God inspires them to your heart.

If you're struggling to *trust* God, tell him why, and maybe talk with a friend. But also take time to *delight* yourself in God through loving, focused praise and prayer. *Commit* all that you're facing to him, then *be still*; let faith in his presence sustain, encourage and transform your desperation into patience for his purpose to be fulfilled.

You might also find the following prayer helps you draw closer to God in response: 'I wait for the LORD, my whole being waits, and in his word I put my hope' (Ps. 130:5).

Dwell with David's faith-building words through your day with an open heart to God, who loves, supports and cares for you – always.

DAY 6

'Wait for the LORD; be strong and take heart and wait for the LORD.'
Psalm 27:14

' . . . yet not my will, but yours be done'. Following on from yesterday, when God says 'no' to removing the difficulty we face while pursuing his will, take time to reflect on the longer view. Jesus faced the horror of his trial and crucifixion because of what lay on the other side; victory over the enemy and spiritual death, resurrection, salvation of humankind to eternal life.

> [Jesus] never lost sight of where he was headed – that exhilarating finish in and with God – he could put up with anything along the way: Cross, shame, whatever. And now he's *there*, in the place of honor, right alongside God. When you find yourselves flagging in your faith, go over that story again, item by item, that long litany of hostility he plowed through. That will shoot adrenaline into your souls!
>
> *Heb.12:2–3, MSG*

Take a few moments to reread and reflect on this truth, your heart open to let God comfort, inspire, strengthen and encourage you, in whatever way he knows best.

Who or what will be blessed because of your obedience to and perseverance with God's purposes? Record your answers so you can remind yourself when you're feeling the strain of your situation in future. Ask God to inspire you creatively as you persevere with his will.

Dwell with David's faith-building words through your day with an open heart to God, who loves, supports and cares for you – always.

DAY 7

'Wait for the LORD; be strong and take heart and wait for the LORD.'
Psalm 27:14

We live in a broken world. We and others suffer terrible difficulty. We can't dictate to God the outcome, but we can ask for help, and wait on him, believing for it in faith. In waiting we become increasingly aware of his presence, keeping company with us through the hardships. God promised never to leave or forsake us.[4] If we reflect on what that implies, we realise there's no greater answer to our prayer.[5]

Waiting on God isn't passive. To 'be strong and take heart' is:

- To keep praying, day after day, laying your pain-filled requests before him;[6]
- To dwell with and fill your soul with truth and guidance from his Word; and to proactively live it out;
- To wait with expectancy that God *will* respond, even if you don't know how or when;[7]
- To give time and space for him to comfort and strengthen you for situations you endure which he may, or may not, resolve;[8]
- To fulfil responsibilities that you're able to.

Which of these especially resonates? Dwell with it now.

Let's pray: Thank you, Lord, for your promise to strengthen all who are weary and lift up all who are bowed down.[9] I commit my situation to you and focus on your presence as we walk through it together.

Dwell with David's faith-building words through your day with an open heart to God, who loves, supports and cares for you – always.

DAY 1

'Your bodies are temples of the Holy Spirit,
who is in you . . . therefore, honour God
with your bodies.' 1 Corinthians 6:19–20

What would you rather do: watch paint dry or study the many and intricate details and dimensions of God's temple in Jerusalem? I've often heard the 'temple' chapters in Chronicles described as 'mundane and laborious', so I'm guessing that some of you will opt for a snooze with the paint. But at the heart of temple architecture, furnishings and ministry, lies a life-transforming principle to embrace.

'The temple I am going to build will be great', Solomon said, 'because our God is greater than all other gods' (2 Chr. 2:5). And it was. Marble steps and pillars, gold plated walls inlaid with carved cherubim, silver and gold utensils and furnishings, and fine linen curtains exquisitely embroidered with blue, purple and crimson yarn. Its lavish wealth and beauty were renowned, but its intrinsic feature and priceless quality were determined by God's presence within; its construction and priestly ministry honouring the holy God it served.

God no longer inhabits a temple of stone but dwells in the living, flesh and bone temples of our lives.[1] It's because God's Spirit lives *in* our bodies that we're to honour him *with* our bodies.

To 'honour' is to glorify, praise, represent and esteem God, in and through your body. As you reflect on these images and ideas, what might this look like in your life?

Dwell with the image of your body as the temple of God's Spirit, now and through your day.

DAY 2

'Your bodies are temples of the Holy Spirit,
who is in you . . . therefore, honour God
with your bodies.' 1 Corinthians 6:19–20

A temple for God's presence fulfilled his longing to dwell among his people – to be at home with them.[2] In fact, Jesus pre-empted Paul's teaching to the Corinthians, saying, 'Anyone who loves me will obey my teaching. My Father will love them, and we will come to them and make our home with them' (John 14:23). Your body is a temple – a home – for God's presence.

Jesus had been talking to his disciples about having to leave them, but promised the coming of the Holy Spirit. The life of God they'd been living *with* for three years, would become the life of God *within* them. The Holy Spirit would empower their actions and prayers. He would help, counsel and intercede for them. He would care for and be present with them. What an awesome, mind-blowing truth. Jesus and his Father want to make their home in your life. Pause for a moment to let that sink in. I hope it puts a smile on your face!

What thoughts or images does the word 'home' inspire? Do they differ from your notion of a 'temple'? Your body is both to God.

How does this make you feel: Excited? Expectant? Astonished? Reticent? Disheartened? Or something else? Talk with him about it.

Dwell with this truth of being God's temple, his home, through your day. Let this awesome reality rekindle your wonder and sink deep into your being.

DAY 3

'Your bodies are temples of the Holy Spirit,
who is in you . . . therefore, honour God
with your bodies.' 1 Corinthians 6:19–20

God called his temple, his home among his people, 'my house of prayer' (Isa. 56:7). Prayer isn't just something we do. Temples of prayerful focus and dependence on God's presence are also who we are.

A curtain separated the Most Holy Place of God's presence from the ministering priest in the sanctuary with its golden altar of hot coals. On these, he sprinkled a unique blend of spices as he prayed;[3] his devoted worship encased by a fragrant cloud, filling the sanctuary and penetrating the place of God's presence beyond the curtain. But this fragrance associated with prayer also permeated his clothing and hair, distinguishing him from others when he emerged.

Dwell with this sensory image of honouring God's presence with devoted prayers of adoring praise. It puts the world and its worries into perspective, distinguishing you from the hurried, anxious pace of life around you. You'll carry a calm poise and inner joy to your relationships, roles and responsibilities; spreading to others the distinctive 'fragrance' of your devotion to God in prayer.[4]

Prayerfully name aspects of God's character, power and purposes, filling the core of your being with adoring prayer. It calms tension, stills racing thoughts, and shapes your response to the world. It will also inspire you how to pray for others through your day.

Dwell with this truth of being God's temple, his house of prayer; it inspires ongoing prayer throughout your day.

DAY 4

'Your bodies are temples of the Holy Spirit,
who is in you . . . therefore, honour God
with your bodies.' 1 Corinthians 6:19–20

Sacrifice. Hmm, perhaps not a favourite topic but it's another distinctive word God used to describe God's home: 'a temple for sacrifices' (2 Chr. 7:12). Although Jesus cancelled the old requirement of offering bulls, sheep, doves, etc. on the altar of burnt offering,[5] Paul teaches us to 'offer [our] bodies as a living sacrifice, holy and pleasing to God' (Rom. 12:1). Sacrifice was and still is intrinsic to temple ministry because as Paul concludes, it's our 'true and proper worship'.

Offering sacrifices to God has been linked with worship since the word first appeared in Scripture.[6] It's relinquishing our natural reactions or personal preferences to keep living in step with God's character and commands. It's how we love him by intentionally living his way of life. And as we surrender *our* way of life, we obtain something far better; a fuller knowledge and experience of God.

Reflect on your understanding of worship. Sung or spoken worship in praise or prayer are valid ways to glorify God, but honouring God with how you live is your 'true and proper worship'.

How might your worship be lived out today?

Prayerfully offer your body – both your inward and outward being – to love, honour and serve God's divine presence within.

Dwell with the image of your body as the temple of God's Spirit. Let it inspire you to worship God by saying 'yes' to whatever he prompts you with today.

DAY 5

'Your bodies are temples of the Holy Spirit,
who is in you . . . therefore, honour God
with your bodies.' 1 Corinthians 6:19–20

I recently attended a black-tie event; my first in thirty years. To cut a long story short, I wore a dress that wasn't what I'd hoped for, and I felt a tad disappointed. Opportunities to dress up are rare and I'd wanted to feel my best, but the Holy Spirit gently convicted me. It wasn't about how I felt about myself but about hosting God's presence. It was about honouring God within me by clothing his temple with qualities reflecting who he is.

The ministering priests in God's temple were set apart from others by their distinctive appearance; a uniform robe of linen with an embroidered sash. Their clothing complemented God's beauty and brought dignity and honour to their service;[7] not because of what they did, but because of whose presence they served.

For today's temple, Paul writes, 'clothe yourselves with the Lord Jesus Christ . . . clothe yourselves with compassion, kindness, humility, gentleness and patience. Bear with each other and forgive one another . . . And over all these virtues put on love' (Rom. 13:14; Col. 3:12–14).

Reflect on each of these descriptions. Have any of these been missing recently?

Talk with God about it.

Would it help to pop Paul's description of clothing on your wardrobe as a gentle reminder of what's most important?

Dwell with the image of your body as the temple of God's Spirit. Let it inspire how you relate to others.

DAY 6

'Your bodies are temples of the Holy Spirit,
who is in you . . . therefore, honour God
with your bodies.' 1 Corinthians 6:19–20

There were numerous gateways into the temple courts, so gatekeepers were allotted to keep watch over the pilgrims, ensuring that only those deemed 'clean' by holy law could enter.[8] Today, it's our eyes and ears that grant the world access to God's living temple; things that spawn thoughts, words and behaviour that may honour him with our bodies or pollute his holy sanctuary. But God's Word provides abundant instructions for living lives that honour his presence as we put them into practice.

Consider the many things you allow entry to God's temple through books, blogs, podcasts, programmes, films, conversations and social media feeds. You can't protect yourself completely from what you see and hear around you, but you can test these things in the light of God's Word. Should any be kept at a distance?

You've also been created with a 'conscience'; one that can be damaged if you keep ignoring it in preference for what you want.[9] How well are you responding to yours?

Whatever you allow to take root in your mind and heart will, in turn, shape your responses.

Ask the Holy Spirit to help you discern the subtler influences that have potential to dishonour and mask who he is.

Dwell with the image of your body as the temple of God's Spirit. Let it inspire greater protection over what you allow to enter and to remain in his holy presence.

DAY 7

'Your bodies are temples of the Holy Spirit,
who is in you . . . therefore, honour God
with your bodies.' 1 Corinthians 6:19–20

The temple was built so that 'all nations' (Isa. 56:7) might encounter God; now he reaches out to others through his home in your life. When we pray for God to reveal himself to the world, you and I are the answer.[10] As we yield to the promptings of his Spirit and obey his Word, his image will imprint itself on our life with increasing measure.[11]

> The physical part of you is not some piece of property belonging to the spiritual part of you. God owns the whole works. So let people see God in and through your body.
>
> *1 Cor. 6:19–20, MSG*

Who are you praying for to come to know God and be saved?

Who mocks you for being a Christian believer?

Who do you know that thinks Christians are hypocrites? (Does this prompt confession?)

Hold these individuals in your heart today. It's not about being perfect or able to offer intellectual arguments to counter unbelief, it's all about Jesus showing himself to them as you yield to how he wants to live his life in you. The more you embrace your awesome dignity as God's temple, the more you'll be inspired to honour his presence.

Take a moment to pray for them now . . . then pray for yourself too.

'I no longer live, but Christ lives in me' (Gal. 2:20). Dwell with the image of your body as the temple of God's Spirit for one more day.

DAY 1

'The joy of the LORD is your strength.' Nehemiah 8:10b

These words may be difficult to hear. In times of distress and heartache, of over-whelming problems and pain, I – we – naturally retaliate, 'What joy is there to be had?' So, let's dig a little into the meaning of our dwelling place this week.

The Israelites' seventy-year exile from God's presence was over, but as they listened to God's law being read,[1] they wept with grief for their faithlessness. And yet, they were still his beloved people; they'd been reunited. If God was filled with joy over their reunion, so should they be too. And so, they were to celebrate the annual Feast of Tabernacles, a festival of thanks for God's past provision in the wilderness, but which also looked expectantly to the coming of the Messiah; when God would 'tabernacle' or dwell with his people.

Jesus the Messiah has since come; God now 'tabernacles' with you and me by his Spirit within us. Today and every day, you can know God's infinite joy, for you and within you. Today – and every day – his joy can give you strength as you believe for his love, forgiveness, compassion, provision, guidance, comfort, peace . . . and so many promises.

Confess to God where you've not walked in his ways. Whatever your circumstances, pleasant or hard, open your heart in faith to know God's immeasurable joy at being united with *you* through Jesus.

Dwell on this verse through your day. Let its truth infuse your heart, mind and soul.

DAY 2

'The joy of the LORD is your strength.' Nehemiah 8:10b

It's helpful to differentiate between the joy of the Lord and the happiness of the world. The joy of the Lord is internal. It doesn't rely on our circumstances; its source is God's presence by his Spirit within. Happiness, however, depends on the nature of our circumstances. Happiness relies on external triggers to promote feelings of pleasure, significance or exhilaration. God's blessing of joy transcends our circumstances, whereas happiness reacts to them.

As happiness relies on external factors, it doesn't last. When its triggers disappear, happiness fades. Joy, however, is the by-product of a spiritual connection with God, so it permanently resides within us as a 'gift' or manifestation of God's Spirit. We can pursue happiness without any guarantee we will feel it, but we can choose the joy of the Lord through the attitude of our heart towards God with us.

Who or what are you looking to for joy or happiness? How does knowing the difference between God's joy and worldly happiness inspire your response?

If you're not sensing God's promised blessing of joy, then remember, it's already within you. Turn to him in prayer now. Open your heart to his presence. Remind yourself of God's character and promises. Receive his loving affirmation and strength.

Dwell on this verse through your day. Let its truth infuse your heart, mind and soul.

DAY 3

'The joy of the LORD is your strength.' Nehemiah 8:10b

Friday is my day off when I often enjoy gardening. I call it my 'Sabbath' as I steer clear of usual 'work', creating space to worship, listen, mull over Scripture and just 'be' with God.

Fridays are also the day I enjoy homemade cake!

During a three-week Daniel Fast,[2] I'd been meditating on Isaiah 58. Two verses struck me the first Friday: 'if you call the Sabbath a delight . . . then you will find your joy in the LORD' (Isa. 58:13b,14a). I was shocked to realise from my yearnings for caffeine and cake that my 'delight' in the Sabbath was linked to my carnal pleasures as much as to delighting in God. There's nothing wrong with enjoying food, but it questioned the reality of my joy in the Lord compared to my joy from physical pleasures. I've also recognised how easy it is to seek joy from my home, work and relationships, more than I do from God.

My point isn't about 'Sabbath' but about knowing the all-surpassing joy of God. If this resonates, take moments when you're able to simply enjoy God's presence and infinite love for you, even when you're feeling stress or heartache. 'Press pause' momentarily on intercession or Bible study; let the world carry on without you and nurture the joy that's inherent in knowing God with you.[3] Might you make this a regular part of your daily prayers?

Dwell on this verse through your day. Let its truth infuse your heart, mind and soul.

DAY 4

'The joy of the LORD is your strength.' Nehemiah 8:10b

Even when life doesn't feel joyful, or we're facing difficulty, we can receive this promise of joy that releases strength. Nurturing our relationship with God when life is going well (see yesterday) is a helpful foundation. We all suffer difficult times when we may only manage to lean on God in faith; believing for his presence in our weeping, unable to pray in words but for the groans and sighs of our hearts.[4] Enjoying the richness of God with us in better days, however, helps ready us to trust him in harder ones.

Remain expectant. Defeat doubt with the truth that God loves you and is for you.[5] Psalm 84 writes about 'people of faith who dare to dig blessings out of hardships'.[6] The joyful expectations of being in relationship with God, transforms arid places with springs of refreshment in God.[7]

James says, 'Consider it pure joy . . . whenever you face trials of many kinds' (Jas 1:2), for as you seek strength and wisdom from God's presence while you're suffering, it helps you overcome bitterness, cynicism or despair, and matures your relationship with him.[8] If you're unhappy or hurt today, know God's presence with you in faith to sustain and guide you through this time. You may not *feel* happy, but as you dwell on God's goodness, his consolation will infuse his joy[9] – his peace, comfort and strength into your suffering.

Dwell on this verse through your day. Let its truth infuse your heart, mind and soul.

DAY 5

'The joy of the LORD is your strength.' Nehemiah 8:10b

Discontent can also undermine our experience of the joy of the Lord and its strength-giving qualities. Scripture repeatedly urges us to give thanks. We're to be thankful in praise as we focus on God's presence, declaring the many facets of his goodness to us in different situations.[10] We are to pray with thanksgiving – even when we're anxious.[11] In fact, Paul teaches us to 'give thanks in all circumstances; for this is God's will for [us] in Christ Jesus' (1 Thess. 5:18). For no matter our changing circumstances, God's presence, promises and kingdom are unshakeable.

Giving thanks doesn't earn God's blessing, but it does open our heart to receive it. It turns our attention away from the people or situations that drain our peace and faith, and back onto God; onto his promises and to how he's providing for us practically and relationally. If you sense you've become joyless, consider five things about God's nature, his gifts, his practical provision, the relationships he's given you, or his beautiful creation, and give him thanks for each one.

I try to do this daily, either last thing at night as I switch off the light, or first thing in the morning as I wake. Perhaps you could adopt this practice too. It invites thankfulness to swell your heart with joy for all that God is and has done for you, even in difficult days.

Dwell on this verse through your day. Let its truth infuse your heart, mind and soul.

DAY 6

'The joy of the LORD is your strength.' Nehemiah 8:10b

A tree is recognised by its fruit. Apple trees produce apples. Pear trees produce pears. Disciples of Jesus are also recognised by the fruit of God's Spirit within them;[12] and the fruit of God's presence is 'joy' (Gal. 5:22). In fact, Jesus described coming into relationship with God as a treasure so precious that it fills the newfound believer with great joy.[13]

As you nurture your devotion to God, as you yield to his ways, as you focus on his presence in difficulty and appreciate all his goodness to you, joy will be a hallmark of his life in you. Remember, joy doesn't equate with happiness. You will still suffer pain, disappointment and grief. But the joy of the Lord will sustain you through difficulty. The joy of the Lord will be your strength. It will uphold you. Reassure you. Protect your heart and mind. It will invigorate you when the trials of the world seek to sap your physical, emotional or mental wellbeing. It will surpass even the God-given pleasures of this world. In turn, your joy may be perceived by others, some of whom might want to experience it for themselves.

Sit with these truths. Ponder them in your heart. Choose to draw near to God in prayer, worship and surrender, and 'He *will* draw near to you' (Jas 4:8, HCSB). Talk to God in prayer and let his joy flood your soul.

Dwell on this verse through your day. Let its truth infuse your whole being.

DAY 7

'The joy of the LORD is your strength.' Nehemiah 8:10b

'Do not be afraid. I bring you good news that will cause great joy for [you and for] all the people' (Luke 2:10). Whatever your fear or hardship, God's joy with you is as relevant today as it was to the shepherds when Jesus was born. Recall what has especially resonated with you this week. Write it down as a reminder for the days ahead, or highlight it in this book.

Psalm 95 invites us to worship God who is our joy. Prayerfully reflect on *each* phrase and respond as you feel led, before moving on to the next:

> Come, let us sing for joy to the LORD; let us shout aloud to the Rock of our salvation.
> Let us come before him with thanksgiving and extol him with music and song.
> For the LORD is the great God, the great King above all gods.
> In his hand are the depths of the earth, and the mountain peaks belong to him.
> The sea is his, for he made it, and his hands formed the dry land.
>
> *Ps. 95:1–5*

And now, let's pray Paul's words together and believe for God's response: 'God of hope, please fill me with all your joy and peace as I put my trust in you. May my joy in you overflow to others with the hope they need too, by the power of your Holy Spirit'.[14]

Continue to dwell on Nehemiah 8:10b for one more day. Let its truth infuse your heart, mind and soul.

DAY 1

'Come to me, all you who are weary and burdened, and
I will give you rest. Take my yoke upon you and learn from me,
for I am gentle and humble in heart, and you will find rest for
your souls. For my yoke is easy and my burden is light.'
Matthew 11:28–30

Jesus.

Hold his precious name in your heart. Whisper it in love.

Now close your eyes and picture him walking through familiar Gospel narratives. Which come to mind? What do you see? What do you feel?

Jesus led a distinct and compelling life. What draws you to him? What particularly inspires you about how he lived life? What is it about him that you'd love to experience in greater measure? Reflect on these thoughts or images for a moment.

I'm drawn to the quality of his character; such kindness, gentleness, goodness, honesty, integrity . . . even when faced with harsh, hostile or deceitful situations. I'm inspired by his insights and wisdom, amazed with the crowds by his abilities, attracted by his intentional pursuit of God's purpose. I long to know more of his joy, his unhurried pace and non-anxious presence; and his prayerful devotion to God. And our dwelling place reminds us that we *can* experience much of his life as we draw close to him, walk alongside him, and so align our lives with his own lifestyle. A lifestyle Jesus tenderly invites us to this week.

Dwell with these words through your day, being mindful that they're Jesus' invitation to *you*.

DAY 2

'Come to me' Matthew 11:28

'Do!' the Pharisees commanded God's people, lumbering them with legalistic demands on how to honour God and live right for him. The impossible burden wearied their souls, drained their joy, and sapped their once vibrant faith. But Jesus says, 'Come'.

The 'noise' of expectations – self-imposed, or from family, friends, church and work – can drown out his loving call. Your hurts, fears, shame and guilt can mask his understanding and compassion. But 'come' invites you to draw near and remain close to him.[1] It's from dwelling in devoted, yielded relationship with Jesus that you'll gain his perspective on life; that you'll learn to prioritise what's important to him. And it's from that place of coming to and remaining with him that his comfort, wisdom, guidance and strength will sustain you; infusing rest and relief to your worn-out soul.

Come.

Jesus invites you to trust him: not only for eternal life in heaven, but to trust him with your life; for 'life . . . to the full' (John 10:10) today.

Take a moment now, but ongoing through your day, to hear, see and accept Jesus' invitation to 'Come'. Set aside your load. You don't even need to pray. Just come.

Sit or walk with him. Nothing else, no strings attached, just come.

Slow your breathing, still those racing thoughts, and come.

'Give ear and come to [him]; listen, that you may live' (Isa. 55:3).

Dwell with his invitation to come to him, be with him, and find rest in his presence as you continue with your day.

DAY 3

'Weary and burdened, and I will give you rest.' Matthew 11:28

Jesus isn't talking about the effect of a hard day's work; Jesus speaks to a sense of overwhelm. Fatigue. Of being worn out or burnt out. An all-consuming load of trouble, hurt, fear or anxiety that weighs you down. Are you struggling to conform to what others perceive as 'proper' Christianity; the very problem Jesus condemned?[2] It may be how to take a Sabbath, a particular style of church worship or an opinion about drinking alcohol, for example. Whatever may weigh you down, it is helpful to discern what aligns with God's Word and what is merely someone else's expectations dumped on you.

Or perhaps you've taken on too much:

- You're weighed down because you felt you ought to say 'yes' to something, though Jesus didn't ask you to.
- You added something to your load that you wanted to do, though it isn't how Jesus called you to serve him.
- Or, you've overcomplicated his calling, which has consequently grown too heavy.[3]

Or perhaps you long to live in harmony with God's presence but life's troubles and temptations are stealing it from you:

- The pain of a longstanding problem.
- Fear for 'tomorrow'.
- Guilt and shame over an ungodly habit.

Come – and talk with God about anything that resonates. Come to him for release and healing.

Dwell with Jesus' promise of rest through your day, and keep listening for what he may continue to reveal.

DAY 4

'Take my yoke upon you' Matthew 11:29

The yoke Jesus refers to enables two people or oxen to carry a heavy load without buckling beneath the weight. Made from a length of wood, carved at each end to fit around the neck and shoulders, the load is carried between them.

To take on a yoke in Jesus' day was to become a disciple.[4] Jesus doesn't offer escape from responsibilities to God, to each other and society, or protection from hard work and problems. But he does offer his yoke – his way of life – as the tool to help us live in this troubled world, with God's sustaining presence.

Jesus chose twelve disciples 'that they might be with him and that he might send them out' (Mark 3:14). Their training involved instruction in various ministries, 'but also continuous association and intimate fellowship with Jesus himself'.[5] For us, that's being with him in prayer, and observing and learning from him as we read Scripture.

Remind yourself what attracts you about Jesus' life, that inspires you to adopt his lifestyle.

Is there balance in your rhythm of 'being with him' and 'being sent out'? Pray about any tweaks you sense may be needed to help you experience more of his life.

Dwell with his invitation to know a deeper 'discipleship-relationship'[6] as you continue with your day.

DAY 5

*'Learn from me,
for I am gentle and humble in heart'* Matthew 11:29

A disciple learned from their teacher's words of instruction, temperament and personality, nature and disposition, and also from how they lived their lives.

Jesus' way of life is beautifully unpacked in his 'Sermon on the Mount' (Matt. 5 – 7). Prayerfully read it through when you're able. Reflect on which teachings especially resonate with your emotions or situations. Dwell with what helps you adopt his lifestyle for yourself.

You can also learn how Jesus lived life by observing his character and personality. Bring to mind a familiar story of Jesus. Watch how he loved people; how he laughed and wept with them, served and reached out to them, including those who made demands of him.

Let God envision your mind and heart, and dwell with what inspires you to adopt his lifestyle yourself.

Reflect on other ways you may learn from and adopt his lifestyle.

By responding to how you discern his leading when praying.
By seeking to be present and responsive to his presence through your day.
By discerning and adopting his principles, perspective and priorities.
By pausing to consider what he would do and say as you face different situations.
By observing him and adopting his ways from further reading of Scripture.

How do these inspire your response?

Continue to dwell with his longing for you to learn from him, keeping an open heart to his leading through your day.

DAY 6

'And you will find rest for your souls. For my yoke is easy and my burden is light.' Matthew 11:29–30

Trained as a carpenter, Jesus knew the difference between an ill-fitting yoke and one that was made to measure. Ill-fitting yokes chafed the shoulders and neck causing pain, swelling and bleeding. Consequently, carrying loads became even harder. But Jesus described his yoke as 'easy', i.e. 'well-fitting'.[7] His yoke, his lifestyle that he invites you to adopt, is tailor-made for you.

We can feel 'stretched' during times he chooses to grow the gifts of God within us, but that's different to taking on something that he never asked us to do. Are there commitments you need and are able to release yourself from? Consider how best you might extricate yourself.

Another key point is his burden is 'light' because his yoke is lined with love. Our primary burden is to love God and to love others with whatever roles and responsibilities he gives us. If you've ever done something difficult for someone you love, you'll know how love lightened the burden. If you reframed a challenging job, relationship, or responsibility as a way for you to love God and others, how does that encourage your attitude towards it?

Prayerfully devote yourself to being true to who God made you to be.

Dwell with this word through your day, and let Jesus dismiss any stress or anxiety with his rest.

DAY 7

'Come to me, all you who are weary and burdened, and I will
give you rest. Take my yoke upon you and learn from me, for
I am gentle and humble in heart, and you will find rest for
your souls. For my yoke is easy and my burden is light.'
Matthew 11:28–30

Imagine being yoked to Jesus. Feel the gentle pull of his shoulders walking with you, supporting you, giving strength and stability when the path gets rough. Feel the lightness in your spirit as you walk in step with him, listening to his laughter, the wisdom of his insights, the comfort of his counsel – seeing his smile and feeling his deep pleasure in working with you.

Apprenticing[8] ourselves to his gentle and humble heart *is* attractive. As we adopt his lifestyle of prayer, sabbath, love, grace, kindness, etc. we know rest and relief from anxious, stressed, hurting, racing thoughts and emotions; we know deep peace and wholeness of wellbeing.

Reread Jesus' words again. Absorb, digest and process each word and phrase.

How are you going to live out what he's been revealing to you this week; one step at a time, week by week, month by month?

Let's pray: Loving Jesus, I sense you reaching out to me with yet more of your abundant life. Inspire my first steps to release me from what binds and restore to me the fullness of life with you.

Continue to dwell with whatever God has been showing you this week,
and receive his promised rest to your soul.

DAY 1

'Our days on earth are like grass; like wildflowers, we bloom and die. The wind blows, and we are gone – as though we had never been here.' Psalm 103:15–16 NLT

There are times I sing worship songs of yearning to be with God in heaven, when in reality, I'm not ready; I'm still clinging to hopes, dreams and loved ones in this life.

So, I admit we're not dwelling in the jolliest place this week. In fact, in the scheme of eternity, we are 'dust . . . we bloom and die . . . as though we had never been here' (Ps. 103:14–16, NLT). Scripture also says that we're 'a passing breeze that does not return' (Ps. 78:39), 'a mist that appears for a little while and then vanishes' (Jas 4:14). But God reminds us of life's frailty so that we won't cling to it too tightly yet use it well.

Being reminded that we *will* have a last day,[1] encourages us to live well, with and for God, as we approach it. This life isn't our destination. This isn't the end. Psalm 103 isn't life-sapping, it's life-giving. It reassures and inspires hope as it envelops this reality in God's compassion, grace, abounding love and forgiveness.[2] Life here is fleeting but you are known, cared for, loved beyond measure and have eternity to press into. No wonder the writer bookends his psalm with praise. Read it now if you're able, in prayerful awareness of God's presence with you.

Continue to dwell with God's Word through the rest of your day.

DAY 2

'Our days on earth are like grass; like wildflowers, we bloom and die. The wind blows, and we are gone – as though we had never been here.' Psalm 103:15–16 NLT

If today was my last day, I would grieve for my loved ones and dearest friends whose flourishing I could not celebrate or struggles seek to relieve. I'd grieve for the grief I'd see in their faces, the hugs that held on without letting go. The tears that flowed unashamedly. I would tell them why I cherished them, and encourage them to keep being all God made them to be. And by golly, I would pray for them, thanking God, that he would be their comfort, help and hope. For my tomorrow, unlike theirs, would be without pain or tears. Tomorrow my heart would be bursting with joy while theirs ached with sorrow.

If they didn't know God, I would use my last opportunity to share Jesus with them, then pray he'd keep calling and drawing them close.

Today may not be your last day, but as you dwell on life's passing, who do you feel prompted to pray for? And who might you open further conversation with about Jesus? Ask the Holy Spirit to bring to mind names or faces of loved ones or friends, people from your past or known only to you at a distance. Open your heart for his love and compassion to guide and inspire.

Dwell with Psalm 103:15–16 in the reassuring light of God's tender love and compassion for you.

DAY 3

'Our days on earth are like grass; like wildflowers, we bloom and die. The wind blows, and we are gone – as though we had never been here.' Psalm 103:15–16 NLT

Forgiving others for the pain and problems they may have caused us isn't easy. But forgiving others isn't just one of God's commands that we seek to obey; it releases us from festering fretfulness that distracts our thoughts, undermines Christ's peace and grace, and often creates stress. It also reminds us that we aren't perfect either; that we may need to seek forgiveness of others too.

If today was your last day, who might you need to forgive, and who would you need to ask forgiveness of? Today may not be your last day, but life is still too short for grudges or broken relationships. Unforgiveness fuels pain, anger, resentment and bitterness. These can cause health issues, affect relationships, and will hold you back from the fullness of life God promised.[3] Seek to release anyone you need to forgive; bless them in prayer, if not in person. And if you've held back from asking forgiveness, too ashamed, too proud, too afraid of a potential rejection, it's time to ask with grace and humility. God's love and compassion in your asking may help heal and free them of the hurt they feel towards you, releasing them to live wholly as God intended.

Dwell with Psalm 103:15–16 in the reassuring light of God's tender love and compassion for you.

DAY 4

'Our days on earth are like grass; like wildflowers, we bloom and die. The wind blows, and we are gone – as though we had never been here.' Psalm 103:15–16 NLT

If today was my last day, would anyone need to know how much I loved, valued and appreciated them?

Life's too short to be so busy with goals, dreams and responsibilities that we forget to encourage others along the way, or to assume they know how much we love and appreciate them. It's too short to be ruled by persistent demands while failing to notice who's dragging their feet, the downcast face, the teary eyes. It's too short to be so distracted that we forget to encourage those who've given of themselves – again – often unnoticed and at personal cost. It's too short to be so tied up with our agenda that we fail to see who's making themselves vulnerable to criticism as they fan into flame God's gifting within;[4] or the one faithfully serving us, year on year, who's growing weary.

Read that paragraph again, slowly. Who comes to mind? What's your next step? A phone call, text, email or a handwritten note? Could you invite the downcast for a coffee or a meal, the weary for a companiable stroll, or for time to share and pray? Ask God to inspire you how to love, encourage and value others today.

Dwell with Psalm 103:15–16 in the reassuring light of God's tender love and compassion for you.

DAY 5

'Our days on earth are like grass; like wildflowers, we bloom and die. The wind blows, and we are gone – as though we had never been here.' Psalm 103:15–16 NLT

If today was my last day, I would rue the days that, with my current level of health and energy, I'd frittered away unproductively. I'd regret letting fear, ungodly habits, busyness or apathy, etc. distract me from fulfilling my God-given potential.

If this resonates, consider how you might put that right:

- Identify the gifts, relationships, tasks and resources God's given you.
- Distinguish between the urgent demands over the gentle pull of what God shows you is important.
- Prayerfully consider what to let go of, and how.
- Prayerfully consider what to take up or give.
- Prayerfully consider how to nurture your gifts, through training, prayer, mentoring, opportunities, etc.

Your days are short but God loves to equip, encourage and work through you,[5] even if *you* feel unable to give anything. He is compassionate; he understands your limitations, fears, sense of inadequacy, or reticence from past failure or negative criticism. But today he wants to assure you that he created you with specific roles in mind,[6] to dovetail with his unfolding story. Open your heart to how the Holy Spirit wants to encourage your response to these prompts. Contentment is felt in being available for God's will. Be inspired as you anticipate pressing onward with him from within or outside your home.

Dwell with Psalm 103:15–16 in the reassuring light of God's tender love and compassion for you.

DAY 6

'Our days on earth are like grass; like wildflowers, we bloom and die. The wind blows, and we are gone – as though we had never been here.' Psalm 103:15–16 NLT

If today was my last day, I would take time to worship in whatever way I could. But today might not be my last, nor yours. And as we race from one thing to another, pausing to speak out our worship of God can slip from the mind.

God is with you in everything. At your desk or while changing nappies. While cleaning streets, toilets or hospital corridors. When teaching, caring, farming, nursing or advising on finances. In retail, politics, retirement and fulfilling roles for church. God is with you in all the ups, downs and busy round and rounds. What could prompt you to 'press pause' at least once in your day, to turn the eyes of your heart on his face and say thank you . . . I love you . . . I worship and praise you – in song, prayer, proclaiming Scripture or in silent adoration?

Psalm 103 inspired one of my husband's favourite hymns; H.F. Lyte's, 'Praise, My Soul, the King of Heaven'.[7] The song on my heart today, however, is, 'Build My Life,' by Housefires.[8] What song might inspire you to worship today as you are present to God's presence with you at home, on your commute, at work, eating lunch or leaving the school gate?

Dwell with Psalm 103:15–16 in the reassuring light of God's tender love and compassion for you.

DAY 7

'Our days on earth are like grass; like wildflowers, we bloom and die. The wind blows, and we are gone – as though we had never been here.' Psalm 103:15–16 NLT

'Don't count the days. Make the days count' said boxer Muhammad Ali.[9] Compared to thousands of years of world history, our days are extremely short. But God lovingly urges us to 'come near' to him (Jas 4:8), to 'make the most of every opportunity' (Col. 4:5), to 'run [the race] with perseverance' (Heb. 12:1), to 'love one another' as he has loved you (John 13:34), to take hold of the 'life . . . to the full' Jesus promised (John 10:10).

When you're mindful of death's inevitability in light of God's eternal life and love, the awareness enthuses a godly response to *today*. Your times are in his hands, he knows the length of your days.[10] You have nothing to fear, but everything to live for. Nothing to hold back, but everyone to love. Nothing to feel insignificant about, but everything God has made you to be and do. Live well *with* God, and live well *for* God, whether it's your last day or the first of many more, and may his love and compassion lift your heart in praise.

Let's pray: 'Oh! Teach us to live well! Teach us to live wisely and well! . . . And let the loveliness of our Lord, our God, rest on us, confirming the work that we do' (Ps. 90:12,17 MSG).

Dwell with Psalm 103:15–16 in the reassuring light of God's tender love and compassion for you.

DAY 1

'The kingdom of God is within you.' Luke 17:21b NIV1984

The kingdom . . .
The kingdom of God . . .
The kingdom of God is within you.

As we begin a new week, take a moment to reflect on these words and phrases – one at a time: How do you understand them? What comes to your mind?

The Pharisees anticipated God's promised Messiah would establish an earthly kingdom to oust their Roman oppressors. But on asking Jesus when God's kingdom would come, Jesus corrected their misunderstanding:

> The kingdom of God does not come with your careful observation, nor will people say, 'Here it is,' or 'There it is,' because the kingdom of God is within you.

> *Luke 17:20–21, NIV1984*

'Within you' can also be translated as 'among you' or 'in your midst'. Either way, it means that God's kingdom is present in the Person and ministry of Jesus. The kingdom of God arrived in the world from the moment of his birth. And it's still here, present by his indwelling Holy Spirit within anyone who acknowledges Jesus as their resurrected King.

The kingdom of God on earth is spiritual, not physical. While you live in this world, you encounter and are transformed by it internally, then express its truth outwardly through how you live.

The kingdom . . .
The kingdom of God . . .
Is within you.

Dwell with this truth with a thankful heart through your day, open to discern what God may say.

DAY 2

'The kingdom of God is within you.' Luke 17:21b NIV1984

God is sovereign over his created world, but human life is currently under the dominion of his enemy.[1] Consequently, the kingdom of God is within us but we can lose sight of its staggering implications. We can succumb to the distractions and temptations of our enemy's broken world, or feel intimidated by his lies and oppression. So be reminded today that the kingdom of God, the rule and reign of King Jesus is – within – *you*.

The Person and ministry of King Jesus is in you by his Holy Spirit. The experience of the divine presence and the power of his enabling – is in *you*.

This is God's provision for your life – all the promises in his Word are '"Yes" in Christ' (2 Cor. 1:20). They are faithfully fulfilled in your King.

This is your guide and rule for life – the reign of King Jesus within you.

This is your purpose and calling – to serve and live for King Jesus.

This is your peace, assurance and security – that your King lives in and with you.

Ponder these awesome facts, conveyed to you through the indwelling Holy Spirit. How do they inform and potentially transform your sense of identity, purpose or value, your uncertainty or fears, your hopes, lifestyle and choices?

Dwell with this truth with a thankful heart through your day, open to discern what God may say.

DAY 3

'The kingdom of God is within you.' Luke 17:21b NIV1984

When the disciples asked Jesus to teach them how to pray, he included the line: 'your kingdom come, your will be done, on earth as it is in heaven' (Matt. 6:10). But it's easier said quickly than prayed sincerely! For as God's kingdom reign is within us, to pray these words personally is to say, 'God, I ask that the culture, outlook and purpose of your kingdom would rule over *my* lifestyle, conduct, responses, time, possessions, resources, opinions, ambitions, etc.' And as God doesn't force his will upon us, we are the answer to that prayer.

Spend a few minutes taking a tour of your life in your mind's eye. Ask God to show you what praying 'your kingdom come, your will be done' would look like for your relationships, homelife, work, finances, drinking and eating . . . and anything else that comes to mind. Then be honest: Are you willing to play your part in praying for more of God's kingdom on earth?

This isn't an exercise to blame, shame or condemn, it's an invitation to admit what you'd struggle to give up or adopt for God to help you embrace his very best life for you. Pray honestly about any fears or uncertainties in making this prayer a reality, and be open to his loving, wise response. You are not alone; the help and inspiration of God's Spirit is within you.

Dwell with your prayer as you continue with your day.

DAY 4

'The kingdom of God is within you.' Luke 17:21b NIV1984

The kingdom of God is within you but its reign over your life and consequently, its influence through your life, will constantly be challenged, and potentially held back, depending on your response.

Whether it's '*my* kingdom come' cravings and pursuits, or other people's pressure to conform to their ideals, Jesus role-models how to use Scripture to defend God's kingdom ways. 'It is written' he defied the 'tempter' in the wilderness. 'It is also written . . . Away from me Satan! For it is written' (Matt. 4:3–10). Whatever the enemy threw at him, Jesus refused to entertain doubts or questions about his Father's provision, protection, promises and purpose for his life. His obedience to his Father's kingdom rule was unquestionable.

Consider what easily tempts you from God's ways. Using a Bible concordance or online search, find out what Scripture verses say about the weaker or less resilient parts of your life, recording them in a small notebook or on a mobile app to keep in your bag, pocket or desk. Use this defence when temptation challenges his rule. But remember. The power of Jesus' response to Satan wasn't just in regurgitating God's Word, but in his desire to yield to it. The more you long for a greater experience of God's kingdom, the more your desire will grow – your heartfelt desire – to conform to King Jesus' reign.

Keep bringing this verse to mind through your day and let it grow your desire to experience more of God's kingdom.

DAY 5

'The kingdom of God is within you.' Luke 17:21b NIV1984

Buckingham Palace in London, England, has a balcony overlooking The Mall, from which, on momentous occasions, the monarch greets thousands of devoted subjects; cheering, clapping, flag-waving and singing the National Anthem. It's the minutest glimpse of worship due to King Jesus. But as the kingdom of God is within us, we don't limit it to certain occasions.

The kingdom of God is present in the Person and ministry of Jesus within you, every moment of your day. It's easy to forget this truth in the busyness or boredom, the stress and strain, in the fun times, or periods of problems and pain, but you can develop the habit of pausing to be present to his royal presence. To let your love well up into grateful praise and adoring worship. I find this particularly helpful when I feel stressed, upset or tempted.

Whether it's spoken, sung, shouted, whispered or silent expressions of love, the King of God's kingdom is worthy of devotion. Picture his smile, feel his love reaching out to you, and know that he delights in your devotion. In focused, adoring worship you'll experience greater fullness of his life pulsating within you, gracing all you are and say with kingdom truth, peace and power.

How could you develop an atmosphere of worship in your home, car and workplace that would help you keep present to the King of God's kingdom within you?

Keep bringing to mind this verse through your day, and when you do, pause to worship.

DAY 6

'The kingdom of God is within you.' Luke 17:21b NIV1984

Bring to mind the people you mix with in person or online. I'd guess they vary from those who are passionate for God to those who don't even believe he exists. But whatever their understanding and faith, you are an ambassador of Christ, the King of God's kingdom.[2] You are in the world but you're no longer 'of the world' (John 17:14–16).[3] By walking in step with God's kingdom ways, you carry it into every room, relationship, workplace and gathering.

The assurance you have from God's kingdom will be sensed in your calm poise. Its wisdom will be heard through your measured, discerning response. The care and compassion of God's kingdom will be felt through your loving kindness. The joy of its good news will infuse your tone and countenance. And the sweet fragrance of faith in Christ's victory will permeate your authority in prayer. You're a living, breathing, love letter from King Jesus, read, felt and understood by others as his kingdom culture is relayed in practice.[4] Never underestimate the effect of your life when yielded to God's kingdom within you.

As you dwell on this truth, let it inspire your response to God's kingdom life and encourage you. Though some will reject God's presence, it may seed a desire in others to seek God for themselves.

Dwell with this truth as you relate with different people through your day.

DAY 7

'The kingdom of God is within you.' Luke 17:21b NIV1984

It is a place, but it doesn't appear on a map.

It's already fully established, but still to be completed.

It's under constant enemy attack, but is the most secure place to be.

It has a King, but his throne is not of this world.

It is near to everyone, yet still far from many.

It is eternal, infinite, yet exists within the fallible, temporary parameters of human life.

It has no beginning or end, but continues to grow.

It is the most valuable treasure that anyone could have, yet comparatively few really want.

What is it? It is the kingdom of God.

The kingdom . . .

The kingdom of God . . .

Is within you.

How has God rekindled a fresh desire to experience more of his kingdom reign in your life this week?

> 'When you come looking for me, you'll find me,' he says. 'Yes, when you get serious about finding me and want it more than anything else, I'll make sure you won't be disappointed.' (Jer. 29:13, MSG)

Recall any steps you still need to take to help that become a reality. And know that your King wants you to experience his kingdom life far more than you can 'ask or imagine' (Eph. 3:20).

Let's pray: Lord, help me to live my life today for the praise of *your* kingdom glory.[5]

Continue to dwell on this verse through your day, let it grow your desire for more of God's reign.

DAY 1

'And Saul's son Jonathan went to David at Horesh and helped him to find strength in God.' 1 Samuel 23:16

Afraid. Exhausted. Confused. Uncertain. Threatened. Hounded. That's how we find David in our dwelling place this week. I imagine all of us can relate to one or more of these feelings or situations ourselves, or for someone else. So, let's begin by immersing ourselves in the story, pausing first, to pray: Father God, I still my mind and open my heart to meet with you in your Word; to find strength in you for myself and/or [name].

David and his men are exhausted. They'd inflicted heavy losses on a band of looting Philistines who'd been raiding the threshing floors of Keilah. David had been guided by God to help the town, but there was no victory celebration. No feast of thanks. No pause to rest and recover. David had exposed his location to his violent pursuer, King Saul, and instead of offering protection and refuge as thanks for David's help, Keilah's inhabitants would betray him. David and his battle-weary men fled into inhospitable wilderness, moving from one place to another with Saul in pursuit; for Saul had come to take David's life.[1]

We feel the pain, terror and confusion, but we dwell with verse 16. What aspects of God's nature encourage and reassure you? Which of his promises are significant to you in this season?

Be mindful of God's presence with you, his nature and promises, as you dwell with this verse through your day.

DAY 2

'And Saul's son Jonathan went to David at Horesh and helped him to find strength in God.' 1 Samuel 23:16

Immerse yourself in the story. Can you feel David's fear; his tight chest, knotted stomach, clammy skin and thumping head? Do you see his haggard face, the dull eyes? Hear the strain in his voice; sense the overwhelm of problems with no relief in sight.

What makes you afraid, even terrorises your thoughts and emotions? How do you relate to David's crushing burdens? Be as specific as you can, and recognise the effect it's having on you.

Now feel the touch of Jonathan's hand on your arm. Take a deep breath.

Sometimes, God's help comes through the company and counsel of a friend.

If you've buried your fears, doubts and worries, or if you're trying to press on by ignoring them, ask God to bring someone to mind you could call on. A trust-worthy friend or leader you can be honest with. Someone who knows you well enough to remind you of what God has said over your life, of the purpose he's called you to, or the promises in his Word that are pertinent to you. Someone who won't judge but who with grace, patience and wisdom will love you, listen to you and discern how they may help you find your strength in God.

As you dwell with this verse through your day, thank God for this friend who can support you. Pray for them as they might now be praying for you.

DAY 3

'And Saul's son Jonathan went to David at Horesh and helped him to find strength in God.' 1 Samuel 23:16

If you're unable to meet with a friend this week, perhaps I can be your 'Jonathan' to help you find strength in God.

David also felt threatened by enemies while in the Desert of Judah, and poured out his longing for the security of God's presence: 'You God, you are my God, earnestly I seek you; I thirst for you, my whole being longs for you, in a dry and parched land where there is no water' (Ps. 63:1). Perhaps, like David, you find yourself in a wilderness; life feels dry, threatened with constant danger. You have called to God for relief, but still feel the scorching heat of your situation. Feel my hand on your arm, hear my voice: God is with you, God sees you, God cares for you. Take a slow, deep breath as you let this truth shift your focus away from your circumstances and onto God with you.

God promises to give you what you need;[2] practically or emotionally, through wisdom or guidance. Thank him in faith for his promise. What other promises can you thank him for, to strengthen your sustaining faith for this time?

If possible, read Psalm 63, adapting its words to reflect your own life and situation; and David's faith will help you to find strength in God too.

Be mindful of God's presence with you, his nature and promises, as you dwell with this verse through your day.

DAY 4

'And Saul's son Jonathan went to David at Horesh and helped him to find strength in God.' 1 Samuel 23:16

David faced many problems. Later in his story, his own men turned against him after their women and children were taken captive by Amalekite raiders:

> David and his men wept aloud until they had no strength left to weep . . . David was greatly distressed because the men were talking of stoning him . . . But David found strength in the LORD his God.

1 Sam. 30:4,6

What a subtle but faith-building change. When the world once again appeared set against him and Jonathan wasn't nearby, David found strength in God for himself.

Friends, podcasts, church services and daily Bible notes can help us find strength in God. We don't graduate from needing their support.[3] But we can't always rely on someone else's faith; we also need to have learned to find strength in God for ourselves.

The following guidelines are familiar, but if you've lapsed in any of them, be encouraged to re-establish them:

- When you pray, spend time listening to God.
- Be open to God speaking to you as you read Scripture.
- Reflect on what you've heard or read in church, a podcast or daily devotional book, and how you can apply it to your life.
- Seek to keep present to God's presence in the busyness or humdrum of your day, the laughter or pain.

Be mindful of God's presence with you, his nature and promises, as you dwell with this verse through your day.

DAY 5

'And Saul's son Jonathan went to David at Horesh and helped him to find strength in God.' 1 Samuel 23:16

Immerse yourself in the scene again, but this time as Jonathan. Feel his love and compassion for his friend; hear his gentle yet affirming tone. See his warmth of expression, mingled with the concern of a slightly furrowed brow. Hear how he affirms God's promise and purpose for David. Dwell with this image with an open heart, for God may call you to be a 'Jonathan' too.

Jonathan didn't help David find strength in himself, in his skills or his men. And Jonathan didn't help David find strength with pleasing platitudes. Jonathan helped David find strength in God by proclaiming truth and reminding David of God's purpose for him; filling David's heart and mind with God's promises, power and faithfulness.

Who has God brought to mind? Whose pain or disillusionment do you hold in your heart? If you're not in touch already, is it time to give them a call, arrange to meet up or plan some online facetime?

As you pray with them, and for them, be open to any words or promises the Holy Spirit inspires to your heart. Affirm what you know to be their God-given calling and gifts. Share life-building truths from God's Word that he cares for them, will never leave them, is for them, etc.

Dwell with this verse through your day, and how God may continue to move your heart to reach out to a friend.

DAY 6

'And Saul's son Jonathan went to David at Horesh and helped him to find strength in God.' 1 Samuel 23:16

As soon as Jonathan left David, the Ziphites betrayed his new location to Saul.[4] But David prayed: 'Surely God is my help; the Lord is the one who sustains me' (Ps. 54:4). His prayer reveals how, during this period of unceasing difficulty, he affirmed his faith that in *God* he would find his strength.

God can use wilderness times to grow our faith too; to refine our character to become more like his and to train us further for his purposes. David's life was tough, but consequently, he learned to trust God's character and promises, despite circumstantial evidence to the contrary.

How might you allow God to strengthen your faith and grow you increasingly into his likeness during this current season of life?

How is God revealing his character and purpose to you in greater measure than you knew before?

How are you encountering him more deeply in prayer, or finding strength from his Word?

Repeat David's prayer as your own: 'Surely God is my help; the Lord is the one who sustains me.' It reaffirms your strength is in God as you wait for his help and/or deliverance; as you root your hope in the unchanging, irrefutable, reliability of his character and Word.

Be mindful of God's presence with you, his nature and promises, as you dwell with this verse through your day.

DAY 7

'And Saul's son Jonathan went to David at Horesh and helped him to find strength in God.' 1 Samuel 23:16

As we dwell in God's Word and hide it in our heart, it becomes a permanent source of help to find our strength in him. This is a key reason for writing *Dwell*. God's Word can be our permanent 'Jonathan' and it can help us *be* a 'Jonathan' too. It's the lamp that lights the way for our feet when the path of life is steeped in darkness.[5] It promises God's counsel and guidance to help us make right decisions.[6] It's the wisdom we need that surpasses worldly opinion and expectations.[7]

As we conclude our week, be encouraged by David's faith-filled words after Jonathan helped him find strength in God:

> I love you, Lord, my strength. The Lord is my rock, my fortress and my deliverer; my God is my rock, in whom I take refuge, my shield and the horn of my salvation, my stronghold. I called to the Lord, who is worthy of praise, and I have been saved from my enemies.

Ps. 18:1–3

Let's pray, asking God to help us be a 'Jonathan': 'Sovereign Lord, please give me a well-instructed tongue as I prayerfully dwell in your Word; one that helps sustain the weary to help them find their strength in you.' (Adapted from Isa. 50:4.)

Be mindful of God's presence with you, his nature and promises, as you dwell with this verse through your day.

DAY 1

'Blessed is she who has believed that the Lord would fulfil his promises to her!' Luke 1:45

Waiting for God to fulfil a promise isn't always easy, especially if it takes weeks, months or even years. We can grow impatient – irritated, frustrated, questioning – which may then morph into discouragement. The nature of our circumstances may sow seeds of doubt over whether the promise is achievable. And slowly but surely, we begin believing our doubts more than our belief in God's faithfulness to his Word, or our belief in his power to fulfil it. But as we dwell with Elizabeth's response to Mary this week, we can stop believing our doubts, stop doubting our beliefs, and return to believing our beliefs.[1] And in doing so we'll experience God's blessing.

Mary was young and unknown, but God looked favourably on her to be the woman in whom he'd conceive his Son; conveying his will to her through an angel.[2] Imagine how she felt while carrying both the blessing and potential burden[3] of the news privately, until she could visit her relative, Elizabeth. Yet, whatever joys and fears she felt, Mary could say: 'I am the Lord's servant . . . May your word to me be fulfilled' (Luke 1:38).

How do God's promises excite or comfort you? Do you fear what others might think or how you'd cope if they were fulfilled? Do you still believe for them, or are you nursing doubts?

Dwell with Elizabeth's words through your day. Be open to how God wants to encourage you.

DAY 2

'Blessed is she who has believed that the Lord
would fulfil his promises to her!' Luke 1:45

Mary was *blessed* because she believed God's promise for the humanly impossible to be fulfilled in and through her. Mary believed that whatever God said to her would not fail to accomplish what he desired.[4]

To capture the essence and meaning of the word 'blessed' in the Bible, we think of:

Contentment. Satisfaction. Fulfilment. Peace. Inspiration. Enrichment. Assurance. Strength.

Reflect on these words, one by one.

How do they make you feel?

What thoughts or longings come to mind?

How might experiencing being blessed in this way transform your emotions and outlook?

How might experiencing being blessed in this way inspire greater trust in God to fulfil his promises to you?

Is God revealing anything new about himself, about you, or about your relationship with and response to him?

Be honest with God if these words feel like strangers in the street rather than friends making a home in your life. Ask him to grow your head and heart knowledge of him, through dependent, trusting faith.

Dwell with Elizabeth's words through your day. Be open to how God wants to encourage you.

DAY 3

'Blessed is she who has believed that the Lord
would fulfil his promises to her!' Luke 1:45

God has made foundational promises in his Word, which are for all of us. These promises affirm different aspects of his character, purpose or power. When you ask to receive such a promise, you ask, already believing for God's response, rather than hoping for it. For example, his promise of unfailing, unconditional love where you feel empty or unlovable,[5] his promise to never abandon you where you feel rejected,[6] his promise of forgiveness where you're convicted and make confession,[7] his guidance where you're unsure,[8] his peace despite difficult circumstances,[9] or his spiritual equipping for the role that he's called you to.[10]

These promises are yours through your life in Christ. Asking helps you to focus on your current need from God, but believing for his answer focuses your mind and unzips your heart to receive and experience it. His promised peace. His promised wisdom, etc.

Do this today. Bring to mind any foundational promises in Scripture that are pertinent to you at the moment. Promises, for example, about:

God's love and character . . .
God's will and purpose . . .
God's power and enabling . . .

Worship God for who he is, declaring aloud your trust in his promise, and thanking him for his presence and faithfulness to fulfil it.

Dwell with Elizabeth's words through your day. Be open to how God wants to encourage you.

DAY 4

'Blessed is she who has believed that the Lord
would fulfil his promises to her!' Luke 1:45

In addition to foundational promises, God inspires certain promises for a specific reason or season. When God called my husband to train for Baptist ministry, we resigned from successful careers, sold our home, said goodbye to family and friends in Guernsey, then moved to London, England. I was excited to be in God's will. His guidance was clear. But I was close to my mum and deeply cherished my island home. As preparations unfolded, I felt torn between the delight and assurance of being in God's will and the sadness of leaving my loved ones, and the security and familiarity my life was rooted in. But during that time, God planted a promise in my heart: 'no one who has left home or brothers or sisters or mother or father or children or fields for me and the gospel will fail to receive a hundred times as much in this present age' (Mark 10:29–30). It was comforting and reassuring. It held me as we settled in England. And it's been fulfilled repeatedly through the homes, church families and work that he's since provided.

What promise has God inspired for yourself, for someone else, or for a certain situation? Let it infuse faith as you pray.

Open your heart to God's blessing, declaring aloud your trust in his promise, and thank him for his faithfulness to fulfil it.

Dwell with Elizabeth's words through your day. Be open to how God wants to encourage you.

DAY 5

'Blessed is she who has believed that the Lord would fulfil his promises to her!' Luke 1:45

Alongside foundational and personal promises, God also makes promises prophetically.

The New Zealand sunlight brightened the YWAM[11] training base. Our tutor, Sophie,[12] had created space for open worship in song and in silence; to love God, be loved by him, and discern what he may be saying. Hours passed, but I clearly recall when I sensed someone approach me. It was Sophie, a gentle smile in her eyes as she offered me a silk, embroidered waistcoat; one she'd been wearing earlier that week.

'God wants you to have this,' she said, 'and to wear it as a mantle of the anointing I have, so that the same anointing will be on you to preach the Word.'

I had never given a talk before, let alone preached.

Months later I returned home to work, marriage, motherhood, then a move to England; the prophetic symbol buried in a drawer. It was fifteen years before I was first asked to preach, followed, in time, by invitations to teach around the UK.

Has God promised you something through a prophetic message, recently or a long time ago; a Spirit-inspired word birthed within you, spoken over you, or given to you through a dream?

Thank God for that promise. Receive it again in faith with an open heart to be blessed as you believe for its fulfilment.

Dwell with Elizabeth's words through your day. Be open to how God wants to encourage you.

DAY 6

'Blessed is she who has believed that the Lord
would fulfil his promises to her!' Luke 1:45

God may ask you to wait patiently for a promise to be fulfilled,[13] but that doesn't suggest waiting passively; you can be actively seeking God for his reasons for the waiting. He may be preparing you in character, skill or experience to cope with the outworking of the promise; there may be circumstances he needs to put in place before releasing the promise to you; he may be purifying your motives, or encouraging increased dependence on him.

Remember Joshua? He was promised victory with a peasant army over professional warriors in the Promised Land, but he still had to train with spear, develop army captains, plan battle strategy and, most importantly, meditate on and observe God's written commands.[14] So, be encouraged as you use this waiting period to listen for further instruction, to yield to God's transforming work in your life, or to gain skill, knowledge or experience through reading, study, volunteering or taking on a new job, etc.

Does having a part to play in the fulfilment of a promise, resonate in your heart? Is there something about God's promise that's nudging you to pursue it more proactively? Thank God for his promise. Seek his will for this time of waiting, and be blessed as you yield to his ongoing work and/or pursue steps towards its fulfilment.

Dwell with Elizabeth's words through your day. Be open to how God wants to encourage you.

DAY 7

*'Blessed is she who has believed that the Lord
would fulfil his promises to her!' Luke 1:45*

I've shared some personal stories this week to affirm our need to believe in God's words to us, whether they're written in our Bibles or prophetically inspired. To believe not just with our head but with a trusting, obedient and, where appropriate, proactive response.

Read back over your journal or bring to mind what God has reminded you to believe for. If action is needed, prayerfully consider what your next step, or steps, might be, and how you plan to move forward. Share this with someone you can be accountable to, as you respond to what God has revealed to your heart. And remember, *blessed* is the one who believes God will fulfil his promises to them. Believing and behaving towards the promise will fill you with his peace, assurance and strength.

Let's pray: Thank you, Father, that you desire to bless me, even as I wait for the fulfilment of your word to my heart, mind and soul. I'm afraid I may have wasted time and emotion wishing for the promise to be fulfilled, when simply believing and acting towards it would bless me in the waiting. I thank you in faith for all you have done and will continue to do in and through my life. I love you. I worship you. I yield my life to your will once again.

Dwell with Elizabeth's words through your day. Be open to how God wants to encourage you.

DAY 1

'So do not fear, for I am with you; do not be dismayed, for I am your God. I will strengthen you and help you; I will uphold you with my righteous right hand.' Isaiah 41:10

No one enjoys the distress, panic, dread and trepidation of being filled with fear. *Pure* fear is God's gift, warning us of an imminent threat of pain, harm or danger, provoking an urgent, protective response. But *anxious* fear is not of God. It's inflamed by negative, untrusting, irrational or unproved assumptions which overwhelm our thoughts and emotions and, in turn, may hold us back from making a choice or taking action. Fear muddies clear thinking, wastes time and can be detrimental to health. No wonder God repeatedly says, 'Do not fear'.

God tenderly spoke the words of our dwelling place to the Israelites, even while warning them of their impending disciplinary exile to Babylon.[1] God's covenant love was and is unconditional. His people need never fear he would abandon them, no matter the nature or cause of their circumstances. God would always be their God and fulfil his promises to strengthen, help and uphold them. Even his discipline was for their good. They could trust him for the future. And so can we. And so can you.

If you're vulnerable to anxious fear, remember, God is with you. You are loved, cherished and cared for. Be comforted and reassured by God's promise to strengthen you. He will be faithful to all he is and has said.

Dwell with God's promise through your day.

DAY 2

'So do not fear, for I am with you; do not be dismayed, for I am your God. I will strengthen you and help you; I will uphold you with my righteous right hand.' Isaiah 41:10

Fear may suggest we think God has abandoned us, leaving us alone to deal with our concerns. Fear can also imply we don't fully believe in who he says he is. But God promised he would never leave us, and he *is* who he says he is. God loves you unreservedly, cares for you immeasurably more than anyone else. He has all wisdom and power to guide, sustain and equip you. God – the Almighty, awesome Lord you know and believe him to be – is with you. Always. Constantly.

Read Isaiah 41:10 again; slowly and aloud if possible. Receive this truth into your heart, mind and soul. Name the source of your fear, then picture yourself placing it in front of God and letting go. Now focus on God with you. If it helps, stretch out your arms to symbolise physically your inner belief and embrace of his presence. Be assured: God – is – with – you. You may also like to close your eyes to irradicate distractions. Delight yourself now in his love and care.

God's presence is your help for whatever you face; ask him for that help now and thank him in faith that he will provide it exactly as he knows best.

Dwell with God's promised presence, help and sustaining strength to dispel your fears through the day.

DAY 3

'So do not fear, for I am with you; do not be dismayed, for I am your God. I will strengthen you and help you; I will uphold you with my righteous right hand.' Isaiah 41:10

Dwelling with our focused attention on God's presence is immensely calming in the moment, but we also need to trust who God says he is, trust what he says he can do, and trust that his ways are right, good and the best way forward. Trust infuses peace, clarifies thinking and enables constructive action. Trusting God is an active decision to live confidently in light of who we know him to be. Trust is a vital component of faith because while many people believe in God's existence, it is trusting faith, i.e. a confident attitude towards his love, care, guidance and enabling, and a committed response, that enables us to experience the power and reassurance of his life.

Name the source of your fear, then picture yourself placing it in front of God and letting go. Now focus on different attributes of God's nature and power that speak into your concerns. If possible, write them down, but either way hold them in mind as you reflect on God's Word to your soul from Isaiah 41:10. Read it again slowly, aloud if possible, including your descriptions of who God is. Receive this truth into your heart, mind and soul.

Dwell with God's promised presence, help and sustaining strength to dispel your fears through the day.

DAY 4

'So do not fear, for I am with you; do not be dismayed, for I am your God. I will strengthen you and help you; I will uphold you with my righteous right hand.' Isaiah 41:10

In trusting who God is, we also trust what he's said and promised.[2] We can't just know his Word; we have to *trust* God to fulfil it if it's to dispel fear and inspire us into action. We have to own personally that 'God *will* fulfil his promise of X Y Z, therefore, I have nothing to fear'.

I haven't space to include every promise that would dispel our different fears. If my examples below fail to speak into your situation, ask God to inspire the word you need to believe for, or ask a trusted friend to help you discern it. For as David says: 'When I am afraid, I put my trust in you. In God, whose *word* I praise – in God I trust and am not afraid' (Ps. 56:3–4, emphasis mine).

Look up the verse(s) that applies to you, and read slowly; if possible, out loud. Read with an open, trusting, receptive heart, mind and soul:

Fear of sudden disaster and ruin – Proverbs 3:25–26

Fear of making the right decision – James 1:5

Fear for making ends meet, putting food on the table, clothing your children etc. – Matthew 6:25,33

Fear of someone/certain people – Psalm 118:6–8

Fear of anything that's threatening to overwhelm you – Psalm 23:4

Dwell with God's promised presence, help and sustaining strength to dispel your fears through the day.

DAY 5

'So do not fear, for I am with you; do not be dismayed, for I am your God. I will strengthen you and help you; I will uphold you with my righteous right hand.' Isaiah 41:10

I'm mindful how this week will resonate with others in *Dwell*. As I write, however, we've endured an exceptionally turbulent few years; nationally, internationally and therefore, personally. Many things continue to induce fear. Consequently, I've no hesitation in writing on fear, worry and anxiety throughout this book, to help us know God's strength, guidance and presence in all we face.

Today, we consider the vital theme of prayer, dovetailing with Day 4, Week 36. Prayer opens our soul to receive God's comfort and strength for life's difficulties, so, 'Do not be anxious about anything, but in every situation, by prayer and petition, with thanksgiving, present your requests to God. And the peace of God, which transcends all understanding, will guard your hearts and your minds in Christ Jesus' (Phil. 4:6–7).

Praying about your fears *and* thanking God for his response shifts your focus from the problem to your Provider. It deepens trust and reassurance in God, and displaces anxious fear with peace.

Share honestly with God about your fears, then thank him in faith for his perfect wisdom in how he'll respond. Pause with the truth that he cares for you.

What else can you thank God for to help focus on his ever-present goodness?

Dwell with God's promised presence, help and sustaining strength to dispel your fears through the day.

DAY 6

'So do not fear, for I am with you; do not be dismayed, for I am your God. I will strengthen you and help you; I will uphold you with my righteous right hand.' Isaiah 41:10

There's a caveat to our dwelling place. We can trust God with our fears when we're seeking his ways and purposes within the circumstances. But we can't trust him for something that doesn't align to his nature and will. Whatever stage we're at on our journey of faith, let's ask God to help us take another step of letting go of what we hold too tightly in this world,[3] to open our hands, hearts, minds and will to the fullness of his very best life for today, and forever.

'Take delight in the LORD, and he will give you the desires of your heart. Commit your way to the LORD; trust in him and he will do this' (Ps. 37:4–5). As you delight in God, meaningfully and consistently, the joy, peace and power of his presence will open your heart to his will. His desires will be your desires, and as you commit to them, you can trust him to fulfil them. How different this is to the angst and fear we carry when we hold tightly to our wants, 'rights' and responses instead of letting go and letting God transform who we are and what we pursue.

Take time to delight in his presence now if you're able.

Dwell with God's promised presence, help and sustaining strength to dispel your fears through the day.

DAY 7

'So do not fear, for I am with you; do not be dismayed, for I am your God. I will strengthen you and help you; I will uphold you with my righteous right hand.' Isaiah 41:10

In his book, *The Me I Want to Be*, John Ortberg aptly says, 'Peace doesn't come from finding a lake with no storms. It comes from having Jesus in the boat.'[4] My desire this week was to introduce ways in which you can know Jesus in your 'boat' too, whatever 'storms' might instil fear. For as Paul teaches: 'God has not given us a spirit of fear and timidity, but of power, love, and self-discipline' (2 Tim. 1:7, NLT). And as Ortberg writes, 'The mind controlled by the Spirit is life and peace . . . [this is] the role he wants to play in our minds: *The Spirit is a non-anxious presence.*'[5]

Reflect on how God has been ministering to you this week. Make a note of verses or practical responses to keep handy for future reference. And if you can, take time to be still and know God with you; his presence that's your help and strength for whatever you face.

Let's pray: 'When I said, "My foot is slipping," your unfailing love, LORD, supported me. When anxiety was great within me, your consolation brought me joy' (Ps. 94:18–19). 'So [I] say with confidence, "The Lord is my helper; I will not be afraid. What can mere mortals do to me?"' (Heb. 13:5–6).

Dwell with God's promised presence, help and sustaining strength to dispel your fears through the day.

DAY 1

'Search me, God, and know my heart; test me and know my anxious thoughts. See if there is any offensive way in me, and lead me in the way everlasting.' Psalm 139:23–24

Every New Year and birthday (in June), I prayerfully review the past six months to help me prepare for the next. When, after years of doing this, I was introduced to the Ignatian prayer of Examen, I recognised similarities with my biannual reviews, but it fine-tuned my practice and encouraged me to adopt it more regularly.

The practice of the Daily Examen[1] helps us prayerfully review the past day to discern God's presence, confess sin and inspire us to grow more like Jesus. Ideally, its five steps are completed in one sitting, but this week, I'll lead you through one step each day, building on what you've learned the day before. Be mindful, however, that the Examen isn't emphasising where you've obeyed or broken God's commands, but on how you've moved towards his life, love, nature and purposes, or away.

David's prayer asks God to search his heart and mind. Inspired by God's faithful presence, David desires to honour God through yielded trust and devotion.[2] Pray his prayer now with an open heart, pausing to reflect on each word to discern how God may speak or inspire your response: Search . . . test . . . know . . . see . . . lead.

Continue to dwell with David's prayer through your day.

DAY 2

'Search me, God, and know my heart; test me and know my anxious thoughts. See if there is any offensive way in me, and lead me in the way everlasting.' Psalm 139:23–24

Step One of the Examen: Thanksgiving

Psalm 139 is a sustained prayer, acknowledging and thanking God for his unfailing presence and infinite yet intimate knowledge. Praise-filled awe and gratitude preceded David's request for God to examine his heart, and giving thanks is the first step of Ignatius' prayer of Examen.

Slow your breathing and still your thoughts as you focus on God's presence. Linger with him in loving companionship.

Ask God to help you discern how his presence walked with you through your day. Replay its many details. Pause with who or what filled you with peace, delight or inspiration. It may be a person or group – what good thing did you receive from them? It may be something you did, or something about your work. How did it enthuse and energise you? It could be a good night's sleep, a compliment, something you ate, watched or any number of the small activities and pleasures of life.[3]

Bring all the details into focus and how they made you feel.

Take time to thank God for what you're especially grateful for and for how you encountered his goodness and love. Be mindful of how your gratitude inspires greater longing for him.

Dwell with David's prayer in a spirit of thanksgiving through your day. Be mindful of how the Holy Spirit continues to inspire your response.

DAY 3

'Search me, God, and know my heart; test me and know my anxious thoughts. See if there is any offensive way in me, and lead me in the way everlasting.' Psalm 139:23–24

Step Two of the Examen: Petition (i.e. Ask)

The prayer of Examen doesn't encourage self-absorbed introspection or overwhelming shame and guilt. Rather, it invites God to *search* us, to guide our thoughts and feelings as we prayerfully review our day. We ask for his help that we might *know* our hearts – ourselves – as he does.

Dwell with this invitation for God to shine his searchlight on your desires, motives and responses, but do so knowing his infinite love for you. There is nothing to fear from asking God to help you *know* your heart – yourself – as he does. There is nothing to fear from what he may ask of you in subsequent steps of this practice. You can trust his searchlight on all that you are because your very best life will be lived and experienced in a close and yielded relationship with him.

Enjoy God's loving delight for you, his vision and potential that he's created for your life. Ask him to lead you today and through this week in bringing clarity to muddled thoughts and emotions.

Dwell with your request for God to help you know your heart as he does. Let it deepen your desire through the day for greater intimacy with him, and for how you may respond.

DAY 4

'Search me, God, and know my heart; test me and know my anxious thoughts. See if there is any offensive way in me, and lead me in the way everlasting.' Psalm 139:23–24

Step Three of the Examen: Review

Test me and know my anxious thoughts David prayed, asking God to show him where his feelings or actions betrayed a lack of trust; a turning away from God rather than a leaning into him. It prompts us to replay the detail of our day, both the mundane and energising parts, the painful or joy-filled moments, where we were doubting or brimming with faith.

The practice of Examen encourages you to pay attention to your emotions in this step. What made you feel bored, elated, resentful, anxious, compassionate, angry, content or confident, for example?[4] What filled you with joy or troubled you? What inspired or challenged you? What gave you a sense of rest and what caused tension? Were you aware of God's presence at particular times more than others?

Ask God to help you discern what he may be revealing. For example, does a repeated sense of frustration suggest you're involved in a role that may need to change? Does concern for someone suggest a prompt to intervene or support?[5] Does anxiety reveal a lack of trust? Ask God to help you understand how your feelings highlight what helped you draw closer to him or turned you away.

Dwell with David's prayer. Let it deepen your desire to yield to God to know him in deeper measure.

DAY 5

'Search me, God, and know my heart; test me and know my anxious thoughts. See if there is any offensive way in me, and lead me in the way everlasting.' Psalm 139:23–24

Step Four of the Examen: Respond

See if there is any offensive way in me David prayed, but the Examen doesn't encourage us to go looking for things that aren't there. Again, we do this in partnership with our loving Father, who delights in our ongoing transformation. We don't need to spend extensive time waiting on him; when we sincerely ask him to search and test us, his leading or conviction will be prompt and specific.

Where is God showing how you've turned away from rather than towards him? What felt like a distancing between you, rather than a drawing closer together? What reflected his beauty and what didn't? What served his kingdom and what served yours? Where did you keep in step with God's ways and when were you not living authentically? Perhaps you were unaware of any selfish, unkind, deceitful, greedy motives, but God searches out everything when we ask him to help transform us.

Respond in prayerful confession for the moments you wilfully or unintentionally turned away. Receive in faith his forgiveness and cleansing, and be mindful to extend this forgiveness to others.[6] Do you feel led to any other response?

Dwell with David's prayer through your day. As it deepens your desire for greater intimacy with God, it gently prompts you to keep in step with his ways.

DAY 6

'Search me, God, and know my heart; test me and know my anxious thoughts. See if there is any offensive way in me, and lead me in the way everlasting.' Psalm 139:23–24

Step Five of the Examen: Renew

As we pray, *lead me in the way everlasting*, i.e. 'God, lead me in righteous ways that honour you', we ask him to help us learn from the Examen and to become a little more like Jesus in the next twenty-four hours. We commit to how God is inspiring further transformation.

The Examen also encourages us to pay attention, with God's help, to how we're feeling about what lies ahead, and to let these feelings turn into prayer in response to any doubts, apprehension or delighted anticipation.[7]

How can you put into practice what you've learned from your Examen? How can you live more authentically as God's treasured friend? What do your feelings suggest about the future that you can pray about before you move into it? Whether you feel concerned or expectant, talk with God about it.

From thanks for who God is at the start of your prayer, give thanks for how he's at work in your life as you incline your heart to his. Ask him to show you and help you to become the person he is calling you to be, and resolve to respond as he leads you.

Dwell with how God is renewing, transforming and guiding you. May it deepen your desire for greater intimacy with God and, in turn, your response.

DAY 7

'Search me, God, and know my heart; test me and know my anxious thoughts. See if there is any offensive way in me, and lead me in the way everlasting.' Psalm 139:23–24

Today you might review what God has highlighted this week, mindful of the stage of Examen and the step of David's prayer that revealed his insights. Ask God for advice, healing, or whatever else you need his help with.

Alternatively, you might like to pray all five steps of the Examen again for the past day, as is the usual practice: Give thanks. Petition. Review. Respond. Renew.

Remember, Jesus wants you to be his friend.[8] Talk with him as one. Talk of your hopes and dreams and whether they align to his. Talk through weaknesses that trip you up and how he may creatively inspire you to resist them in future. Ask for wisdom and guidance, believing he will give it to you. Trust also for his peace to fill your heart as you yield to his presence. And remember, to keep giving thanks.

Let's pray: Thank you, Lord, that you desire for me to draw closer and become more like you, each and every day. I am warmed and inspired by your unrelenting pursuit for my devotion. I turn to you now and commit myself to walking in step with you in the coming day.

David longed to honour his all-powerful, all-knowing, ever-caring God, as I'm sure you do too. Dwell with his prayer with an open heart for one more day.

DAY 1

'Whatever is true, whatever is noble, whatever is right, whatever is pure, whatever is lovely, whatever is admirable – if anything is excellent or praiseworthy – think about such things.'
Philippians 4:8

For nine months I'd been struggling with a distressing problem, which at times distracted and consumed my thoughts. There were times when anxious or irrational thoughts robbed me of peace, my focus on God's presence, my assurance of his loving care and my confidence in his truth. They deprived me of sleep, and their stress-induced repercussions undermined my health.

Life can easily do that to us, and not just with problems. We can know God's reassurance in moments of being present to his presence, but as we brush up against temptations, distractions or difficulties, our thoughts can overwhelm and take over. But this doesn't reflect God's promise of abundant life in Christ.[1] When the Holy Spirit prompted me to dwell with these words from Paul, they helped to change my thought patterns and recentre my awareness and focus on God with me.[2]

What thoughts are you often consumed by? Are they worries, longings, cravings – or something else? Talk with God about them.

Acknowledge the positive influence of good and happy thoughts too. Thank God for what births them.

How are your thoughts informing your feelings? How do they feed what you talk about? Are there signs that they're influencing your conduct or choices?

Dwell with Paul's words through your day, familiarising yourself with their rich implications.

DAY 2

'Whatever is true, whatever is noble, whatever is right,
whatever is pure, whatever is lovely, whatever is admirable – if
anything is excellent or praiseworthy – think about such things.'
Philippians 4:8

The problem I mentioned yesterday confirmed my need for divine reprogramming to 'reset' my thought life to 'factory settings', i.e. 'Creator settings'; to the way God intended me to process life with him.

The original Greek for 'think about' implies concentrated focus. Water follows the path of least resistance, and in doing so, begins to wear a groove into the surface. It takes effort to reroute water from this groove until it carves a new course. It's the same with your thoughts. Paul understood their powerful influence, but he didn't merely suggest some lovely things to ponder. To *think about* suggests more than *keep in mind*. It's 'to take into account . . . reflect upon and then allow these things to shape your conduct. The Bible is not concerned with mental reflection for its own sake, but only as it promotes behaviour'.[3]

I'll unpack the meaning of Paul's examples over the next few days, but for now, I'll leave space for the Holy Spirit to guide your heart.

Read Paul's words again, slowly. Ask God to highlight which word or phrase he wants you to dwell on for the rest of your day. Consider how you could concentrate on the good thing you need to focus on, rather than on what's unhelpful.

Dwell with Paul's words through your day, let God use them to reset your thinking.

DAY 3

'Whatever is true' Philippians 4:8

Problems, tension, temptation and sheer busyness can unsettle our feelings and shift our thoughts away from God. But Paul suggests a few ways to help reset and reroute our thought-life as God intended. Keep in mind, however, that for wholesome, godly thoughts to break the influence of negative ones, we mustn't just 'think about such things', we must 'put [them] into practice'; and as we do, God's promised peace will be restored (v. 9).

When my thoughts were consumed with my problem, I found myself making assumptions about what might have happened or could happen. That habit was promptly challenged when instead, I thought about what was *true*. No longer would I entertain thoughts about the 'ifs' and 'possibilities', the 'might' or 'might not be's'. Recognising what a time-waster that is and how my random 'I wonder if' thoughts depleted energy and emotion, I focused instead on whatever I knew to be *true*. I dismissed unreliable, deceptive or misleading thoughts and adopted God's truth from his Word.

Do you find yourself making assumptions or getting caught up in an endless cycle of 'ifs' and possibilities? Instead, reflect on what you know to be true:

- About the situation consuming your thoughts
- Of the character and promises of God which are pertinent to your situation or temptation.

How might truth shape your thoughts, feelings, words and responses?

Dwell on this truth throughout your day. And if your thoughts spin off in the wrong direction, break their hold with a prompt return to *whatever is true*.

DAY 4

'Whatever is noble, whatever is right' Philippians 4:8

To fill your mind with *noble* thoughts is to dwell on what's beautiful and honourable. You are the temple of God's Holy Spirit. You live and move in the world but you don't have to let your thoughts drift with the flippant, shallow or ungodly. As you set your thoughts on 'things above',[4] God's holy ways will dignify and beautify what you say, how you say it, and what you do.

Reflect on this as you see your life as a temple of God's presence, moving among your friends, family, church, workplace and other activities. The Holy Spirit within you is the atmosphere of your life in Christ. How do these images inspire or challenge what you allow to fill your mind – and in turn, what then flows out?

To think about *whatever is right* is to consider how best to live for God and for others; how to conform to God's standards rather than others'. Dwelling on *right* thoughts may challenge and change your response, but in turn, you will know peace.

Ask the Holy Spirit what *right* things he wants you to think about. For example, if you feel tempted to criticise, judge or neglect reaching out to someone with love, what *right* thoughts from God's ways would cause you to speak and act differently?

Continue to dwell on whatever is *noble* and *right*, yielding to how the Holy Spirit may nudge and refine how you speak and live.

DAY 5

'Whatever is pure, whatever is lovely, whatever is admirable'
Philippians 4:8

Pure things are fitting for God's temple. Ask God to highlight any soiled or shabby thoughts you allow in his presence. What *pure* thoughts would dispel those unwholesome ones?

Whatever is *lovely* promotes peace. It fills the mind with attractive qualities: kindness, patience, humility, compassion, generosity and forgiveness, etc. To think on *lovely* things calls forth love instead of dislike; assurance instead of fear; a measured response instead of hasty reactions or lack of self-control; awareness and understanding in place of resentment or criticism. These transformed thoughts in turn flow out to comfort, encourage and reassure others with God's loveliness.

What 'unlovely' thoughts have made a home in your life? Reflect on what the opposite would be and how that now shapes your response.

When something is *admirable* it has a good name. To think about *admirable* things refuses to entertain what is false, demeaning, or which undermines. It's thinking on that which is well-spoken of, but also, to then speak well of. It promotes constructive words instead of destructive ones.

Do you entertain thoughts of gossip and slander, or do you easily malign someone's good name? What *admirable* thoughts would God want you to think and, in turn, speak about instead? If you can't think of anything good to say, then it's best to keep silent.[5]

Continue to dwell on these *pure*, *lovely* and *admirable* thoughts, yielding to how the Holy Spirit may nudge and refine how you speak and live.

DAY 6

'If anything is excellent or praiseworthy – think about such things.'
Philippians 4:8

Paul sums up with two qualities that should grace our thoughts and, in turn, how we speak and live. No matter who we're talking to or what we're dealing with, we can ask God to help us discern what is *excellent or praiseworthy*, rather than fill our minds and souls with negativity.

Western culture loves to gossip rather than encourage, pull down rather than promote, judge rather than commend, shame rather than keep silent. But God loves to call out the good. As his people, we are to stop wasting time on thoughts that tear ourselves or others down. Instead, we're to love, be inspired by and encourage what we can. No matter how small the *excellent or praiseworthy* qualities may be, we're to think about and promote them. It expands God's life within us and encourages those we praise. It promotes a sense of being loved, appreciated and accepted. It nurtures a sense of value and worth.

Ask God for discernment about lives and situations that occupy your thoughts negatively. Ask him to help you see and understand as he does. Open your heart to his love, compassion and goodwill to all people. His longing for them to know him for themselves.

Who can you encourage? Build up? Promote?

Dwell with whatever is *excellent or praiseworthy* through the rest of your day. Refuse to let pride or negativity steal God's goodness, peace and love from your thoughts, words and actions.

DAY 7

*'Whatever is true, whatever is noble, whatever is right,
whatever is pure, whatever is lovely, whatever is admirable – if
anything is excellent or praiseworthy – think about such things.'*
Philippians 4:8

Dwelling on Scripture as described through *Dwell* is invaluable to retraining our thought-life which then influences our feelings and, in turn, our words and how we live. This week, however, Paul has honed in on some key ways we can reset unhelpful thought patterns to reroute their flow in the way God intended.

Read through Paul's list once more. Which words have most inspired your thought life and response this week? It takes time to ingrain these new habits, but regularly returning to this truth will have the desired effect and in turn, you will know God's peace (v. 9).

Take time to be present with God.

Let his thoughts fill your thoughts. Let his presence infuse peace, reassurance and comfort. Let his love transform your thinking about yourself – and others.

And now, let's pray: Lord, I'm amazed by the power of my thought-life to distract me from your presence and love, and in damaging how I feel about myself or others. I choose to fill my mind with beauty rather than ugliness, grace rather than unkindness, peace rather than conflict, love rather than fear . . . Jesus, please inhabit my thinking with your goodness in each task, conversation and activity of my day. I yield my wandering thoughts to your loving kindness.

Continue to dwell with this verse through your day. God may yet inspire and encourage you.

DAY 1

'Come and have breakfast.' John 21:12

Whether you're feeling stressed by demands at work, content with a full and productive life, or isolated with little to do, Jesus invites you to sit with him on the beach. Revisit the story now as you prepare to meet God in it this week.

It was early morning. The air, cool. Water lapped against the boat of seven exhausted men.

> Jesus stood on the shore, but the disciples did not realise that it was Jesus.
> He called out to them, 'Friends, haven't you any fish?'
> 'No,' they answered.
> He said, 'Throw your net on the right side of the boat and you will find some.' When they did, they were unable to haul the net in because of the large number of fish.
> Then the disciple whom Jesus loved said to Peter, 'It is the Lord!' As soon as Simon Peter heard him . . . he wrapped his outer garment round him . . . and jumped into the water. The other disciples followed in the boat, towing the net full of fish . . . When they landed, they saw a fire of burning coals there with fish on it, and some bread.
> Jesus said to them, 'Bring some of the fish you have just caught.' So Simon Peter climbed back into the boat and dragged the net ashore. It was full of large fish, 153, but even with so many the net was not torn. Jesus said to them, 'Come and have breakfast.'

> *John 21:4–12*

Dwell with the imagery of this story through your day.

DAY 2

'Come and have breakfast.' John 21:12

Today, we ask the Holy Spirit to help us imagine being part of the story, using our senses to engage with it.[1] Read slowly and expectantly as it unfolds – God wants to meet with you through it.

How do you feel after a long night's work but with an empty net at your feet?

Look, a figure has appeared on shore in the dim light. He calls out, 'Throw your net . . .'

'Really?' you silently question, water spraying as you cast out the net yet again.

But something's different. Something has changed.

Feel its weight as you spot silver flashes of squirming fish.

Your friends groan as their unwashed bodies heave the net into the boat.

Take a fish. What does it feel like in your hands?

Another shout, but this time from the boat. Peter jumps into the water.

What do you feel as you help bring the boat to shore, see fish already baking on hot coals and smell fresh bread?

The fire pops and snaps. Will you draw close to its warmth?

Now look at Jesus. Look into his eyes. What do you see? What do you feel?

Someone's counting the fish; another, guts a few to supplement the meal. Hear the sizzle as they're placed on the coals.

Now, 'Come and have breakfast.'

'Come' Jesus says.

What stirs within as you immerse yourself in the story?

How is God revealing himself to your heart?

Continue to dwell with God meeting with you in this story through your day.

DAY 3

'Come and have breakfast.' John 21:12

'Christians read the Bible not as a document from history, but as a world into which they enter so that God may meet them there.'[2] Ask God to help you meet with him in his Word. Close your eyes and recall the details of the story. Reread it if you have time; slowly and with anticipation.

Where are you in the story today? In the boat or onshore?

Who are you in the story; an observer, yourself, or one of Jesus' disciples? Do you sense a connection with any of them?

What happens in the story that particularly resonates or speaks to your own feelings or situation? Self-effort and empty nets? Passionate yearning for Jesus? Provision? Care? Friendship?

The first time I encountered God using this practice in this passage, I entered the story as Peter, but promptly and unexpectedly found myself engaging as 'the disciple whom Jesus loved' (vv. 7,20). God highlighted feelings and attitudes of vulnerability and negativity about myself in that powerful encounter with him. The second time I did this, however, I was back as Peter, nursing a deep sense of shame and failure.

We will all engage differently with God through this story; be open to how he moves you through it in ways you may not anticipate. Remember, he wants to meet with *you*. He's waiting to speak to *your* heart, mind and soul, even after you've finished reading.

Continue to dwell with God meeting with you in this story through your day.

DAY 4

'Come and have breakfast.' John 21:12

Remember that this practice is about meeting God through story. It's about being open to God dwelling in you as you dwell in his Word. Ask God to continue guiding your prayerful engagement with him through his Word. Don't force anything to happen, let God meet with you as he chooses.

How are you *feeling* in the story? Be specific. What thoughts or emotions are stirred as you engage with it?

Here are some suggested responses to ponder if you'd value some help, but don't let my list dissuade you from how God may be ministering his Word to you already, sinking it deep into your soul: Discouragement. Despair. Hesitancy. Faith. Passion. Strength. Self-effort. Need. Awe. Cared for. Seen. Loved.

What has been unearthed in you that you need or want to talk to God about?

What kind of fatigue or soul weariness, disillusionment, or frustration has the Holy Spirit touched on? What fears or shame has he unearthed? What dreams and longings has he sparked or rekindled? How has he reassured you?

Sit around the fire with Jesus, alone now. Feel the warmth of the flames on your body and the warmth of his unconditional love in your soul. You are safe to talk with him about anything. In fact, he wants you to. Listen to his response.

Continue to dwell with God meeting with you in this story through your day.

DAY 5

'Come and have breakfast.' John 21:12

Once again, if you'd value it, I've suggested some ideas to help you meet with God in the story today. Choose one or more, then talk through your responses with God and give space to listen too. Alternatively, skip these suggestions and continue to meet with God in his Word as he leads.

- Imagine you'd been up working all night. How would you be feeling by early morning? And how would you feel if, despite your hard work, you had nothing to show for it? Nothing to feed your family table or to pay tomorrow's bills? Talk with God and listen for his reply.
- What might 'throwing your nets' look like for you? What is Jesus prompting you to do, to 'catch the fish' that you can't see but are in abundance very close to you?
- Which, if any, of the disciples do you resonate with most – named or unnamed? Reflect on why that might be.
- Where in your life do you need to discern God's presence and recognise his voice guiding and caring for you today?

Feel the warmth of the fire, your aching limbs and hunger pangs. Smell the baking fish and fresh bread. Jesus cares for you. He loves you unconditionally. He knows what you need. Spend time with him by the fire. What would you say to him? Listen for his response.

Continue to dwell with God meeting with you in this story through your day.

DAY 6

'Come and have breakfast.' John 21:12

It is customary to use Ignatian contemplation in one sitting, rather than over seven days. But we're here to dwell. To remain with God and glean all we can as we meet with him in the story this week. Today, you might choose to a) use one or both of the ideas (1/2) below to help unzip your whole being to God with you, b) dwell with your response to God's revelations so far, or c) re-engage with him in the story from a different viewpoint.

1. Three years previously, Jesus had called his disciples away from fishing, but twice told them to return to Galilee once he had risen from the dead.[3] Evidently, however, they also returned to their fishing boats. What have you returned to from your life before following Jesus? If so, what brought you here? Was it circumstances, your own choice, or did someone persuade you? What made you agree?
Be honest about where you are, doing what you're doing. Ask God to help you move forward into his purposes.

2. What, if anything, do you like about early mornings? How do you feel emotionally when you wake up: upbeat or low, expectant or despondent, assured or afraid, refreshed or exhausted? Might Jesus be speaking to you in the early hour but you've not recognised his presence or his voice? Ask him what he might say.

Continue to dwell with God meeting with you in this story through your day.

DAY 7

'Come and have breakfast.' John 21:12

Look back over your week's journaling, or recall how God has been meeting with you through this story. Reflect on the key things he's revealed to you:

- About God himself: How does that reassure and deepen your faith? Dwell with these truths and how you'll continue to let them grow your faith.
- About you: How has identifying your feelings helped you understand why you respond in certain ways? Ask God to help you apply his truth to your work, relationships or problems; embrace God's best for you to let it continue transforming your life.

If it would help to talk and pray with someone about your encounter with God, arrange a time to call or meet up.

Let's pray: Thank you, Jesus, for seeking out your friends in their old, familiar place; for reaching out to help them so they could know your presence, be assured of your provision and have their hearts rekindled as they drew close to you. Help me, Jesus, to know you with me now. To discern your voice. To follow your guidance. And to rest in your provision and loving care.

Continue to dwell with God meeting with you in this story through your day.

DAY 1

'Be still, and know that I am God; I will be exalted among the nations, I will be exalted in the earth.' Psalm 46:10

As I write, wars and political crises rage on in many places around the world. Natural disasters have devastated countless lives and continue to threaten others. Global powers are in conflict over nuclear programmes with flashpoints increasingly perilous.[1] The COVID-19 disease and the repercussions of the pandemic are an ongoing threat to many. The climate warming emergency is a looming menace, already affecting more than 40 per cent of the world's population.[2] And the impact of rapidly escalating living costs threatens many of our business and personal budgets, with special concern for those with limited income.

I'm sorry to sound so gloomy at the start of our week, but it's for reasons like these that Psalm 46 was written; a psalm aimed to gather communities facing chaos and crisis to proclaim their confidence in God – their 'ever-present help in trouble' (v. 1). But it's also a psalm whose truths speak powerfully into our personal heartaches and problems; helping us face them with faith in who God is, and in his presence with us.

Whether you're anxious about world events or more troubled by personal crises, know and open your heart to the reassuring truth of God – with – you.

Continue to dwell on God's Word to you through the rest of the day.

196

DAY 2

'Be still, and know that I am God; I will be exalted among the nations, I will be exalted in the earth.' Psalm 46:10

The root of the phrase 'Be still' means: Release. Let go. Quiet. Leave off! Enough! God rebukes the source of chaos and crisis to stop its roaring rage. He commands it to 'know' – to acknowledge, learn, recognise, honour and respect – that he has ultimate power and authority. Troubles will exist until Jesus returns, but dwelling with God's truth nurtures faith in his infallible character and overruling sovereignty. It infuses comfort, peace and reassurance.

We believe, despite today's heartache, that God's eternal reign will be established on earth without tears or pain.[3] But the future isn't our only hope and reassurance. God is present now: working through us to help those in need; counteracting evil with love, kindness, forgiveness, humility, generosity, manifested through his people; at times, intervening miraculously. And God's Spirit dwells in you, with wisdom, guidance and strength to help you endure this fallen world. Whichever of these gifts you need today, ask God, and still your soul with him as a gesture of faith to receive.

Which global or national issues cause you particular concern for the effect they've had on yourself or others, or the effect they may yet have? Picture yourself handing these things to God, then dwell on his Word instead of the source of your fears.

Continue to dwell on his Word to you through the rest of the day.

DAY 3

'Be still, and know that I am God; I will be exalted among the nations, I will be exalted in the earth.' Psalm 46:10

In his build up to verse 10, the psalmist proclaims God's power over nature (vv. 1–3), over those who attack the place where he dwells (vv. 4–7) and over the raging, warring world (vv. 8–11).

Bring to mind a people group or country suffering the effects of drought, earthquake, tsunami, hurricane, famine. Holding the truth of verse 10 in your heart, ask God to intervene; for his power to be exalted. Pray for the workers alleviating the disastrous consequences on those effected, and for those suffering. Be open to how you might be part of the answer to your prayer.

Verse 9 speaks prophetically of the coming of God's kingdom when there will be no more war.[4] But for today, in line with verse 10, name any warring people groups or nations that burden your heart. Pray for God's love, humility and wisdom to influence their leaders. These may feel like impossible prayers but let faith arise as you hold on to verse 10, and ask God to be exalted. Pray also for the people oppressed and grieving by the effects of war, that they will experience God's provision and comfort through community support and humanitarian aid. And pray for yourself too; as you yield to God's loving kindness in any tense or broken relationships.

Continue to dwell on his Word to you through the rest of the day.

DAY 4

'Be still, and know that I am God; I will be exalted among the nations, I will be exalted in the earth.' Psalm 46:10

Following on from yesterday, we now reflect on God's power over the attacks on his dwelling place. For the psalmist, this was the city of Jerusalem with its temple (vv. 4–7). Today, however, God dwells by his Spirit in the living temple of your life. 'God is within [you], [you] will not fall; God will [help] you at break of day' (v. 5).

God's protective care is a familiar theme in Scripture. There are many sources of comfort or perceived security we can turn to, but ultimately, God is your true source of life. He has planned your days and promised to remain with you and sustain you through heartache, deprivation and pain.

Who or what makes you feel threatened? What is the worst thing that you dread?

Do you believe God will remain with you and help you, even in these scenarios? Do you trust his promises for today as well as the future glory awaiting you?

Speak to God about these things. If tears flow, give them their needed release. And be still. Let the truth of his presence, even if you can't *feel* it, still your racing thoughts as you acknowledge God with you now. Exalt all that you know about him over your fears.

Continue to dwell on his Word to you through the rest of the day.

DAY 5

'Be still, and know that I am God; I will be exalted among the nations, I will be exalted in the earth.' Psalm 46:10

On Day 1 I mentioned that Psalm 46 was written primarily for a community to express confidence in God in crisis, but in turn, it's a personal comfort for our own problems. Whatever troubles you're dealing with, the assurance of verse 10 ripples through your inner being as you dwell on the descriptions of God in preceding verses; descriptions that comfort, inspire and embolden faith.

God is your:

- Refuge – a shelter.
- Strength – your empowering for action.
- Ever-present help in trouble – he is *always* present to support, provide and guide you; he is enough for every situation you face.
- River – as in life-giving. It is metaphorical for 'the continual outpouring of the sustaining and refreshing blessings of God'.[5]
- Fortress – a stronghold; an impenetrable place of security.

This is who God wants you to know him to be. Eugene Peterson translates Psalm 46:10 as: 'Step out of the traffic! Take a long, loving look at me, your High God' (MSG).

Which of the descriptions of God especially resonate? 'Be still' and take a long, loving look at God through this lens. Open your heart to all he wants to reveal or infuse to your inner being.

Continue to dwell on his Word to you through the rest of the day.

200

DAY 6

'Be still, and know that I am God; I will be exalted among the nations, I will be exalted in the earth.' Psalm 46:10

The Westminster Shorter Catechism (written in 1646–1647), opens with the question:

'What is the chief end of man?'

Answer: 'Man's chief end is to glorify God, and to enjoy him forever'.[6]

When we react to a problem with fear, anger or irrational behaviour, our human nature takes centre stage. But as we still our thoughts and reactions before God, to know and acknowledge him – his character, power and purposes – we exalt him. Our words, attitudes, actions, priorities, tone of voice and body language exalt his love and peace over hatred and tension, his salvation and truth over misunderstandings or deceit, his wisdom over confusion, etc. In fact, it's often in times of crisis and hardship that our reflection of God's presence proves especially distinctive. Some may observe or even ask how we can be so assured or measured in our responses when we're facing our own storm. And as our lives exalt God's presence, some may be drawn to want to know him too.

How can you exalt God through your responses to world events?

How is your devotion to, dependency on and knowledge of God honouring him through your response to personal problems?

Ask God to give you further insight into how he might make himself known through your life.

Continue to dwell on his Word to you through the rest of the day.

DAY 7

'Be still, and know that I am God; I will be exalted among the nations, I will be exalted in the earth.' Psalm 46:10

Being still is about being open to God; a leaning in with spiritual ears to hear what he might say. Listen again to Psalm 46:10 as if it were God's audible voice to your heart, mind, body and soul: 'Let be and be still, and know (recognize and understand) that I am God. I will be exalted among the nations! I will be exalted in the earth!' (AMPC).

Open your heart to his presence. Open your mind to his nature, truth and promises. There's so much to be afraid of in this world, but God offers you his presence as your safe place. Your security. Tremble no more. Receive his peace.

How is God moving in your life? What is he saying to you?

Even if you don't feel or discern his presence, know and acknowledge that he is with you, and *will* be exalted in your life and in the world. Rest in that profound truth.

Let's pray: Almighty, loving God, how awesome is your presence. You are my shelter and my security. Your blessings continually flow into my life. Your power overrules the ways of the world. You are my hope for today and forever. I choose to yield and draw close to your presence. Be exalted in my life.

Continue to dwell on his Word to you through the rest of the day.

DAY 1

'The gracious hand of his God was on him. For Ezra
had devoted himself to the study and observance of the
Law of the LORD, and to teaching its decrees and laws in Israel.'
Ezra 7:9b–10

Enshrouded in Anglo-Saxon paganism, the seventh century, brutally warring Northumbrians were described as hard-hearted, stubborn and unreachable for Christ. But Brother Aidan's heart was warmed to minister God's life and Word among them; a ministry that birthed many Christian communities in Northern England. Aidan[1] was known for his prayerful meditation on God's Word. This was the source of his effective work and ministry. And this is why he chose to base himself on the barren island of Lindisfarne. Cut off twice daily by tidal flows from Northumbria's mainland, the solitude served his reflective study away from ministry demands.[2]

Aidan's inspirational story sheds light on the person and work of Ezra, the priest. Ezra returned from Babylonian exile to find God's people lapsed in their commitment. Like Aidan, however, he was devoted to prayerful meditation on God's Word,[3] and as a result of his study and application of Scripture, his life and teaching were powerfully influential in drawing God's people back to himself.[4]

Picture Ezra seeking insights as he prayerfully pored over his scrolls, Aidan meditating on Scripture. See and feel their subsequent reflection of God's love, gentleness, wisdom and generosity, interacting with those they walked and talked with, drawing them to God. How does this inspire you?

Continue to dwell and pray on these words and images through your day.

DAY 2

'The gracious hand of his God was on him. For Ezra
had devoted himself to the study and observance of the
Law of the LORD, and to teaching its decrees and laws in Israel.'
Ezra 7:9b–10

Whenever I read *devoted* it catches my heart; a gentle yet passionate word, steeped with loving commitment. Devotion is birthed from heartfelt desire. It's a focused determination of the inner being; of a heart, mind and will that's prepared to commit to a project, cause or relationship. Devotion flows from being inspired, rather than doing something because we ought to.

Devotion to Scripture is birthed from desire too; from the ache of a heart to engage with its author. No one can make you long for God; no one can force it upon you. But desire to encounter God in his Word will strengthen and grow as you reflect on the immense unchanging nature of his love for *you*.

Hold that thought in your heart and mind today. Ask God to help you 'grasp how wide and long and high and deep is the love of Christ, and to know this love that surpasses knowledge – that you may be filled to the measure of all the fullness of God' (Eph. 3:18–19). If it helps, write out some verses that speak of his love; put your name in them and hear God speak them to you. I've included some suggestions in the endnotes.[5]

Dwell with Ezra's response to God's love that inspired his devotion to God's Word.

DAY 3

'The gracious hand of his God was on him. For Ezra
had devoted himself to the study and observance of the
Law of the LORD, and to teaching its decrees and laws in Israel.'
Ezra 7:9b–10

We don't know when and where Ezra studied God's Word but we do know how Aidan lived out this vital practice. Dismissing the comforts of Northumbria's royal court, Aidan chose to base himself on Lindisfarne because of its isolation; walking three miles across low tide puddles and sandflats to prayerfully meditate on God's Word. Equipping himself in the quiet for his effective ministry.

Where might be your 'Lindisfarne', a place where you could set aside a few minutes or more, to prayerfully study God's Word and meditate on your response? It's a place where you turn off all the beeps and vibrations of media notifications, or better still, where you leave your mobile or screen 'on the mainland'. It's a place where you can shut the door to the world; literally, or by closing your eyes.

And what is 'low tide', the signal that beckons you to be in God's Word? An alarm, perhaps. Time after breakfast, lunch or tea. Your commute. Hearing the closing music to a favourite programme, prompting you to switch off and 'switch on' to God's Word. Or maybe, when your baby sleeps; a few precious minutes to dwell on God's Word before you have to catch up elsewhere.

Dwell with these words and thoughts through your day, let God inspire ideas that fit *your* life and situation.

DAY 4

'The gracious hand of his God was on him. For Ezra
had devoted himself to the study and observance of the Law
of the LORD, and to teaching its decrees and laws in Israel.'
Ezra 7:9b–10

God's Word is 'alive and active' (Heb. 4:12) – it takes a lifetime to unpack its treasures that help grow our relationship with its author. So, the length of time we spend studying isn't the key. What's important is that our choice to study God's Word is birthed from desire (see Day 2), otherwise we might only open our Bible to tick off a daily reading plan, to lead a group or to preach, if we open it at all. These are good and necessary reasons to study Scripture, but they won't inspire a passionate pursuit and response to God in his Word.

You don't need to be a priest, monk or theologian to *study* it, which means, to seek and enquire. Whether you have a few minutes or an hour, ask God to enlighten your reading by his Spirit,[6] to help you discern insights and to understand and apply what he wants to teach you. As I've written elsewhere: 'Five minutes focused immersion in the word is far better than fifty minutes distracted skim reading.'[7]

Are there any extra resources you could buy or ask for as a gift to help your understanding? A study Bible, Bible handbook or commentary?

Dwell with this verse through your day, and how Ezra and Aidan were shaped and empowered through their study of God's Word.

DAY 5

'The gracious hand of his God was on him. For Ezra
had devoted himself to the study and observance of the Law
of the LORD, and to teaching its decrees and laws in Israel.'
Ezra 7:9b–10

'When you read the Word, say, "God speak to me and whatever you tell me,
I will do it" ... Do the Book. Do it!'[8]

This eager anticipation to hear from God in his Word then respond to what he
says, sums up Ezra's devotion to study *and* observance. God's Word was Ezra's
rule of life. It formed his opinions, moulded his temperament and conduct, and
guided his words and choices.

Putting into practice what you've learned from prayerful meditation on Scripture:

- Teaches you how to live as Jesus did and adopt his lifestyle.[9]
- Demonstrates to God and to people that he truly is your Lord;[10] affirming
  what you know and say in action.[11]
- Strengthens and equips you for the trials and afflictions of life.[12]
- Releases freedom and blessing in your life, i.e. peace and fulfilment.[13]
- Grows your faith and experience of God's promises. It's as you act in re-
  sponse to God's promises that you encounter their fulfilment, which in
  turn, deepens your trust.[14]

Open your heart to God. Is there anything specific you feel nudged to put into
practice today?

Dwell with this verse through your day, and how Ezra and Aidan were
shaped and empowered through their study of God's Word.

DAY 6

'The gracious hand of his God was on him. For Ezra
had devoted himself to the study and observance of the
Law of the LORD, and to teaching its decrees and laws in Israel.'
Ezra 7:9b–10

Ezra and Aidan shared their lives and taught God's Word with people who didn't have copies of Scripture themselves; much like many of our friends, perhaps. Having devoted themselves to the study and observance of God's commands, they were able to communicate them in a way others could understand and apply to their own lives.[15]

God's Word doesn't change but culture does, and we're all called to convey God's Word in meaningful ways to others.[16] Picture the faces of people you know. Hold each individual or group before God for a few moments; family, friends, colleagues, acquaintances and followers on social media. Ask God to inspire you how to convey truth and wisdom from his Word that will be relevant to their understanding of Christianity, their background and current situation, their relationships, problems, worries, etc. But also consider how your conduct and lifestyle choices might convey God's ways to others, as you continue being transformed in response to his Word.

If you're a parent or carer of children, what time can you commit to help them learn from God's Word? Ask God to show you how your choices and lifestyle can teach them too.

Dwell with this verse through your day, and how Ezra and Aidan's teaching was made effective by first devoting themselves to living out what they'd learned.

DAY 7

> 'The gracious hand of his God was on him. For Ezra
> had devoted himself to the study and observance of the
> Law of the LORD, and to teaching its decrees and laws in Israel.'
> Ezra 7:9b–10

Through his Word, God comforts us in distressing times, shapes our conduct, helps us with difficulties and guides us through uncertainty. We don't just study it to know and talk about it; we study it to let it support, guide, influence and transform our lives.

As we conclude our week, pray about and commit to how you've felt led in your:

- Devotion to God's Word;
- Study of his Word;
- Application of his Word;
- Teaching his Word through your life as well as your words.

Some of us can devote ourselves to prayerful meditation, twenty, thirty or sixty minutes a day. Others to a half hour a week, or less. But we can all devote ourselves to prayerfully dwelling with just one verse at a time. God never condemns, but let the passion and influence of people you know who are steeped in Scripture inspire you to switch off your phone or screen, close your eyes to distraction and meditate on just a few words, even now.

Let's pray: Loving God, thank you for your precious Word and the rich blessing of discerning your messages to my soul through its pages. I open my heart to know you more and my life to be transformed by its truth.

Continue to dwell and pray on these words and images through your day.

DAY 1

'Always give yourselves fully to the work of the Lord.'
1 Corinthians 15:58b

If you serve the people of God's church, paid or unpaid, full- or part-time, this word is for you. Likewise, if you're a retail assistant, social worker, politician, cleaner, doctor, refuse collector, teacher or charitable volunteer, etc. The 'work of the Lord' isn't reserved for certain individuals, roles, giftings or responsibilities, it's something we're all called to do; and to give ourselves to it *fully*.[1]

But what is this work? Ultimately, as Jesus explained, it's 'to believe in the one he has sent' (John 6:29). This is our essential, life-giving foundation necessary for every *work of the Lord*. All that we do for the Lord is to be immersed in our belief that Jesus reconciled us to our loving Father. It's from this devoted relationship that we live a life infused with and radiating our knowledge of him; a holy life of love, forgiveness and service that seeks to live by God's ways and commands.[2] And to this *work* we give ourselves *fully*.

Your belief isn't just what you think or speak about, it's how you live out your life in Jesus; and this kind of belief is the work God has called you to. If you tend to work *for* the Lord rather than working *out of* your loving, yielded relationship with him, let this truth release you from any strained effort, and instil his joy and peace.

Embrace God's love for you as you dwell with this verse through your day.

DAY 2

'Always give yourselves fully to the work of the Lord.'
1 Corinthians 15:58b

The work of Jesus was to reveal God's life and fulfil his purpose.[3] That must therefore underpin the nature of our work too, no matter who we are or what we do in the everyday ordinariness of life.

Our work for the Lord is:

- To yield to the transforming power of the Holy Spirit that gradually conforms us into his likeness.
- To align what we say and do with his teaching on how to live God's kingdom life, that conveys truth and releases kingdom blessings.

In short, it's to yield to God's divine, spiritual life infusing and permeating our everyday, ordinary lives as we love and serve others.

To this *work* we're to give ourselves *fully*. It's not something we dip into from time to time; we give ourselves to God's work willingly, diligently, passionately and energetically through prayerful discernment, reading his Word and responding to his nudges. Some may be driven by status, wealth or pleasure, but we are compelled by God's love, truth and abundant life.

Hold your roles and responsibilities in mind and picture the transforming effect of God's love, holiness, grace, compassion and generosity, infusing them. How does this inspire and encourage you?

Dwell with your response to God's *work* through your day, and how you'll pursue it *fully*.

DAY 3

'Always give yourselves fully to the work of the Lord.'
1 Corinthians 15:58b

I'm a parent, grandparent, homemaker, writer and speaker. I've been an investment banker, church administrator, house group, worship and prayer leader. And I'm still learning how delighting in Jesus infuses his life into the ordinariness of changing nappies, packing lunchboxes, washing windows or doing the food shop; into different roles, responsibilities and ministries. It's awareness of the awesome, amazing, beautiful presence of Jesus that inspires a passion to give myself fully to his life that may, in turn, make him known.

'Seek his face always' the psalmist writes (Ps. 105:4). *Fixing* our eyes on Jesus infuses wisdom to direct, contentment in all circumstances, peace that overrules emotional turmoil and assurance that we're valued no matter what we do. *Walking* in step with Jesus ignites proactive compassion; raising our voice for the marginalised and oppressed, and giving to the poor. *Delighting* in Jesus shines his presence into whatever we're doing. In short, enthusiasm to commit fully to the Lord's work is birthed from a passion for Jesus; loving him, being with him, adoring him. All these come first. Knowing Jesus is the purest inspiration to giving ourselves fully to God's work.

Still your busy thoughts. Switch off distractions. Release discouragements. Ask the Holy Spirit to inspire images of Jesus from the Gospels, to warm your heart's response.

Dwell with the image of who Jesus is as you commit yourself fully to his work today.

DAY 4

'Always give yourselves fully to the work of the Lord.'
1 Corinthians 15:58b

A few years after God clearly called me to teach his Word, I ran in the opposite direction. As the build-up of fear got the better of me, I settled for a place of comfort; a place without pre-event nervous nausea, and at times, panic-stricken tears. A place where I didn't have to stand in front of a sea of faces willing my mouth to moisten, or deal with any critical feedback and my sense of inadequacy. A place where I didn't have to be away from home or navigate driving through unfamiliar towns. I said 'no' to what God had clearly willed, in preference for making life feel easier.

But just as God rescued and recommissioned Jonah,[4] God reached out to me too. His conviction was pure. I confessed my rebellion, recommitted myself *fully* to his work, and trusted for him to reopen doors.

If you've said 'no' to God too, be reassured. God is the redeemer of your mistakes and the giver of second (third, fourth . . .) chances. Talk with him if you've been settling for less than giving your best, or if you've buried the dreams he placed in your heart. Admit where you may have run away from his purpose, given in to discouragement, or settled for an easier life. Listen for how he might speak to your heart, then recommit yourself fully to his work.

Dwell with God's inspiration to recommit yourself fully to his work in and through your life.

DAY 5

'Always give yourselves fully to the work of the Lord.'
1 Corinthians 15:58b

There've been times I've given myself to the Lord's work but felt discouraged. Times when I've given out so much with little or no monetary income, igniting fears for future security. Times when it's just jolly hard work and exhausting; when despite knowing I'm doing his work, I'm faced with overwhelming obstacles. When I've yielded to Christ's loving humility but have been shamed, blamed and rejected. And times when, despite offering love and asking forgiveness, it's been painfully hurled back in my face. But you know what? Jesus' work for God was hard too, to the point of excruciating. And Jesus is with me – and with you.

'With your help I can run through a barricade; with my God I can scale a wall' (Ps. 18:29).⁵ Let this truth encourage you to persevere. If you're seeking to yield to God's character and giving yourself fully to his work, be confident of his help to break through, overcome or endure the struggles you face. Do the odds feel stacked against you? 'With my God . . .' Are you facing what seems like an impenetrable 'barricade' of obstacles? 'With my God . . .' Is your nose up against the rough 'wall' of a deadline, exam, problem or pain? 'With my God . . .'

Open your heart to God's wisdom, guidance, sustaining strength, peace, enabling, creativity and more. Know that with God, you can overcome whatever threatens to defeat you.

Dwell with God's presence and help as you give yourself fully to his work today.

DAY 6

'Always give yourselves fully to the work of the Lord.'
1 Corinthians 15:58b

When I feel apathetic about the Lord's work or tempted to do my own thing, I remind myself of three things:

1. 'throw off everything that hinders' (Heb. 12:1a). For example:
   - Fear.
   - Cynicism: Paul urges us not to 'quench the Spirit' but to test what God is saying so we can embrace and pursue what is good (1 Thess. 5:19–22).
   - The stuff of this life that steals my time, attention, energy, gifting and resources away from God's life that is truly life.
   - . . . whatever the Holy Spirit prompts to my heart.

   Do any of these nudge you for a response?

2. 'and the sin that so easily entangles' (Heb. 12:1b).
   To *entangle* is to knot, ensnare, restrain, control or tightly constrain. If you've tried to untangle a knotted ball of string, you'll know what that means. The string is present but the knots prevent its usefulness. God's life resides within us by his Spirit, but its power and effectiveness can be held back by sin. What are the *knots* that constrain your work for him, and how does this image encourage you to untie them?

3. I remind myself of how God has ministered through people who've given themselves fully to his work. If you haven't time to read books, look up a personal bio online of your modern or ancient hero of faith; not merely to be inspired by them, but to enthuse your own response.

Dwell with these images as you commit yourself fully to God's work today.

DAY 7

'Always give yourselves fully to the work of the Lord.'
1 Corinthians 15:58b

A familiar quote says, 'Pray as if everything depended on God and work as if everything depended on you.'[6] That is such good advice. Giving ourselves fully to the Lord's work doesn't rely solely on self-effort, but neither does it rely solely on God's transforming and equipping power. It's a beautiful harmonious relationship of the two.

Therefore, 'stand your ground. And don't hold back. Throw yourselves into the work of the Master, confident that nothing you do for him is a waste of time or effort' (1 Cor. 15:58, MSG); 'be steadfast, immovable, always excelling in the work of the Lord [always doing your best and doing more than is needed], being *continually* aware that your labor [even to the point of exhaustion] in the Lord is not futile nor wasted [it is never without purpose]' (1 Cor. 15:58, AMP).

Reread these different translations, slowly; aloud if possible. Hear God's loving encouragement to your soul. Reflect on how you feel led to respond then commit yourself to pursuing it.

Let's pray: Jesus, you inspire and enthuse me with who you are. Forgive me and protect me from diminishing the dreams you've placed in my heart and from growing cynical or lazy with what you've called me to be and do. I commit myself again to your transforming and influencing work. Thank you for your encouragement, that whatever the nature of my work, when I invest it for your kingdom, it's never wasted.

Dwell with this verse through your day, knowing God's delight in your response.

DAY 1

'And he will be called Wonderful Counsellor, Mighty God, Everlasting Father, Prince of Peace.' Isaiah 9:6

'My name is Anne with an "e".'

It may sound odd but that's how I often introduce myself, and I'm not alone. I met another 'Anne' recently who introduced herself the same way! That 'e' is important to me, as my parents specifically chose their preferred spelling of it. They also gave me a second name, Catherine, after my paternal grandmother; so that name is deeply special and meaningful to me too. But names in the Bible weren't just identifiers or parental preferences; they often carried powerful connotations – in fact, they always did when they were names God gave for himself.

Similarly, Jesus is given a variety of names in Scripture, names which proclaim truth and descriptions about him.[1] They define the qualities of God's inherent character and nature, his roles, abilities and purpose. They reveal who he is to the world – and to you, personally. So, they're not just names to know or memorise. These names help you meet with who he is, but also help you pray for others.

How have you experienced Jesus in the ways these names suggest on first reading? Which one or more names mentioned especially resonates with you today?

Embrace what the Holy Spirit may be revealing to you, and thank Jesus for who he is.

Continue to dwell with these names of Jesus throughout your day. Let them build your faith, encourage your heart and continue to guide and empower you in prayer.

DAY 2

'And he will be called Wonderful Counsellor, Mighty God, Everlasting Father, Prince of Peace.' Isaiah 9:6

Feeling terribly sick while undergoing cancer treatment, Darlene Zschech wrote a song (with Martin Smith) about God's greatness.[2] When interviewed, she said, 'A lot of people bring their theology down to their experience, but I believe you've got to take your experience up to what the Word of God says.' [3] Whatever experience you or others are going through, I pray that Isaiah's prophetic description of Jesus will help you engage with who he is.

God revealed his names to his people as they needed them – especially at times of deep crisis.[4] When Isaiah prophetically described the names and nature of the Messiah, whose reign would be universal, powerful nations were attacking the Israelites. Destruction and captivity were imminent. But God never lost sight of his purpose to save and restore.[5] If you're suffering distress, remember, this isn't your only reality. You may have to live *with* difficulty, but you can choose to live *by* faith in the nature of who Jesus is.

Messiah *has* come. Focus on these descriptions of Jesus. Whatever calamity you or others face, rest in the assurance that Jesus fulfils what these names suggest. As you prayerfully reflect on and proclaim them, they will raise your expectation of who Jesus wants to be for you and for others.

Continue to dwell with these names of Jesus throughout your day. Let them build your faith, encourage your heart and continue to guide and empower you in prayer.

DAY 3

'And he will be called Wonderful Counsellor, Mighty God, Everlasting Father, Prince of Peace.' Isaiah 9:6

Jesus is Wonderful. There is nothing dull about him! He is exceptional. Distinguished from all the kings of the earth. Though he was born as a human child he was conceived by God's Spirit. He was both God and man. He is God's Son. He is God. His life from conception to resurrection was wonderful. Ascended Lord and King, he *is* wonderful.

If the world would believe in who he is, it would marvel at the wonders he has done. It would marvel at his wonderful love. It would marvel at the mystery of his godliness. But you *do* believe in who he is. Take a moment to praise him with this name: Wonderful. Exceptional. Distinguished. Delight in his wonderful love for you and those you pray for.

His name, and therefore his nature, is Wonderful Counsellor. He rules and reigns with God's supernatural wisdom and justice. And he knows our hearts and our circumstances better than we do. No one is able to teach us as he can; teaching us God's ways so 'we may walk in his paths' (Isa. 2:3).

Whatever you face today, know Jesus as your Wonderful Counsellor. Ask him for the counsel you need, and listen for any response he may wish to give – for you, and/or for those you pray for.

Continue to dwell with your Wonderful Counsellor through the day. Let him build your faith, encourage your heart and continue to guide and empower you in prayer.

DAY 4

'And he will be called Wonderful Counsellor, Mighty God,
Everlasting Father, Prince of Peace.' Isaiah 9:6

His name, and therefore his nature, is Mighty God. He has ultimate strength and power to execute God's plans; to save souls and establish his kingdom. He has authority over angel armies and has defeated our spiritual enemy. You will face problems in this world but be reassured, know his peace – for Jesus has 'overcome the world' (John 16:33).

It was customary for kings to command their armies from a hillside. Battle would ensue in the valley beneath, but by placing themselves higher up they oversaw the entire scene, rather than just a part. They could devise battle strategy and issue commands, or send help and reinforcement precisely where it was needed. If you feel alone in your battle, in a valley of darkness and despair, look up. Jesus is with you and watching over you. He knows the brokenness around you and within you. And Jesus, Mighty God, has all power and authority to help. Ask him for the might of his Person and provision that you need. Ask him for the 'sword' of his Word you can use in prayer for yourself or for others.[6] You are not alone. Trust him to sustain and equip you, and listen for any response he may wish to give – for you, and/or for those you pray for.

Dwell with your Wonderful Counsellor and Mighty God through the day. Let him build your faith, encourage your heart and continue to guide and empower you in prayer.

DAY 5

'And he will be called Wonderful Counsellor, Mighty God, Everlasting Father, Prince of Peace.' Isaiah 9:6

His name, and therefore his nature, is Everlasting Father. He is one with his Father, expressing his nature perfectly.[7] What tenderness and compassion he imparts to us. As a father is concerned for his children, as he cares for, disciplines, provides for and protects them, so Jesus' rule will convey this nature too; forever and unfailing.

Have no fear in approaching him, no matter where you are in life or what you've done. He loves and delights in you, today and forever. Unconditionally. Have no doubts about his compassionate care as you draw near. You may be suffering calamity, but he comes to you with sustaining wisdom and strength, the comfort of his presence and his promise never to leave. Know that his rule in your life is caring; his discipline is always for your very best.[8]

Be released today from praying for all your needs, and instead, picture yourself with Jesus as Everlasting Father. You may see yourself walking with him, sitting with him – you may even see yourself being embraced by him. Dwell with what's comfortable and meaningful for you. He knows your practical needs,[9] so for today, simply be open to his Fatherly love and care.

Dwell with your Wonderful Counsellor, Mighty God and Everlasting Father through the day. Let him build your faith, encourage your heart and continue to guide and empower you in prayer.

DAY 6

'And he will be called Wonderful Counsellor, Mighty God, Everlasting Father, Prince of Peace.' Isaiah 9:6

His name and therefore his nature, is Prince of Peace. *Prince* implies an administrator. *Peace* means wholeness. To respond to our Prince of Peace is to live in harmony with God and to be people of peace towards others. It's to be at ease, rather than restless, 'being at rest both spiritually and emotionally'.[10] Jesus administers the benefits of wholeness and well-being to individuals who've accepted his reign, even when our circumstances are anything but peaceful.

Isaiah warns of losing his peace when we turn our back on his ways.[11] To experience his peace, we yield to him. While suffering the pain of a relationship breakdown, I lacked peace if I focused on the other person's faults; it made me arrogant, angry, self-righteous and bitter. But when I yielded to Christ's love, grace, kindness and forgiveness – for my own faults too – I knew deep, life-enriching peace, even within my heartache.

If you lack peace, ask the Holy Spirit to show you why. It may be rooted in a lack of trust, or an aspect of your life that you've yet to submit to his ways. Open your heart to Jesus to help you encounter his wholeness of well-being. Believe in faith for his response as you rest in the knowledge that he's with you.

Dwell with your Wonderful Counsellor, Mighty God, Everlasting Father and Prince of Peace through the day. Let him build your faith, encourage your heart and continue to guide and empower you in prayer.

DAY 7

'And he will be called Wonderful Counsellor, Mighty God, Everlasting Father, Prince of Peace.' Isaiah 9:6

As God's people we know but also worship Jesus by these names, so to conclude our place of dwelling, I've collated some prayers and truths for you to reflect on, respond to and pray for yourself or for someone else.

Wonderful Counsellor

I will praise the LORD, who counsels me; even at night my heart instructs me.

Ps. 16:7

Mighty God

Who is this King of glory? The LORD strong and mighty, the LORD mighty in battle.

Ps. 24:8

Everlasting Father

the LORD is compassionate and gracious, slow to anger, abounding in love . . . As a father has compassion on his children, so the LORD has compassion on those who fear him . . .

Ps. 103:8,13

Prince of Peace

Peace I leave with you; my peace I give you. I do not give to you as the world gives. Do not let your hearts be troubled and do not be afraid.

John 14:27

Reflect and pray further on whichever truth or prayer especially resonates. How does it reassure you and bring you hope? Worship Jesus for who he is under the banner of this name. You may like to use Handel's *Messiah* to help you.[12]

Continue to dwell with these names of Jesus throughout your day. Let him build your faith, encourage your heart and continue to guide and empower you in prayer.

DAY 1

'Lord, teach [me] to pray' Luke 11:1

Do you ever struggle to pray? Perhaps you've prayed repeatedly about something but feel discouraged by God's apparent lack of response. You're so overwhelmed emotionally that you've no words or energy to pray. The issue at hand for yourself, someone else, the nation or the world is so vast and complex that you're not sure how to start praying. Or perhaps you do pray, but it's a hard slog; something you feel you ought to do but struggle to be inspired by. You may have other reasons, especially if you're struggling with prayer right now.

One of the ways we dwell with God's Word is to hold a theme in our hearts, and let God respond through various Scriptures. Being in his Word in this way is what we'll enjoy this week; reading and responding to what God says when we're struggling to pray. The disciples were inspired by how Jesus prayed; perhaps by his words, demeanour, his natural flow and the reality of his relationship with his Father. It's no wonder they asked him to teach them.[1] Each day we'll consider a different reason why prayer might sometimes feel tough. But even when prayer is faith-filled and flowing, asking Jesus to teach us to pray is a prayer we can all ask daily.

For today, dwell with the disciples' request; let it focus your mind on Jesus as you wait for him to help you to pray for the uppermost things on your heart.

DAY 2

'Lord, teach [me] to pray' Luke 11:1

Needs for prayer bombard my mind, a stream of seeming impossible situations burdening my heart. Wars, refugees, climate change, living costs, humanitarian catastrophes . . . plus news updates from missionaries or aid organisations, and the needs of my own family, friends, church and country. But as the wind in my prayer sails threatens to flag, God's sovereignty comes to mind. It's time to shift my focus onto the answer instead of the problem: 'Lord, teach [me] to pray'.

When the disciples asked Jesus to teach them to pray, he immediately focused on 'Our Father in heaven' (Matt. 6:9). There's never a better place to start praying, whether we're upbeat and full of faith, or crushed by weighty problems. We draw close to God as we gaze on the beauty of his holiness, righteousness, love, compassion, justice, mercy, sovereignty and power. And as we draw close through attentive faith, we know him with us.

If you're struggling to pray because of overwhelming gloom and fear of personal or global issues, shift your attention away from the problems onto who God is – and onto God with you. If it helps, read Psalm 145; prayerfully attentive to each description. Alternatively, you may like to worship God and build your faith through song; for example, with 'Way Maker' by Leeland.[2]

Dwell with your request for help to pray. Keep an open heart and mind to how God may shape his answer.

DAY 3

'Lord, teach [me] to pray' Luke 11:1

I was a sham. At least, that's what I'd begun to believe. I was taking my first tentative steps into a wider teaching ministry, but had been feeling disconnected from God's close and tangible presence which I'd previously enjoyed. It was a bleak time. No one, not even my husband, knew how spiritually low I felt, but I hung onto my faith by reading and praying a verse of Scripture that for some reason was on my heart.[3]

For many weeks that one verse sustained me; it was something tangible I could read and thank God for in faith, despite my insecure feelings. And then, one day, a beautiful handmade card arrived; a stunning photograph of my favourite landscape and a verse addressed to 'Anne'. Yes, very personal. And yes, it was the verse I'd been clinging to those past weeks. God came to me through that Scripture.[4] Although I couldn't feel him, he drew close and restored my faith.

Praying God's inspired Word builds faith and infuses peace. You won't always *feel* his presence, but as you hold tightly to his truth, even when you feel blue, it will be life to you; eternal spiritual strength and protection to guard your heart, mind and soul. If God hasn't inspired a specific word, you can still pray Scripture that magnifies him in your situation.

Dwell with your request for help to pray. Pray God's Word, do what it says, and know how deeply he loves and cares for you.

DAY 4

'Lord, teach [me] to pray' Luke 11:1

I felt drained by the sheer slog of it. God seemed to be in heaven while I tried but failed to get him to hear, let alone answer my prayers from my bedroom. Time dragged as requests from Christian charities, persecuted believers, news-feeds and country profiles overflowed my notebook into a lever-arch file. I could never pray long enough to cover it all and felt uninspired and unenergised as I tried: 'Lord, teach me to pray.'

'Pray in the Spirit on all occasions with all kinds of prayers and requests' (Eph. 6:18).

This answer to my call for help made a home in my discouraged soul. It released me from guilt and my sense of failure. It cut through my inadequate under-standing and ideals. It allowed me to say 'no' to the impossible expectation that I can pray for everyone and everything. Scripture teaches *all* of us to pray for leaders, for the poor and oppressed, etc. But God also burdens each of us with specific passions and burdens. We're called to be faithful to that, while freed from the needs he's empowering others to pray for. And we pray effectively as *he* leads. Perseverance is vital, but striving opposes dependence on the Holy Spirit.

What's on *your* heart to pray for? Still your thoughts, discern his leading, and God will breathe his will and purpose through your yielded heart.

Dwell with your request for help to pray. Keep an open heart to how the Holy Spirit will continue to lead and empower you.

DAY 5

'Lord, teach [me] to pray' Luke 11:1

He was shorter than me but was always my 'big brother' and I, his 'little sis'. He excelled as a head chef and skilled carpenter, at water sports and renovating motorbikes. He was a caring, friendly man, but he was also an alcoholic; an addiction that could transform him into an angry, bitter and, at times, violent apparition of himself. Battling periods of binge-drinking and suicidal attempts with periods of being dry, his marriage, health and job opportunities deteriorated. And tragically, aged 43, he died.

There are times when you're so close to a situation emotionally or so distraught by its unfolding effects that you feel too overwhelmed to pray. But the Holy Spirit who leads you in prayer will, at such times, pray on your behalf. For 'the Spirit helps us in our weakness. We do not know what we ought to pray for, but the Spirit himself intercedes for us through wordless groans' (Rom. 8:26).

Dwell with this promise as you hold your situation in your heart. If it helps, stand tall with arms stretched wide, or sit with cupped hands on your lap as you ask and trust the Holy Spirit to intercede. He hears your sighs. He sees your tears. He feels your pain for yourself or those you pray for. As you trust the Holy Spirit is fulfilling his promise to pray, be present to God with you.

Dwell with your request for help to pray and know God's peace as you trust for the Spirit's response.

DAY 6

'Lord, teach [me] to pray' Luke 11:1

She was unable to drive. Walking wasn't easy. She believed in God but hadn't grasped his gift of friendship-discipleship. She attended a weekly church ladies' group, but her lipstick smile and blue eyeshadow failed to mask the loneliness in her soul. And despite many months of praying for her, nothing changed. Feeling discouraged, I asked, 'Lord, teach me to pray.'

> Suppose a brother or a sister is without clothes and daily food. If one of you says to them, 'Go in peace; keep warm and well fed,' but does nothing about their physical needs, what good is it? In the same way, faith by itself, if it is not accompanied by action, is dead.
>
> *Jas 2:15–17*

I felt compassion and had faith to pray, but was also called to be part of God's answer. She couldn't drive – I could. She struggled to walk – I had a strong arm. She didn't know God personally – I could introduce her. She was lonely – I could visit. And so began my friendship with Beatrice.[5]

Might you be part of God's answer to your prayer? Perhaps you feel led to join an aid agency, to support victims of sex trafficking or to give up your job to serve overseas. But my response with Beatrice was no less significant. Never play down the importance of whatever God asks you to do in being part of his answer to prayer.

Dwell with your request for help to pray. God might reveal how to partner with him for the answer.

DAY 7

'Lord, teach [me] to pray' Luke 11:1

There are days when time doesn't allow for prayer, or you're so exhausted you keep falling asleep, or you're feeling too unwell to discern what words to say. But be encouraged. When Jesus was teaching his disciples about prayer, he said: 'your Father knows what you need before you ask him' (Matt. 6:8). On these days, you can thank God that he knows what you need, then pray the gift of Jesus' own prayer that he's given you to use with faith and expectancy.

Let's pray his prayer now, slowly and from the heart. Either pray the words as written, or give pause between each line and let the Holy Spirit inspire you to adapt them for yourself or a situation on your heart:

Our Father in heaven,
hallowed be your name
your kingdom come,
your will be done,
on earth as it is in heaven.
Give us today our daily bread.
And forgive us our debts,
as we also have forgiven our debtors.
And lead us not into temptation,
But deliver us from the evil one.

Matt. 6:9–13

Now close with a short prayer of thanks, praise or loving adoration . . .

Amen

Dwell with Jesus' prayer through your day: this is his answer to help you.

DAY 1

'Give thanks to the LORD, for he is good;
his love endures for ever.' Psalm 107:1

The warmth of spring sunshine kisses splashes of pink and blue flowers, stretching up towards a clear sky. It is quiet, but for the flapping and spray of two sparrows taking a bath; a peaceful haven to prayerfully reflect on God's Word. But I'm feeling the pressure of pressing deadlines and the angst of a problem refusing to be resolved.

My Bible lies open at Psalm 23. I begin to pray, asking God to be all it promises for my unsettled situations. I ask him to be my guide, my provider, my carer and protector, then fret that he might not answer. Ha, but I am surely mistaken! The psalm wasn't written as a request. It's author, David, was declaring its truths as something he knew and experienced. 'The LORD is . . . I lack nothing . . . he leads . . . he refreshes . . . He guides' (Ps. 23:1–3).

And so, I start over, this time thanking God that he is all this to me already. And his peace and assurance infuse my soul.

This is our place of dwelling this week; the place of thanksgiving that unlocks our soul to experience what's already ours. But for today, dwell on this verse and respond as you feel led.

Give thanks . . .

He is good . . .

His love endures for ever . . .

Where do these words start taking your thoughts and prayers? Dwell with them in your heart and mind through your day.

DAY 2

'Give thanks to the LORD, for he is good;
his love endures for ever.' Psalm 107:1

Still your heart, and pray: I thank you, heavenly Father, that you are good; that whatever I'm facing, your goodness will sustain me. Your goodness will guide me in your ways and will. Thank you for your love, Father. Your unconditional, unfailing, everlasting love.

When life's stresses and strains begin to consume your thoughts and rule your emotions, you can find yourself in an endless spin of 'ask, ask, ask' in prayer. To counter this, I encourage the habit of starting your day, your time of prayer, your next task, meeting or conversation, by pausing to turn your attention onto God, and saying, 'Thank you, for [name something relevant].' It breaks any cycle of domineering thoughts or worries, and opens your heart to receive in faith what is already yours to experience.

This isn't my own idea, it reflects Paul's counsel to pray when you're worried, and not just pray, but to 'present your requests [with thanksgiving]' (Phil. 4:6).

Pray about something on your heart now, and as you do:

Thank God that he hears your prayer.

Thank God that you can trust in his goodness for the right response to your prayer.

Thank God for his love, not just for you, but for others for whom you pray.

Dwell with God's Word through your day, Give thanks . . . He is good . . . His love endures for ever . . . See how it inspires your response.

DAY 3

'Give thanks to the LORD, for he is good;
his love endures for ever.' Psalm 107:1

Still your heart, and pray: I thank you, heavenly Father, that you are good; that whatever I'm facing, your goodness will sustain me. Your goodness will guide me in your ways and will. Thank you for your love, Father. Your unconditional, unfailing, everlasting love.

Yesterday, Paul encouraged us to pray with thanksgiving, something Jesus role-modelled in what appeared to be an impossible situation.[1] But thanksgiving threads its way through Scripture, characterising all of a believer's life. Whether it's thanking God for the food you eat, for the work of your hands, or for who he is, Paul says, 'whatever you do, whether in word or deed, do it all in the name of the Lord Jesus, *giving thanks* to God the Father through him' (Col. 3:17, emphasis mine). Giving thanks 'in whatever you do' opens your heart to experience God's peace, guidance, insight, wisdom, etc. It turns your heart to who he is and inspires a yielded response.

How do you already give regular thanks to God, and what do you forget to thank him for? Even if you're not grateful for a situation, thank God for a facet of his character that supports you in it, or a promise pertinent to it. How could you nurture thanksgiving in your varied situations and responsibilities?

Dwell with God's Word through your day, Give thanks . . . He is good . . . His love endures forever . . . See how it inspires your response.

DAY 4

'Give thanks to the LORD, for he is good;
his love endures for ever.' Psalm 107:1

Still your heart, and pray: I thank you, heavenly Father, that you are good; that whatever I'm facing, your goodness will sustain me. Your goodness will guide me in your ways and will. Thank you for your love, Father. Your unconditional, unfailing, everlasting love.

When praying God's Word with thanksgiving as described on Day 1, it encourages faith because we're praying prayers focused on God's nature, promises and his desire for his 'good' in all situations.[2]

To introduce this week, I related my story about Psalm 23. Below are a few more suggestions to encourage you to adopt a short passage as a prayer of thanksgiving. Believe in faith for God's Word, prayed in context, to become a reality in your life:

- When you're worried about provision, thank him using the words of Matthew 6:25–33; thanking God for his promise that as you sincerely seek his kingdom and righteousness in your life, you need not fear the future.[3]
- When you're not sure how to pray, or feel overwhelmed with requests for prayer, thank God that he already knows what you/they need. Be reassured from Jesus' teaching.[4]
- When you need guidance and wisdom, pray James 1:5,[5] thanking God as you believe for the fulfilment of this promise.

Dwell with God's Word through your day, Give thanks . . . He is good . . . His love endures for ever . . . See how it inspires your response.

DAY 5

'Give thanks to the Lord, for he is good;
his love endures for ever.' Psalm 107:1

Still your heart, and pray: I thank you, heavenly Father, that you are good; that whatever I'm facing, your goodness will sustain me. Your goodness will guide me in your ways and will. Thank you for your love, Father. Your unconditional, unfailing, everlasting love.

Psalm 107 celebrates God's intervention in human predicaments such as captivity, wanderings, bondage, sickness, storms, hunger and calamity. It declares God's goodness and loving mercy, given to all who humbly seek him; inviting us to thank God for his redemption and ongoing care. Thanking God is, in effect, grateful praise. To recall how God has sustained us, answered prayer and guided us in the past, reassures and builds faith.

So today, give thanks for those times when you've experienced God's presence through his peace, strength and guidance, the empowering of his Spirit, or his divine intervention.

You may like to:

- Give thanks of praise in words of prayer;
- Use or adapt relevant Scripture to form your grateful praise;
- Sing out a new song, or sing along to one you're familiar with, to express your thanks, praise and worship.

Whatever you choose, lift up your heart from today's concerns, and thank God for his goodness and steadfast love, for all he's been and done for you in the past.

Dwell with God's Word through your day, Give thanks . . . He is good . . . His love endures for ever . . . See how it inspires your response.

DAY 6

'Give thanks to the LORD, for he is good;
his love endures for ever.' Psalm 107:1

Still your heart, and pray: I thank you, heavenly Father, that you are good; that whatever I'm facing, your goodness will sustain me. Your goodness will guide me in your ways and will. Thank you for your love, Father. Your unconditional, unfailing, everlasting love.

Or course, we don't just thank God for his goodness when we're worried or tackling problems. We have an abundance of precious and wonderful gifts to thank him for; our homes, loved ones and friends, the beauty of his world, food in our cupboard, clean water in our taps – the list would be endless. Delight God with an outpouring of heartfelt thanks for whatever you're especially grateful for today.

If you've time, reflect on these alternative translations too, pausing to respond with prayerful thanks as the Holy Spirit highlights different words or phrases to your heart:

'Give thanks to the LORD, for he is good! His faithful love endures forever.' (NLT)

'Say thank you to the Lord for being so good, for always being so loving and kind.' (TLB)

'Oh, thank GOD – he's so good! His love never runs out.' (MSG)

'O give thanks to the LORD, for He is good; For His compassion and lovingkindness endure forever!' (AMP)

'Shout praises to the LORD! He is good to us, and his love never fails.' (CEV)

Dwell with God's Word through your day, Give thanks . . . He is good . . . His love endures forever . . . See how it inspires your response.

DAY 7

'Give thanks to the LORD, for he is good;
his love endures for ever.' Psalm 107:1

Still your heart, and pray: I thank you, heavenly Father, that you are good; that whatever I'm facing, your goodness will sustain me. Your goodness will guide me in your ways and will. Thank you for your love, Father. Your unconditional, unfailing, everlasting love.

We've been reminded this week that it's God's good and loving design for your life to overflow with thanksgiving in all your circumstances.[6] This doesn't suggest you must thank God for pain and problems, because they don't come from him. Rather, Scripture encourages you to thank God for his goodness and love *in* your blessings as well as *in* your difficulties. Thanking God for his presence *with* you to steer and sustain you through whatever you face. Thanking him that problems don't have to overwhelm you with fear, anger, or discouragement.

How might you nurture this characteristic of thanksgiving beyond this week? Not just in a time of prayer, but throughout your day?

What aspect of God's goodness and love are you experiencing today? Spend time now in grateful praise.

Let's pray: Thank you, loving Father, for your presence and promises in all that I currently face. I open my heart to your peace and strength, grace, wisdom and guidance.

Dwell with God's Word for one more day, Give thanks . . . He is good . . . His love endures forever . . . See how it inspires your response.

DAY 1

'Love the LORD your God with all your heart and with all your soul and with all your strength.' Deuteronomy 6:5

Imagine walking into a room and commanding someone to love you. It just wouldn't work, would it? And yet, that's exactly what God does in his greatest of all his commands.[1]

But to love is to first be *stirred* to love; it's a heartfelt, enthusiastic, devoted, proactive response to whoever or whatever inspired you. When God *commands* us to love him, he's urging us to know him for himself. 'We love because he first loved us' (1 John 4:19). When we know who God is personally – rather than through hearsay – thankfulness, desire and devotion overflow in loving response.

Knowing God nurtures an intimate relationship:

- Of mutual loving delight;
- Where God helps, enables, provides for and encourages you;
- By which you choose to be moulded by his character and to serve his purposes.

Give a moment to let these truths sink deep into your soul to inspire your love response.

How do you 'hear' this command? If God's tone of voice sounds cool, aloof, forceful or officious, release that. Hear it instead being spoken from the one who loves you even more than you can imagine.

Reflect on words that describe who God is in ways you're especially grateful for. Then express your love through thanks and worship.

Dwell with this understanding of God's greatest command, now and through your day.

DAY 2

'Love the LORD your God with all your heart and with all your soul and with all your strength.' Deuteronomy 6:5

Still your thoughts, focus on God's presence, and hear his longing for you to love him, inserting your name into the square brackets:

[. . .] I am your greatest treasure. I created you, body and soul. You're a living being because of me. I know you intimately and passionately. I created you to know me, to delight in a loving relationship with me, and to live life in its beautiful, wonderful abundance that I intended. The pain and problems you face in the broken world were not my original intention, but I am with you constantly, to sustain, guide, comfort and help you endure or overcome.

I cherish who you are, [. . .]; your voice, personality, talents and interests. I am your forever friend, Father and King. Yes. Forever. Unlike your loves in the world that will falter, fade or fail you, and one day, be no more, I am yours for eternity.

My greatest, deepest desire is that you'd love me too. I long for you to love me in sincere, heartfelt response to your understanding of who I am and my immeasurable love for you.

Know me, [. . .]. Know me and so love me.

Know me and therefore love me with all your heart, soul and strength.

With your entire being.

Know and therefore love me more than anyone or anything else.

Dwell with God's desire for you to love him, now and through your day.

DAY 3

'Love the LORD your God with all your heart and with all your soul and with all your strength.' Deuteronomy 6:5

To love God with *all* our heart, soul and strength is to devote our whole being to him. Anything less leads to split loyalty and devotion, a shared giving of our limited time and resources and a divided set of values and goals. It's impossible to love both God and someone or something else with 'all' that we are.[2] A divided devotion underrates God's character, nature and promises at best; and at worst, disdains them. It's the half-hearted, lukewarm love God despises, because this isn't love in its truest sense.[3]

Ask God to search your heart for places where your love might be divided.

Reflect on why those things or relationships arouse your desire and response towards them, more than towards God.

Talk with him about it, and let him show you how they can and will let you down in ways that he never will. Listen to how he will fulfil your needs in those areas, far beyond what anyone or anything else is capable of.

Believe in the truth that God's 'goodness and love' will pursue you all the days of your life (Ps. 23:6). Believe that he is for your very best, and not against you.[4] Know that he will never reject or abandon you.[5]

Now, rest in these truths, and let God minister his love to your soul.

Dwell with God's desire for you to love him, now and through your day.

DAY 4

'Love the LORD your God with all your heart and with all your soul and with all your strength.' Deuteronomy 6:5

Love relationships deepen when people spend undistracted time together. It's the one thing to prioritise with God too, to nurture and inspire our loving response. David, the man after God's heart,[6] prayed for only 'one thing'; to live close to God's presence (Ps. 27:4). Jesus role-modelled prioritising time with his Father, teaching us to do likewise,[7] emphasising the need for this only 'one thing' by honouring Mary, who sat at his feet, listening to him.[8]

God understands every demand on your time. He understands your health and sleep needs. He cares passionately for the children or dependants you love and care for. But he still longs for you to encounter him in deeper measure to inspire your love response. There are responsibilities you can't avoid, while some may be distractions or excuses. Talk with God about them all. He will help you find space in your head and heart to focus on him, in full busy days, or for short or longer private moments. Be open to his insights and ideas.

Ultimately, though, you have to want to be with him; not because you ought, but because you truly believe he's the very best thing in your life. So, whenever that desire begins to fade, turn to Day 2, and hear again God's loving words to your soul.

Dwell with God's desire for you to love him, now and through your day.

DAY 5

'Love the LORD your God with all your heart and with all your soul and with all your strength.' Deuteronomy 6:5

The 'first' thing we're to pursue to help us love God with all that we are, is to 'seek first his kingdom and his righteousness' (Matt. 6:25–33). This means seeking to yield to Jesus' lifestyle and commands in all we say and do. Paul encourages this with his excellent advice:

> Whatever you do, whether in word or deed, do it all in the name of the Lord Jesus, giving thanks to God the Father through him … Whatever you do, work at it with all your heart, as working for the Lord, not for human masters . . .

Col. 3:17,23

You love God:

- As you speak his truth and love to and over yourself.
- As you prayerfully seek to see others with his love, grace and understanding; as you lean on God to help you hear them as he does.
- As you seek to imbue every conversation, email, social media post or text with his gracious words.
- As you let his priorities permeate your routines and activities, and as you depend on him to enable, guide and transform your life.
- In short, you love God by seeking to bring the whole of your life into the orbit of the nature of his love; love that purifies, radiates and empowers.

Reflect on how loving God can enrich what you say, do and 'message' today.

Dwell with God's desire for you to love him, now and through your day.

DAY 6

We dwell with the following passage in Week 7, but it's a key part of our reflections this week too. It helps us understand the nature of God's love and shows us how he loves us which, in turn, inspires a deeply grateful and loving response. But it also shows us how to love others as we love ourselves, which is the second most important command God's given us.[9]

Prayerfully read and reflect on these words that describe how God loves you:

> Love is patient, love is kind. It does not envy, it does not boast, it is not proud. It does not dishonour others, it is not self-seeking, it is not easily angered, it keeps no record of wrongs. Love does not delight in evil but rejoices with the truth. It always protects, always trusts, always hopes, always perseveres.

> *1 Cor. 13:4–7*

How do these words inspire your love response to God? Express it to him now.

Reread the passage, picturing faces of people you know or who you're acquainted with. This is God's second greatest priority for you. Although no one has seen God, if you love others as he loves you, God's nature and truth will be revealed through your life.[10]

Dwell with God's desire for you to love him, now and through your day.

DAY 7

'Love the LORD your God with all your heart and with all your soul and with all your strength.' Deuteronomy 6:5

We're all on a journey of growing our love response to God. No one loves him perfectly. But as we grow our knowledge of him, his perfect, unfailing love inspires us to deepen and strengthen our loving, yielded response.

Immerse yourself in all that God has inspired to your heart this week, then pray through your response to these questions he might ask, inserting your name in the square brackets:

[…], is your love of my presence enthusing you to share your time with me?
[…], is you love of my character inspiring you to adopt it as your own?
[…], do you trust me for peace, joy, value and well-being?
[…], does your love for my purposes spur you on to pursue and fulfil them; with all that you are and all that you have?

Consider these prompts, be honest in your response, and let God minister encouragement, inspiration and affirmation to your heart.

As you're open to God in prayer, are there other prompts he may raise for you to consider?

Whom have I in heaven but you? And earth has nothing I desire besides you.

Ps. 73:25

We can easily skim past confessions like these without pausing to make them our own. But today I invite you to reflect on these words, and when you're ready, to pray them for yourself.

Dwell with God's desire for you to love him, now and through your day.

DAY 1

*'Jesus grew in wisdom and stature,
and in favour with God and man.' Luke 2:52*

I enjoy growing vegetables from seed. It takes weeks of tender care to complete the growth cycle from germination to seedling to plant and fruit. Leaves unfurl and flourish, stems grow tall; sometimes reaching more than a metre. By the time bean pods, courgettes and onions start to swell, I've long forgotten the tiny seeds from which they grew. But the divine seeds within us need to grow too, just as they did in Jesus.

It's easy to forget that Jesus had to grow, as we've scant detail of his upbringing.[1] Yet, his early years were vital[2] and it's no different for you and me. We'll never mature perfectly as Jesus did, but God's life in us continues to grow as we yield to his ways and fulfil our God-given potential in different seasons.

Picture the boy Jesus, maturing to teenager then adult; mentally, physically, spiritually and socially.

Now picture God's life in you by his Spirit: from seed – to seedling – to flourishing, fruit-bearing plant. Life passes through seasons; perhaps you've experienced many harvests, you're nearing another, or are clearing up from the most recent. Perhaps you sense your growth is being held back for some reason. Once again, prayerfully ask God to speak to your heart as you immerse yourself in this image.

Dwell with these words and images through the rest of your day.

DAY 2

'Jesus grew in wisdom and stature,
and in favour with God and man.' Luke 2:52

Jesus grew in *wisdom*. It has been said that 'Knowledge is knowing that a tomato is a fruit. Wisdom is knowing not to put it in a fruit salad'.[3] It's what we do with our knowledge that makes us wise, our proactive response inspired by a worshipful, yielded, reverence of God.[4]

Jesus was raised to grow his knowledge of God through Mosaic Law, the ancient prophets, the history of his people and the Psalms. But this knowledge didn't make him wise; wisdom came from his prayerful application of it; from how he yielded to its teachings, lived it out in practice and, in turn, taught others to apply it too.

What steps could you take to continue growing in your knowledge *of* and *about* God? Listening and talking to God in prayer and reading Scripture are key, but you can also make use of the rich and varied resources on offer, free or to buy. For example, different Bible translations (hard copy or online), Sunday preaching, conference teaching, Bible-study notes or groups, commentaries, devotional books or podcasts about faith, etc.

Whatever you use to help you grow in knowledge, remember to keep it in balance with growing in wisdom too, i.e. by putting it into practice out of reverence for God. What knowledge of God do you have that you haven't yet applied?

As you dwell with Luke 2:52 through your day, be open to how God may further inspire you.

DAY 3

'Jesus grew in wisdom and stature,
and in favour with God and man.' Luke 2:52

Jesus grew in *stature*. I've often wondered why Luke mentions physical growth, but as I've dwelt with this verse, God has inspired a number of thoughts; I've included two here:

1. Our body isn't separate from the spiritual life it houses. Many of us suffer chronic health conditions, and not all of us can afford or have access to high-quality food. But in caring for these physical 'temples' of God's Spirit, we can ask: Is God nudging me to 'grow', i.e. mature my choices in caring for my physicality through rest, exercise, diet, suncream, etc.?

2. Body language is the conscious or often unconscious physical communication of attitudes, feelings or intentions. Scripture says, 'For as he thinks in his heart, so is he' (Prov. 23:7, AMPC). As I've prayerfully pictured Jesus maturing into adulthood, I've sensed how his growing wisdom shaped his body language. Jesus conveyed a non-anxious presence; an inner poise gracing his physicality as wisdom reassured him of who he was in God, how he should live and how he should treat others. Am I growing in sensitivity to how my body communicates God's love, grace, etc.?

Jesus honoured the woman who 'did what she could' to worship him (Mark 14:7–9); and that's all he asks of us as we worship him with our body. Pray on these thoughts and any others God may inspire.

As you dwell with Luke 2:52 through your day, be open to how God may further inspire you.

247

DAY 4

'Jesus grew in wisdom and stature,
and in favour with God and man.' Luke 2:52

Jesus grew in *favour with God*. In Scripture, 'favour' implies God's grace, affirmation, support, kindness, generosity, provision, goodwill, etc. It can also be translated as the beauty of his nature gracing our lives. In short, Jesus grew spiritually. I certainly long for this growth in my life, and can start by asking for it.

The priestly blessing includes the line, 'the LORD make his face shine on you and be gracious to you' (Num. 6:25), which can also translate, 'the Lord show favour to you'. Ask for God's favour on you now; generally, or on something specific. You may like to pray this blessing over someone else too.

But we can't just ask, we also have to yield. Although we aren't perfect, God obviously won't favour wilful disobedience. Be encouraged by Solomon's teaching that as you choose to love and be faithful to God's ways, his favour *will* rest upon you.[5]

God loves you. He is for you. He delights in you. He cares for you. Rest in and receive his love now. As your appreciation for God's love grows, you will also grow in your response. Prayerfully reflect on how you might grow your faithfulness to his love and nature, his priorities, perspective and purposes.

As you dwell with Luke 2:52 through your day, be open to how God may further inspire you.

DAY 5

*'Jesus grew in wisdom and stature,
and in favour with God and man.' Luke 2:52*

Jesus grew in *favour with man*. Jesus engaged with people from many walks of life. With adulterers and prostitutes cloaked in shame. With despised tax collectors and ostracised lepers. With Jew and Gentile believers and non-believers. With Pharisees, Samaritans, Galileans, with rich and poor, country and townsfolk. With jealous religious leaders and commanding Roman officials. In all these relationships and encounters, he remained true to God's love and faithful to his ways. Jesus was certainly rejected by some, but warmly welcomed by thousands.

Peter writes: 'Live such good lives among the pagans that, though they accuse you of doing wrong, they may see your good deeds and glorify God on the day he visits us' (1 Pet. 2:12). Your responsibility is to love others and remain faithful to God. Their response to your love and faithfulness is their responsibility. Open your heart again to the proverb introduced yesterday: 'Let love and faithfulness never leave you; bind them round your neck, write them on the tablet of your heart. Then you will win favour and a good name in the sight of God and man' (Prov. 3:3–4).

Love: How you might grow your expression of love to God and to others?

Faithfulness: to God's presence, God's character, God's truth, God's commands, God's priorities, God's purposes. Reflect on how God may be prompting you to grow in faithfulness.

As you dwell with Luke 2:52 through your day, be open to how God may further inspire you.

DAY 6

'Jesus grew in wisdom and stature,
and in favour with God and man.' Luke 2:52

To be alive is to grow. I may shrink a little as I age, but while I'm alive, my nails will keep growing. Similarly, to 'grow' in our life in Christ is ongoing.[6] We can never say, 'I've made it! I'm fully mature. I've got it sussed!' Michael Green sums this up brilliantly: 'The Christian life is a developing life, for it consists in getting to know at ever greater depth an inexhaustible Lord and Saviour.'[7]

Peter wrote about growth, concluding: 'grow in the grace and knowledge of our Lord and Saviour Jesus Christ' (2 Pet. 3:18a). Without growth, Peter says, our knowledge of Jesus will prove 'ineffective and unproductive' (2 Pet. 1:8); our salvation is secure, but our fruitfulness and experience of Christ's promise of an abundant spiritual life will shrivel.

Peter gives examples of how we grow: in faith, goodness, knowledge, self-control, perseverance, godliness, mutual affection and love.[8] Open your heart to these descriptions. Picture how you've seen it at work in what you've read about Jesus. Be encouraged where you see them growing in your life already. Prayerfully discern how God wants to help you grow them further.

And finally, let this truth build your faith and your sense of purpose and value to God: he wants you to grow to make you increasingly effective and productive in your deepening knowledge of him.

As you dwell with this verse through your day, be open to how God may further inspire you.

DAY 7

'Jesus grew in wisdom and stature,
and in favour with God and man.' Luke 2:52

Grow, i.e. 'continue to work out your salvation' (Phil. 2:12). Salvation isn't to be worked 'for'. It's a gift. But this gift of spiritual life is expressed through an *ongoing* process of growth. To be honest, I get disheartened when I daily realise how I've slipped up, or at times, let myself and God down badly. But even Paul felt this. 'Not that I have already obtained all this,' he writes, 'or have already arrived at my goal, but I press on to take hold of that for which Christ Jesus took hold of me' (Phil. 3:12).

This is his encouragement as we conclude this week. Be encouraged at how you've grown already, but keep on keeping on. Keep close to God, yielding to him, pursuing his character and likeness.

With this in mind, I leave you with some words from transformed slave trader and composer of the hymn, *Amazing Grace*, John Newton:

I am not what I ought to be . . . I am not what I wish to be . . . I am not what I hope to be . . . Yet . . . I can truly say, I am not what I once was . . . and I can heartily join with the apostle, and acknowledge, 'By the grace of God I am what I am'.[9]

Adapt these words into your own prayer of thanksgiving.

As you dwell with this verse for one more day, be open to how God may further inspire you.

DAY 1

'Do not worry' Matthew 6:25

What do you tend to worry about? Rejection? Redundancy? Health tests? War? The Economy? Natural disaster? Failure? Finances? Or maybe God's forgiveness? God's faithfulness? What personal worries would you add to this list? If you're like me, you find it easy to obey, 'Do not murder' (at least, in practice if not in your heart![1]), but struggle to obey, 'Do not worry.' But worry isn't good for our health and it doesn't get us anywhere. As a number of people have suggested, it's like sitting in a rocking chair with plenty of motion but without any progress. And Jesus said, 'Do not worry' because it conflicts with faith.[2]

Worrying suggests we struggle to believe God's promise to provide for us or equip us. It suggests we don't trust in his unfailing love and infallible character. Worrying suggests we don't like handing God control; we struggle to trust in his higher ways, purposes and understanding, preferring to know all the answers in advance. But as worry seems to have a life of its own, how do we *not worry*? This week we're going to dwell on some guidelines from God's Word that will help us receive Christ's command and then, do something about it.

Are you worried about something? Is anxiety consuming your thoughts, straining your heart and gnawing at your soul? Listen to Jesus speaking to you: *Do not worry [insert your name]*

Dwell on this clear yet gentle command through the rest of your day and open your heart to God's peace.

DAY 2

'Do not worry' Matthew 6:25

Jesus is saying 'do not be anxious'; don't be fretful or filled with angst and dread. But how do you *not* worry? You choose which voice you're going to listen to: the voice of your problem, fear, etc. or the voice of God's Word.

Whatever happens in life, you can determine what you let your mind dwell on. Paul writes, 'take captive every thought to make it obedient to Christ' (2 Cor. 10:5). In other words, surrender your thoughts about the problem to God's promises and character; his forgiveness when you've messed up, his presence when you feel abandoned, his provision when you're in need, his right hand holding you when you feel everyone's against you. God's presence, his goodness and love are always with you. Choose to focus on this, and not on the source of your worry.

When you focus on your problem, it has power over your thoughts and emotions. But when you focus on God's reassuring voice through his Word, it calms fretful thoughts; it instils peace, confidence, wisdom, guidance and more.

What are you worried about today, and what does God say about this in his Word? Ask someone to help you if you're not sure where to find the relevant promise or characteristic of God to focus on.

Dwell on this clear yet gentle command through the rest of your day: *Do not worry* [insert your name], as you fill your thoughts with God's nature and promises.

DAY 3

'Do not worry' Matthew 6:25

How do you *not* worry? You choose to trust God more than your own understanding.

Worry erupts when you can't see the way forward or a possible resolution. But trusting God means believing he will fulfil what he's promised, that he'll remain true to who he is, that his wisdom, insight and understanding are infinitely greater than yours, and that he'll work for the good of everyone involved. You don't need to know the answers to stop your worries. You need to trust God. It's like handing God the steering wheel of your life, trusting his navigation and destination (see Day 3, Week 43).

Name what's worrying you, then prayerfully respond to this reflection based on Proverbs 3:5–6:

Trust
In God (not someone or something else)
With all your heart (not just a bit)
Trust that his way is best, that he loves and cares for you, that he will intervene or help you endure.
Trust in his character – and his promises.
Believe in his wisdom and insight instead of relying on your limited understanding.
Ask him to highlight if your priorities or perspective may not align with his.
Yield to his loving care for you – and for all people.
Yield to his good and righteous will and ways.
And he *will* direct you.

He will lead you in wise and godly decisions and responses.

Dwell on this clear yet gentle command through the rest of your day: *Do not worry* [insert your name], but trust in God's higher ways and understanding.

DAY 4

'Do not worry' Matthew 6:25

How do you *not* worry? You pray. But you don't just pray an endless repetitive cycle of *requests* about the issue. Rather you pray with thanksgiving.

Paul writes, 'Do not be anxious about anything, but in every situation, by prayer and petition, with thanksgiving, present your requests to God. And the peace of God, which transcends all understanding, will guard your hearts and your minds in Christ Jesus' (Phil. 4:6–7). Prayer with thanksgiving is an antidote to worry, as it releases God's peace. This isn't suggesting we can't repeat our prayer; elsewhere Jesus teaches us to pray and 'not give up' (Luke 18:1–8). But praying with thanksgiving guards us against praying prayers that lack hope for God's response; prayers that leave us feeling just as anxious after praying as when we started.

Jesus said that our Father already knows what we need when we pray,[3] so begin by presenting your worry to God, then thank him that he knows what you need. It's so reassuring. You can then thank God for his love, goodness and wisdom, etc. as you trust him for how he chooses to respond.

What are you worried about? Pray about it now, thanking God that he knows what you need, and will provide what he knows is best in your circumstances.

Dwell on this clear yet gentle command through the rest of your day: *Do not worry* [insert your name], but keep praying whenever the worry returns, with thanksgiving.

DAY 5

'Do not worry' Matthew 6:25

How do you *not* worry? You choose to develop an increasing awareness of God's presence.

The 'practice of the presence of God'[4] is concerned with being mindful of and responsive to God's presence through the day; not just in focused prayer. When you worry, it suggests you're no longer integrating your everyday life with your life in Christ. When you worry, you're focusing on the here and now, rather than letting the presence of God's Spirit infuse your thinking and being. It is a 'practice' as it doesn't come easily with busyness and distractions. But developing greater awareness of God's presence – of, for example, his love, strength, comfort and guidance – is a marvellous remedy to worry.

What pushes aside your sense of God with you? What drowns out his voice in your everyday? What practical steps could you take that would help you keep focused on God with you? One idea might be silencing or stopping notifications on your phone.

When worry next threatens your peace and joy, pause momentarily. Focus your attention on God with you. Whisper or speak silently: *Jesus*. If it helps, reach out a hand; an outward physical gesture can sometimes reiterate to your inward being what you're choosing to focus on and receive.

Dwell on this clear yet gentle command through the rest of your day: *Do not worry* [insert your name], pausing often to be present to God with you.

DAY 6

'Do not worry' Matthew 6:25

How do you *not* worry? The context of our verse provides our next answer: 'Do not worry . . . But seek first his kingdom and his righteousness, and all these things will be given to you as well' (Matt. 6:25,33).

Worry suggests we've got something out of sync; that our values, perspective and priorities aren't aligned with God's. When you're seeking to know and fulfil God's purposes, you have nothing to worry about for provision for fulfilling his will, for equipping for the tasks and roles he calls you to, for step-by-step guidance to pursue his purpose, and for comfort and peace when you face obstacles or problems, intrinsic to this fallen world. And although you'll never be perfect, as you seek to live God's way of life, the more you'll experience his presence. God's kingdom is already 'within you' (Luke 17:21, AMPC), but it's as you adopt its goals and way of life that his peace, power and provision dispel your anxiety.

What goals and values do you hold most dear? How do your worries reflect what you've put first in your life? How is the Holy Spirit helping you to realign your priorities and lifestyle to God's?

Dwell on this clear yet gentle command through the rest of your day: *Do not worry* [insert your name], but prioritise God's will and holiness, and all that you need will be given to you.

DAY 7

'Do not worry' Matthew 6:25

As you follow God's guidelines to stop worrying, you will in turn become a non-anxious presence to an over anxious world.

John Ortberg writes:

> Imagine not being afraid any more. Imagine facing financial difficulties or an irate boss with inner poise and resolve. Imagine receiving bad news and generating constructive ways to solve the problem rather than spiralling through the worst-case scenarios. Imagine facing rejection and obstacles without giving in to discouragement. Imagine acknowledging the mistakes you have made, moving confidently into the future. Imagine doing all this with God as your partner and friend. Now imagine people around you coming to you when they are upset or discouraged because they find that your peace of mind is contagious.[5]

Peace rather than worry is both attractive and influential. It dispels panic, confusion and irrational responses. It calms, comforts, consoles and reassures. It offers considered ways to move forward. You host the peace, character and countenance of Jesus. As you learn to stop worrying, you will bring his life into the relationship, into the room, into social media; into every place you inhabit during the day.

Take time to pray for people you know who are suffering with worry and anxiety. Pray with an open heart to know how you might be part of the answer to that prayer.

Continue to dwell on this clear yet gentle command through the rest of your day: *Do not worry* [insert your name].

DAY 1

'I remember my affliction and my wandering . . . and my soul is downcast within me. Yet this I call to mind and therefore I have hope: Because of the LORD's great love we are not consumed, for his compassions never fail. They are new every morning; great is your faithfulness.' Lamentations 3:19–23

Rumbling storm clouds hang suffocatingly low over your life. Tears drench your pillow. Disappointment claws at your heart. Anxiety churns nausea in the pit of your stomach. Whatever plight you feel and face – or may one day have to endure – Jeremiah, the writer of Lamentations, offers hope to permeate your darkest of days.

Passages of lament in Lamentations,[1] Job and Psalms help us express pain, fear or confusion to God. But they also conclude by clinging to the truth of God's unfailing love and goodness.

It's vital we express our hurt to God, and we'll do so through this week. Even if you're in a happier season of life, use this time to be present to the pain of others in your friendship circles, wider community, nation or overseas. God will speak to and through you on their behalf, but will also strengthen your familiarity with prayers of lament, to shape your own expression in a future season of hardship.

For today, reflect on each word and phrase of this week's dwelling place.

Dwell with this unchanging truth about God, and open your heart to his presence with you, no matter what you face.

DAY 2

'I remember my affliction and my wandering . . . and my soul is downcast within me. Yet this I call to mind and therefore I have hope: Because of the LORD's great love we are not consumed, for his compassions never fail. They are new every morning; great is your faithfulness.' Lamentations 3:19–23

When God hasn't answered our prayer as we'd hoped, prayed and possibly begged him to, the acute sorrow, anger or disappointment can be excruciating. But what do we do with that pain? Confused or angry with God, we can distance ourselves, or even turn our back on him. We might ignore, stifle and attempt to bury our pain as we keep praying, reading Scripture and serving God as if nothing had happened. But in doing so we may become defensive, react angrily and transmit our hurt onto others. Alternatively, we can be transparent and honest with God, just as his Word encourages us to.

Prayerfully expressing lament helps us face our feelings to know God with us in our pain or disappointment, and to find strength and peace through renewed hope in who he is. It turns raw emotions into worship and trust.

If you're nursing any doubts about God, struggling to believe in his presence, attempting to numb soul pain with self-soothing activities, or pretending the issue doesn't exist, be honest with yourself and with God, and ask him to help you face it *with* him this week.

Dwell with Jeremiah's faith-filled truth through the rest of your day.

DAY 3

'I remember my affliction and my wandering . . . and my soul is downcast within me. Yet this I call to mind and therefore I have hope: Because of the LORD's great love we are not consumed, for his compassions never fail. They are new every morning; great is your faithfulness.' Lamentations 3:19–23

When my brother died from a long battle with alcoholism, I waited a wretched thirty-six hours for a flight to be with family. During this limbo period of isolated grief, my wordless prayerful lament poured out from my heart – to my fingers – and onto the piano keys, playing, 'Blessed Be Your Name'.[2] I wept as I played, unable to sing; the grief so raw I felt I was bleeding internally. But as I chose, by faith, to turn my heart onto God's goodness, his peace infused my soul in those vulnerable hours.

Turning to God, and not away, is the first stage of lament.[3] At other times I've scribbled in a journal, turned to a psalm or dropped to my knees in silent awareness of God's presence. Whatever weight of fear, sorrow or confusion we carry, God is with us, so we choose to approach, rather than run elsewhere.

How might you turn to God today? Might you adopt one of the ways I've described above? Climb a hill to connect with him in creation? Hold your baby and know that God holds you?

Whatever way you turn to God, do so with an open heart, and dwell with Jeremiah's truth through your day.

DAY 4

'I remember my affliction and my wandering . . . and my soul is downcast within me. Yet this I call to mind and therefore I have hope: Because of the LORD's great love we are not consumed, for his compassions never fail. They are new every morning; great is your faithfulness.' Lamentations 3:19–23

When we lament, we may express sorrow or regret, but God takes lament further, welcoming expressions of anger, disappointment, frustration, questions and complaint. His people have done so for centuries; pouring out raw emotion to him about their situations, and even about him.

This is the second stage of prayerful lament. But to complain to God isn't a long-winded, whining whinge. It's being honest and transparent with him about the source of our distress. It's being specific about the nature of our angst; our thoughts, feelings and frustration when he remains silent or doesn't intervene. It's a crying out of our need and longing for his love, power, wisdom and provision to help us.

If you're dealing with the fallout of unanswered prayer, unexpected tragedy, dashed hopes or unfulfilled expectations, don't be afraid to share what you're feeling with God. Be honest with him about every aspect of your anger, disappointment, dejection, frustration, shock, fear, sorrow and pain.

Whatever you pour out to God, do it with an open heart, and dwell with Jeremiah's truth through the rest of your day.

DAY 5

'I remember my affliction and my wandering . . . and my soul is downcast within me. Yet this I call to mind and therefore I have hope: Because of the LORD's great love we are not consumed, for his compassions never fail. They are new every morning; great is your faithfulness.' Lamentations 3:19–23

Lament isn't reserved for dealing with uninvited problems; ours or those of others. Lament is also a powerful prayer when we know we've messed up; when we've fallen short of God's ways, let ourselves down, hurt others, missed opportunities, or damaged our health, wealth or relationships . . . and so the list could go on.

Our lament overflows as regret, shame and guilt. It expresses any fear we have of missing out on God's favour and forgiveness. But we don't leave it there. We trust in God's unfailing goodness and mercy. We ask forgiveness. We ask for guidance. We ask for restoration where possible, and for God to pull us out of our pit of despair; to place our feet back on the solid ground of his path for our lives.

Asking God is the third stage of the prayer of lament. Whether we're asking for healing, wholeness, restoration or provision for a self-inflicted problem, or for one inflicted upon us by our broken world and imperfect people, we acknowledge our weakness and desperate need. And we remain in a place of receptivity for his response.

Ask God specifically for what you need today with an open heart to receive, and dwell with Jeremiah's truth through your day.

DAY 6

'I remember my affliction and my wandering . . . and my soul is downcast within me. Yet this I call to mind and therefore I have hope: Because of the LORD's great love we are not consumed, for his compassions never fail. They are new every morning; great is your faithfulness.' Lamentations 3:19–23

'Dad's died.'

My stomach tightened. Gripping the phone, I slumped into a chair. My voice broke and tears flowed. Dad was 85 but death wasn't an imminent expectation. He collapsed of a heart attack within a few hours of our regular Saturday chat. I wept as an uninvited, relentless loop of memories flooded my soul. I wept in anguished lament that despite forty years of prayer, Dad never said 'yes' to Jesus. But as I was honest with God, his whisper broke through to my heart. Trust. Trust God with the words I'd shared with Dad. Trust God with his final moments. Trust and leave the judgement of the living and the dead in the hands of the only Judge who knows all things.

Trust is the fourth stage of our prayer of lament. We trust God with what we've asked of him, we trust him to fulfil his promises and stay true to his character, and trust that he is with us, no matter what we feel. We won't always understand why God allows something, but we can trust in his unfailing love.

Thank God for a promise or particular aspect of his nature you can trust in, as you dwell with Jeremiah's truth through your day.

DAY 7

'I remember my affliction and my wandering . . . and my soul is downcast within me. Yet this I call to mind and therefore I have hope: Because of the LORD's great love we are not consumed, for his compassions never fail. They are new every morning; great is your faithfulness.' Lamentations 3:19–23

'There is . . . a time to weep and a time to laugh, a time to mourn and a time to dance' (Eccl. 3:1,4).

Let's not rush the four steps or skim through other Bible passages of lament. Let's give them time. They are God's gift to help us process our pain in his presence, to mature spiritually and renew hope. God knows how we feel, but urges us to express it so he can meet us in our angst, walk with us through it, and help transform it into something good.[4]

Our world, its people, our health and conduct are unreliable. But God remains consistent, no matter what we or others endure. Sit with Jeremiah's words again and receive into the depths of your being the hope they instil. Know God with you in your pain. This may be the last day of our dwelling place, but you can dwell with this week's reflections for as long as you need.

Let's pray: Holy Spirit, Comforter, I open my heart to your presence. Thank you that you're with me. And thank you that you know what I need right now, in this moment.

Be mindful of God's presence with you as you dwell with Jeremiah's truth through your day.

DAY 1

Read Luke 15:1–7

When we feel like a lost sheep we may be isolated from the flock, confused, afraid or missing the sense of our shepherd's protective care. We may have wondered away gradually, or simply not followed. But whether we feel near or far from our Shepherd today, we begin our week's reflections using Ignatian contemplation, to immerse ourselves in the Parable of the Lost Sheep.

God desires to meet with you through his Word as you prayerfully use your imagination to engage your five senses with the story. Ask him to help you discern what he wants you to. Be mindful of thoughts or feelings that arise.

Jesus travels to Jerusalem as the cooler rainy season nears its end. Vast crowds follow him, but when the Pharisees and teachers of the law begin muttering criticisms, he tells them this story:

> Suppose one of you has a hundred sheep and loses one of them. Doesn't he leave the ninety-nine in the open country and go after the lost sheep until he finds it? And when he finds it, he joyfully puts it on his shoulders and goes home. Then he calls his friends and neighbours together and says, 'Rejoice with me; I have found my lost sheep.' I tell you that in the same way there will be more rejoicing in heaven over one sinner who repents than over ninety-nine righteous people who do not need to repent.

Luke 15:4–7

Dwell with the imagery of this passage through your day.

DAY 2

Read Luke 15:1–7

In her book, *Deeper Still*, Linda Allcock introduces 'a five-step "meditation tool" to help us fill our hearts with truth, so we can feed on that truth day and night'.[1] As this reflects the ethos of *Dwell*, I'm delighted to introduce you to this practice of biblical meditation; though I highly recommend reading her book where she explains the steps in detail (see endnotes and Bibliography). The names of each step are: Lord. Look. Turn. Learn. Live. So today we start with: Lord.

Meditation Tool, Step One: *Lord*[2]

Still your thoughts and focus on your Lord. Humbly acknowledge how awesome he is, and how utterly dependent you are on him for understanding of his Word. You may like to humble your posture before him too.

Set aside any agenda or need that you'd like God to speak to you about, and resist a closed mind if the parable is overfamiliar.

Ask God for insights and guidance from his Word. Be expectant that God will give you fresh revelation in whatever way he chooses.

Prayerfully hold the parable in your heart and mind, acknowledging God as its author. Thank him that he wants to speak with you through his Word.

Continue to dwell with the imagery of the story, and any thoughts or emotions that it's aroused.

DAY 3

Read Luke 15:1–7

Meditation Tool, Step Two: *Look*[3]

Linda poses three questions to help you look at the passage intently and with an open heart to discern God-given insights: '1. What does this teach [you] about God? 2. How do [you] glimpse Christ's ministry and gift of salvation through it? 3. What did it mean for the first hearers – and for [you]?'[4] Prayerfully mull on the story and questions. Where do your thoughts and emotions lead you? What insights might the Holy Spirit prompt?

Using Linda's tool, I was surprised to relate to the lost sheep. I'd approached the parable as a story that reached out to people who didn't know God, but many, if not all the 'tax collectors and sinners' listening were Jewish. They were already members of God's family, but had wandered away from him. This comforted and encouraged me that God doesn't leave me to my wilful ways, but comes looking for me. He doesn't simply wait to welcome me back when I repent and return to him, he loves me so much that he actively seeks me out. And when I say 'yes' to returning to the fold of yielded devotion, he doesn't drag me back, but carries me.

I also glimpsed Christ's destination; his sacrifice, which would bring us back to God's fold. And I sensed God's call on my life to search for lost sheep too.

Dwell with either the lost sheep or whatever else resonates, attentive to all that God wants to reveal to you through your day.

DAY 4

Read Luke 15:1–7

Some readers will have gleaned a number of insights, feelings and thoughts from dwelling with this passage; remind yourself of them now. To conclude yesterday's second step of her meditation tool, Linda encourages you to prayerfully ask God to highlight 'one truth' he wants you to focus on.[5] Jump ahead to that now.*

Other readers may still be waiting to discern God's leading; the following suggestions may help, but please don't force an idea. God may simply be enjoying your presence with him in his Word, engaging with the full picture for the time being:

Immerse yourself in the passage again as per Day 1, or take a look at the words and phrases you feel drawn to ponder on further: tax collectors and sinners – gathering round Jesus – Pharisees and teachers of the law – muttered – lost – find – joyful – shoulders – goes home – rejoice – sinner – righteous.

Reflect on those which resonate with how you feel about life or God at the moment. Now join with the other readers in the following prayer to discern what God wants you to focus on:

*Loving God who searches for lost sheep, which one truth that you've shown me do you want me to dwell on further? I wait now for your Spirit to prompt my open heart.

Dwell with your 'one truth' through your day. Be open to how God will continue to speak through it.

DAY 5

Read Luke 15:1–7

Meditation Tool, Step Three: *Turn*[6]

Recall the 'one truth' that especially resonates, then consider what other voices, expectations or temptations lure you away from it.

How does your 'one truth' inspire or challenge? And what may be the consequences of turning away from it?

Take time to reflect on these questions, now and through your day (adapted from more detailed explanations in Allcock's book). As Linda says, they will help you discern where your heart naturally inclines, then help you turn it back towards God.[7]

'The heart is deceitful above all things and beyond cure. Who can understand it? "I the LORD search the heart and examine the mind"' (Jer. 17:9–10). Using Linda's tool and seeing myself as the lost sheep, I sensed that when God comes searching for me, the pleasure of an ungodly habit or attitude may tempt me to run away out of fear, embarrassment, or to enjoy my guilty pleasure. With the parable in mind, ask God to show you why, or where, he may search for you. Confess where you've turned away from his truth, and prayerfully commit to how you will turn towards it in future. Then, rest in the reassuring joy of being restored; of being carried on his shoulders.

Dwell with your 'one truth' through your day. Be open to how God will continue to speak through it.

DAY 6

Read Luke 15:1–7

Meditation Tool, Step Four: *Learn*[8]

This part of the meditation suggests helpful ways to memorise a verse or passage of Scripture. As *Dwell* is an example of such an aid, we'll skip straight on to the next step, but do take a look at Linda's book for further inspiration.

Meditation Tool, Step Five: *Live*[9]

Linda offers a number of ways we can live out the 'one truth' we've been meditating on, which we haven't space to unpack here. But we can prepare ourselves to live it out by considering potential situations which may challenge our adherence to our truth. Bring one to mind now. How could you choose to live out your truth in that situation? How might seeking to live by your truth, inspire, guide or reassure you? Be encouraged to turn and run towards God, instead of running away.

Finally, are you willing to leave the comfort of the sheepfold to search for friends who don't yet know God's love and mercy? If so, what steps can you take to live out this truth with someone who's come to mind?

Solomon, Jesus, Paul and James encourage us to live out God's Word and not just listen to it.[10] Let's dwell with how we can do that too.

DAY 7

Read Luke 15:1–7

As we draw this week's place of dwelling to a close, prayerfully imagine yourself in the scene, one more time. Be mindful of thoughts or feelings that arise as you engage with the unfolding story.

I've shared some of the ways I've been led in response to this passage, but take a few moments to review how God has been speaking to you, and how you feel prompted to respond in the days ahead. You may also like to prayerfully read through Psalm 23, reflecting on and receiving your Shepherd's care, provision and protection. How do these beautiful words inspire your response?

Also take time to pray. First, for yourself, and how you wish to yield or respond to God's leading. Second, for other 'lost sheep': family or friends who have wandered away from God, or who've yet to believe in Jesus' gift of eternal life.

Let's pray: Loving Shepherd of my soul, I am once again amazed at your desperate search for folk like me who get lost along the way, and for those who've yet to be welcomed into your fold. Thank you for all you've revealed to me and your promises to my soul.

Dwell with this story through the rest of your day.

DAY 1

'Open my eyes that I may see wonderful things in your law.'
Psalm 119:18

I wonder what range of feelings you have as you open your Bible to read. Expectant? Hopeful? Exhausted? Stressed? Distracted? Numb? Fed up? I've felt all these and more over the years, but have adopted a practice that raises my anticipation of meeting with and hearing from the Author of its pages. Placing my Bible on my lap, I take a moment to still my thoughts and focus on God with me. Then I pray this wonderful prayer from Psalm 119. And as I've learned how much God delights to answer this prayer, it's a wonderful place to dwell in this week, to embed it within our being as we seek God in his Word. Whether your Bible reading comprises a few verses, a chapter or more, I trust this prayer will unlock your heart to encounter more of God in his Word and inspire your response.

Of course, this isn't a formula, so do take care, as I still have to do, not to merely repeat the prayer by rote; especially when you've been praying it for some time. But every time you pray it, ask with an expectant heart; one that sincerely longs for God to speak to you afresh through what you're about to read.

Use this prayer if you've more reading planned, but keep praying it through the day too. It's a prompt to keep open to God's ongoing inspiration from his Word.

DAY 2

'Open my eyes that I may see wonderful things in your law.'
Psalm 119:18

Before you start reading your Bible, remember: this is God's message to *you*. That may sound obvious, but as there's immense variation in the styles and genres of its different writers, it's worth pausing to honour their source. God's Word is his revelation of himself working for, with and through his people. But it's also his means to speak into your everyday life, and help you to know him through its pages. God's words are intended to speak to you, whatever your background, education or culture.

Praying Psalm 119:18 before you read any Scripture focuses your attention on God. It slows your thoughts as you spend time with him in his Word, protecting your reading from simply being a task to complete. It opens your heart and mind to his voice, and shuts the door to distractions. It invites his words to sow wisdom, guidance, divine power and seeds of transformation. In short, praying Psalm 119:18 invites a conversation. It stills your spiritual ear to hear God, and inspires prayer in response to his living text.

As you open your Bible, ask the Holy Spirit for insight, even when your reading leaves you with questions. Trust and believe him to grow wisdom and understanding within you as you commit to praying this God-given prayer.

Use this prayer if you've more reading planned, but keep praying it through the day too. It's a prompt to keep open to God's ongoing inspiration from his Word.

DAY 3

'Open my eyes that I may see wonderful things in your law.'
Psalm 119:18

Praying these words will inspire you to read for life change and not just for knowledge.

Anyone might read the Bible with an intellectual interest, where the words simply become head knowledge. But God's desire is to put his Word in your mind and write it on your heart.[1] When you're open to this, the Holy Spirit draws your reading of Scripture into your inner being where it may guide, transform and empower you. It's his precious gift when you seek hope, comfort or direction on a particular issue.

But the Holy Spirit may also want to speak or reveal things to you from the Word beyond what's immediately on your mind, or what you think you need or want from it. Praying Psalm 119:18 will encourage this yielded reading, with reverence, sensitivity, surrender and expectation. So, as you pray this prayer, receive it as a conscious reminder to read for more than consolation or counsel about pressing issues. Open your mind and heart to perceive and receive what God will teach, challenge, inspire, comfort, discipline or empower you with today. As you read with increased awareness of his desire to speak through his living Word, you may be surprised and, I'm sure, delighted at what he reveals.

Use this prayer if you've more reading planned, but keep praying it through the day too. It's a prompt to keep open to God's ongoing inspiration from his Word.

DAY 4

'Open my eyes that I may see wonderful things in your law.'
Psalm 119:18

My greatest experience of being strengthened in my inner being has been through reading, meditating on, praying and responding to God's Word. Of course, I've appreciated spiritual encounters in private and corporate prayer and praise, and can recall significant moments when God's touched me emotionally or prophetically through ministry events. But by far my most consistent experience of God's strength, guidance and comfort has been through dwelling in his Word, which invites greater awareness of his character, wisdom and promises dwelling with and within me.

Praying Psalm 119:18 will remind you that this can be your experience too as you take time to be in his Word with an open heart and mind; even when you ask God to meet with you through one verse. The Bible teaches us to build ourselves up in our faith.[2] Your faith may swell under the anointing of the Spirit in worship, or as people pray for and counsel you. But your faith will steadily grow through prayerful meditation on and response to God's living Word.

What or who do you rely on to help you know God? I hope my experience will encourage you to use Psalm 119:18 to open your heart to his living Word in greater measure too.

Use this prayer if you've more reading planned, but keep praying it through the day too. It's a prompt to keep open to God's ongoing inspiration from his Word.

DAY 5

'Open my eyes that I may see wonderful things in your law.'
Psalm 119:18

God doesn't just open our eyes to 'see' wonderful things, but to inspire us to respond to what he has revealed. It's the 'doing' of those things that empowers his living Word in us. It's the 'doing' of the Word that converts a shallow reading of the text to a deeper transformation; that shifts your response from the Word serving your immediate needs to God being Lord of your life. And it's the experience of God that you gain from your response that infuses your life with hope, wisdom, comfort and testimony to pass on to others.

In response to your praying Psalm 119:18 this week:

- What insights has God given you from his Word that resonate with personal situations, guiding, comforting, reassuring, or which spark conviction? Is any further response needed?
- Isaiah writes: 'The Sovereign LORD has given me a well-instructed tongue, to know the word that sustains the weary. He wakens me morning by morning, wakens my ear to listen like one being instructed' (Isa. 50:4). Who are the 'weary' God is calling you to 'sustain' through insights he's given? We'll think on this more tomorrow, but does anyone come to mind whom you might pass on some comforting revelation from God's Word?

Use this prayer if you've more reading planned, but keep praying it through the day too. It's a prompt to keep open to God's ongoing inspiration from his Word.

DAY 6

'Open my eyes that I may see wonderful things in your law.'
Psalm 119:18

The Old Testament explains the vital priestly role of knowing Scripture so, in turn, they could guide others. They didn't just read from God's law; they explained it to the people so they could understand and apply it to their own lives.[3] You are now part of God's royal priesthood. You can draw near to God through Jesus, but are also called to share his truth with others. As you share insights from Scripture that the Holy Spirit inspires, you may help someone else to understand and apply it for themselves.

You may not be called to teach God's Word as a theologian, preacher or writer, and it isn't always necessary or appropriate to quote chapter and verse. But you have friends, family, colleagues, or a social media feed that will benefit from the wisdom God gives you; the truth that shapes your conduct, the comfort and strength that sustains you in difficulty, and your eternal assurance which moulds your perspective on life.

As you pray Psalm 119:18 today, be open to how God may inspire you to help others understand and apply his Word in their family, friendships, church, workplace or online. Then respond as you feel prompted.

Use this prayer if you've more reading planned, but keep praying it through the day too. It's a prompt to keep open to God's ongoing inspiration from his Word.

DAY 7

'Open my eyes that I may see wonderful things in your law.'
Psalm 119:18

Praying Psalm 119:18 awakens our anticipation for God to speak to our heart through his Word, to deepen our knowledge of him and nurture relationship. As God's glorious presence imparts truth from his Word to our soul, we are strengthened and sustained for our journey of life with him.

As we close our week, you might like to design a bookmark using this prayer, reminding you to keep praying it each time you read your Bible. What else might prompt you to pray this prayer if you read on an electronic device? Keep pen and notepad handy, too, or be willing to write notes in your Bible itself, believing that God will speak to you as you've asked him to.

Let's pray it again together using alternative translations:

'Open my mind and let me discover the wonders of your Law.' (CEV)
'Open my eyes so that I may contemplate wonderful things from Your instruction.' (HCSB)
'Let me see clearly so that I may take in the amazing things coming from Your law.' (VOICE)
'Open my eyes [to spiritual truth] so that I may behold Wonderful things from Your law.' (AMP)

Use this prayer if you've more reading planned, but keep praying it through the day too. It's a prompt to keep open to God's ongoing inspiration from his Word.

DAY 1

'Like a city whose walls are broken through is a person who lacks self-control' . . . 'But the fruit of the Spirit is . . . self-control.'
Proverbs 25:28; Galatians 5:22–23

It's a tragic headline that announces the downfall of a prominent politician, sportsperson, celebrity or, indeed, a Christian leader; to hear of behaviour and/or addictions that disqualify their good reputation. One act, perhaps, just one moment lacking self-control; of being unable to delay future gratification for pleasure 'now' that destroyed their life-work. Some may gloat over another's downfall, but we feel sorrow and pain for the individual, families or friends concerned. After all, how can we judge someone else's failings when we're flawed ourselves, and with our own areas of weaker self-control?

I'm acutely aware of how and when I'm more vulnerable to temptation. Some of my weaknesses may be similar to yours; others will likely be different. So, let's begin by doing two things – not to shame or condemn, but to inspire your response this week.

1. Recall a situation when you lacked self-control and the consequences that ensued.
2. Consider, and preferably write down, any areas in your life where self-control is often weak or lacking.

Our sorry experience suggests we struggle to govern ourselves; perhaps you're still reaping the fallout from point 1. But be encouraged. The source of this godly character trait is already within you by the Holy Spirit. This week we're dwelling with how God can help it grow and bear fruit.

Dwell with God's Word through your day, and his Spirit of self-control present within you.

DAY 2

'Like a city whose walls are broken through is a person who lacks
self-control' . . . 'But the fruit of the Spirit is . . . self-control.'
Proverbs 25:28; Galatians 5:22–23

The analogy of a lack of self-control to *a city whose walls are broken through*
paints a picture of life that lacks adequate defence against temptations; one that's
subdued, disgraced or overpowered by these destructive forces. Lacking self-control
ultimately stunts our growth in becoming more like Jesus, and diminishes
God's empowering through our lives. But allowing ungodly character traits or
unrestrained appetites to fester can also harm our peace, health, self-worth or
relationships. It can rob us of achieving dreams and goals and fulfilling our
God-given potential. We might suffer consequences from wasting time, reduced
job performance or, indeed, for overworking. No wonder Proverbs paints such a
stark picture of a lack of self-control! But be encouraged. God's Spirit in us can
help strengthen or rebuild those gaps in our 'walls'.

Identify possible triggers that weaken your resolve in the areas you struggle with
self-control. Be honest with God about these provocations that arise from certain feelings, people, situations or places. You may also discern that certain areas
of weakness are due to offers of short-term gain. Such insights and awareness
can fuel your desire for the greater blessing of God's abundant life. Talk honestly
with God about this and thank him for how he wants to rebuild and strengthen
your 'broken walls'.

Dwell with God's Word through your day, and his Spirit of self-control
present within you.

DAY 3

'Like a city whose walls are broken through is a person who lacks self-control' . . . 'But the fruit of the Spirit is . . . self-control.'
Proverbs 25:28; Galatians 5:22–23

The indwelling Holy Spirit sows Christ's character like a seed within us. The seed becomes fruit as we yield to his ways instead of our natural responses, and as we nurture this growth, we become more like him. That's why self-control is intrinsic to our devotion. It's about how we *respond* with his love, patience, kindness, gentleness, etc., rather than *reacting* with the flesh. It's our spiritual defence against letting our feelings take control, rather than the nature of his life within.

Biblical self-control isn't about willpower or obeying rules. It's about experiencing more of God's peace, joy, contentment and enabling. When we focus on what we can get from giving in to temptation or allowing ungodly behaviour, we simply fuel our desire for it. But when we fix our heart on the promise of abundant life in Christ, we take our first step in strengthening our defensive 'walls' to temptation.

How do you long to see God's nature and power grow in your life? Be specific. How does a lack of self-control hold that back? Keep your desire in mind next time temptation threatens to stunt or rob its growth.

Dwell with God's Word through your day, it will inspire you to yield to his Spirit of self-control present within you.

DAY 4

'Like a city whose walls are broken through is a person who lacks self-control' . . . 'But the fruit of the Spirit is . . . self-control.'
Proverbs 25:28; Galatians 5:22–23

'Christian religion is not obedience to a legal system, but devotion to a Person.'[1] Pause with that thought for a moment. Let it feed your soul.

Building on our reflections, Paul writes: 'do not grieve [cause grief to, fret or vex] the Holy Spirit of God, with whom you were sealed' (Eph. 4:30, my addition). It's a deeply moving thought that we cause God sorrow. Some translations write 'holy' Spirit[2] (lower case 'h'), as it's describing God's living presence, not just a title for the third person of the Trinity. God's Spirit is our most intimate connection with him. He loves us more than we can fully comprehend, and we love him in response as we choose his 'holy' ways. To misuse our words and conduct offends God's presence and undermines his reputation. When we relate to the Spirit as a person, however, we're more likely to take care not to grieve him.

Reflecting on your weaker areas of self-control, prayerfully consider how giving in to ungodly words, actions or habits may grieve him. Listen for his loving response.

Picture yourself being faced with one of your temptations. How might God's love strengthen your resolve to love him in response by choosing his ways instead of your own?

Dwell with God's Word through your day, it will inspire you to yield to his Spirit of self-control present within you.

DAY 5

'Like a city whose walls are broken through is a person who lacks
self-control' . . . 'But the fruit of the Spirit . . . is self-control.'
Proverbs 25:28; Galatians 5:22–23

Self-control invites a deeper experience of God's life and keeps us from being
unfruitful. It helps form Christ's character in us, his 'love, joy, peace, forbear-
ance, kindness, goodness, faithfulness [and] gentleness';[3] i.e. self-control devel-
ops Christ-like maturity.[4] It frees us from worry, a guilty conscience, and helps
us to love and persevere. Self-control is also beneficial to our health, finances
and jobs. It deepens our relationships and can make us more effective leaders as
we inspire rather than demoralise followers or employees. It can help us achieve
our goals and to become the person we've the potential to be.

Read that paragraph again. What especially resonates; what benefit from the
Spirit's fruit of self-control do you long for? How would rebuilding your 'broken
walls' free, fulfil and enable you to live into the vision God has for your life? Talk
with God about this and be open to discern his response.

The advantageous consequences of self-control are important to keep in mind
whenever temptation strikes. What practical thing could you do to remind
yourself of them when needed, to encourage you to honour God by yielding to
his Holy Spirit?

Dwell with the inspiration of rebuilding your walls and growing the fruit of
self-control, thanking God for how he's inspiring you.

DAY 6

'Like a city whose walls are broken through is a person who lacks self-control' . . . 'But the fruit of the Spirit . . . is self-control.'
Proverbs 25:28; Galatians 5:22–23

Godly self-control, as with all fruit of the Spirit, is nurtured through habits which keep us present to God's presence. Habits of reading, reflecting on, dwelling with and responding to God's living Word;[5] of talking with, confessing and listening to God in prayer;[6] of praise and worship;[7] of being in the company of other believers;[8] and of sharing what we have with others.[9] These aren't just spiritual activities, or a list of 'to-do's' to tick off once completed. Engrained godly habits hold greater power to resist temptation than sheer willpower. They strengthen our defensive walls against temptation when we might otherwise default to unhelpful, unhealthy or unholy reactions to stress, boredom, anger, cravings, enticement, etc.

Casting your eye again over the life-enriching habits above; do any need resurrecting? If so, what steps can you take to restore and develop them?

If you're responsible for discipling others, are you tending these habits yourself as much as for them?

As essential as these habits are, however, they're not an end in themselves. Primarily, they help deepen our love for and devotion to Jesus. That comes first, the love that in turn douses temptations' flames and nurtures the fruit of self-control. A love that keeps on growing with the years.

Dwell with God's Word through your day, thanking him for his Spirit of self-control, present within to help you.

DAY 7

'Like a city whose walls are broken through is a person who lacks self-control' . . . 'But the fruit of the Spirit . . . is self-control.'
Proverbs 25:28; Galatians 5:22–23

The fruit in my kitchen basket is to be eaten, not admired. Similarly, the spiritual fruit of self-control helps nurture the nature of Jesus that others are starving for. We bear fruit to nourish and share his life with them. And the more we live like Jesus, the more we glorify God.

There's a quiet, unobtrusive beauty and winsome humility when Christ's life is lived out through someone unaware of their spirituality; vastly different to the counterfeit, subtle or blatant attention-seeking niceties, motivated and manufactured by self. In who do you see Christ's character gently and faithfully revealed? Thank God for their inspiration, take note of what inspires your own devotion to Jesus, and pray for them.

Let's pray, adapting and quoting some words from Romans 7:15–25: Father God, I long for a greater experience of your life in and through me; to beautify my character with Jesus and nourish others with who you are. Yet, like Paul, 'what I want to do I do not do, but what I hate I do' . . . in my inner being I delight in your ways but the war of sin wages against it. How wretched I would be if I were left to my own devices. But thanks be to God, who delivers me through Jesus Christ our Lord!

Dwell with God's Word through your day, and his Spirit of self-control present within you.

DAY 1

'Peace I leave with you; my peace I give you. I do not give to you as the world gives. Do not let your hearts be troubled and do not be afraid.' John 14:27

'Peace' may not describe how you're feeling today. You may be anxious and distressed. Your thoughts may be racing incessantly from one to another, or you're overwhelmed by the effect of a hurt, incident or future concern. You may be suffering strain and stress; you may have lost your appetite, or be struggling with headaches and nausea. Or you may simply be feeling unsettled, disconcerted and unnerved for no discernible reason.

'Do not be afraid'.[1] Healthy fear triggers an urgent response to flee or avoid danger. Fear is also natural when we face pain or hardship; Jesus was afraid when anticipating the horror of torture.[2] But an underlying persistent sense of dread, distress and apprehension is not from or of God. The fruit of the Spirit – the outworking of God's life in you – is the peace seen and conveyed in Jesus, who carried it into storm-tossed boats and baying-for-blood crowds.[3] We live in a troubled world, but we carry God's peace from his Spirit too.

Peace be with you, [insert your name].[4] As you read these words, hear Jesus saying them to you with loving care and affirmation.

Dwell with Jesus' promise of peace to help you experience it through your day.

DAY 2

'Peace I leave with you; my peace I give you. I do not give to you as
the world gives. Do not let your hearts be troubled
and do not be afraid.' John 14:27

When I'm feeling agitated, my husband is the first to know; if not from my
irritable responses, then from the outpouring of my distress in the hope that he
can help me. Caffeine, namely English Breakfast tea, is another antidote. And
if I wake feeling trepidation, it can feel safer and more appealing to bury myself
beneath the felt comfort of a snug duvet than to sit up and pray; to focus my
heart and mind on God.

The world may offer peace through being with friends, the comfort of food,
receiving approval, etc. Such peace offers ease, relief and reassurance, but its
source assures it will only be temporary. As we focus in faith on God's Spirit in
and with us, however, on his nature and his promises, we know peace regard-
less of our circumstances. Peace that's beyond our understanding,[5] ministering
God's wholeness, hope and assurance to the core of our being. Peace that displaces worry and angst. Peace that prevails as dignity, serenity and inner calm,
despite life's difficulties.

What unsettles you? Who or what has caused inner turmoil or uncertainty?

Focus on God's peace-filled presence. If it helps, open your hands as a gesture of
wanting to receive; repeating the name of your Prince of Peace: Jesus.

Dwell with Jesus' promise of peace to help you experience it through
your day.

DAY 3

'Peace I leave with you; my peace I give you. I do not give to you as the world gives. Do not let your hearts be troubled and do not be afraid.' John 14:27

I know I have God's peace because his Spirit dwells within me. But knowing it doesn't always mean feeling it. I have to allow God's peace to 'rule' in my heart (Col. 3:15).

When troubles ignite envy, anger or hurt, robbing us of Christ's gift, we're to choose responses of peace to overrule. We choose God's nature over the attitude or feeling that undermines his peace; kindness instead of defensiveness, humility instead of self-justification, forgiveness instead of anger, honesty instead of lies . . . The problem may not resolve and the world may not respond with peace, but as we walk in step with God's Spirit, *we* will know peace.

'Turn from evil and do good; seek peace and pursue it', David taught in Psalm 34:14, echoed centuries later by Peter (1 Pet. 3:11). Identify any feelings, attitudes or actions you need to turn from which deny your experience of God's peace. Your problem may be painful and complex, but how can you seek good in what you say and do in response? Ask God to help you know how to 'seek' his peace through how you live and relate to others in your difficulty, and choose to pursue it in the coming days.

Dwell with Jesus' promise of peace to help you experience it through your day.

DAY 4

'Peace I leave with you; my peace I give you. I do not give to you as the world gives. Do not let your hearts be troubled and do not be afraid.' John 14:27

A complex problem unexpectedly surfaced after Dad died, with potential implications that troubled me by day and woke me at night. God graciously inspired timely Scriptures of love, encouragement, wisdom and reassurance to my heart, but as my sense of God's peace continued to yo-yo, I remembered an unused journal I'd received for Christmas. I needed God's Spirit-breathed word written down in one place where I could access it with ease. It became my specific 'sword of the Spirit' (Eph. 6:17) for the situation; easily 'drawn' when fear and trouble threatened God's truth and peace.

The more you dwell in God's Word and let it dwell in you, the greater will be your instinct to let his peace-giving truth infuse your heart. Would a specific journal for the purpose help you too? Either way, ask God to help you discern his words that speak into your place of unrest. As you're inspired with a Scripture, dwell with it. Pray it. Believe it. Proclaim it. Receive its promise and reassurance. This isn't a positive thinking exercise; it's releasing the power of God's living, active, powerful truth to restore his peace to your soul.

Dwell with Jesus' promise of peace to help you experience it through your day.

DAY 5

'Peace I leave with you; my peace I give you. I do not give to you as the world gives. Do not let your hearts be troubled and do not be afraid.' John 14:27

'You will keep in perfect peace those whose minds are steadfast, because they trust in you' (Isa. 26:3). If we're to know God's peace, we need to trust him.

When you focus on your circumstances they assume power over your thoughts, feelings and behaviour. But a steadfast mind never wavers from who God is and what he does; an immoveable, unshakeable faith that fills you with his peace.

A steadfast mind trusts God, even when you've no idea how or when the issue you face will be resolved; if, indeed, it will be. It trusts him for his forgiveness and redemption, even though you've messed up, and peace is threatened by felt shame and blame. It trusts him to help you; to guide and provide for you. A steadfast mind trusts God's promises from his Word for your situation. It trusts his mercy, his love for and presence with you. And a steadfast mind trusts God's loving care and grace for *all* people.

Reread the paragraph above, inserting your name where I've written 'a steadfast mind' or referred to a steadfast mind as 'It', and adapting each phrase personally; i.e. engage with this truth for yourself. For example, '[Anne] trusts God's goodness, even when she doesn't know how [X Y Z] will be resolved.' How are you inspired to respond?

Dwell with Jesus' promise of peace to help you experience it through your day.

DAY 6

'Peace I leave with you; my peace I give you. I do not give to you as
the world gives. Do not let your hearts be troubled
and do not be afraid.' John 14:27

The peace we receive and enjoy from our life in Christ is a precious gift, but it's not just for us. We are also promised joy when we carry it into relationships, work or situations we face and intentionally seek to minister peace to others.[6] Plus, of course, we're called to help others find peace with God through Jesus, the true peacemaker between heaven and earth.[7] We promote God's peace through our own testimony, attitudes and conduct. There is rich joy to be known in sharing what we've received.

Whose faces or what situations – local, national or global – is God bringing to your mind as you reflect on this? Ask him how you might bring peace through prayer, words and practical involvement.

Who or what has unsettled your promised peace from God? Pray for them now. Consider how you can reach out with peace. And whatever their reaction, if your heart is right with God, you will be filled with his peace.

What holds you back from introducing God's life and peace to others? Talk with God about that now, and let his peace overrule your fear.

Dwell with Jesus' promise of peace to help you experience it through your day.

DAY 7

'Peace I leave with you; my peace I give you. I do not give to you as the world gives. Do not let your hearts be troubled and do not be afraid.' John 14:27

'Do not let your hearts be troubled' by grief, fear and difficulty. 'Do not' invites us to continue to choose God's peace beyond this week, rather than passively assume it. I've offered some suggestions to help you but God will speak to you personally, so keep listening for his insights.

And remember:

as you look to Jesus for peace, instead of from someone or something else;
as you pursue peace through yielding to his character and ways;
as you respond to God's Word dwelling within you;
as you trust God in all your circumstances;
and as you seek to convey his peace to others,
you will continue to live in and out of God's promised peace for you.

As we draw this week to a close, I'd like to pray for you using the words of 'the priestly blessing'. Still your heart as you hear me read them over you and be still with God in response:

> The LORD bless you and keep you; the LORD make his face shine on you and be gracious to you; the LORD turn his face towards you and give you peace.

> *Num. 6:24–26*

Dwell with Jesus' promise of peace to help you experience it through your day.

DAY 1

'Sow righteousness for yourselves, reap the fruit of unfailing love,
and break up your unploughed ground; for it is time to seek
the LORD, until he comes and showers his righteousness on you.'
Hosea 10:12

When we slip up, wilfully or unwittingly, the intense pain of our shame can debilitate rational thinking and rob our peace. We may feel choked by self-reproach; humiliated, anxious and filled with regret. We may feel too flawed to be liked and may even despair that God could ever restore us to his or other people's favour. Even without such remorse, we know that we're all susceptible to the pervasive nature of sin. No one is completely free of the weeds that sin sows in our hearts, minds and lives. So, wherever our devotion to God lies today, our word this week is for us all.

Despite the Israelites' prevalent waywardness, Hosea's book conveys God's persistent love and longing for them to turn back to him.[1] God was, is and will always be for his people. And that includes you and me.

Nothing can separate you from God's love.[2] Nothing can rob his passion for you. This is Hosea's message to you this week, whatever you've done, minor or major. Open your heart to him. Let him love you into his safe, reassuring presence. From there you can move into all that his Word holds for you.

Dwell with God's Word from Hosea through your day, spoken to you in love.

DAY 2

'Sow righteousness for yourselves, reap the fruit of unfailing love, and break up your unploughed ground; for it is time to seek the LORD, until he comes and showers his righteousness on you.'
Hosea 10:12

God's people were consistently disloyal to him, refusing to acknowledge him as their source of agricultural and horticultural abundance. Leaders, prophets and people knew God's ways but had turned away from them. They indulged in sexual and magical practices, and sacrificed to pagan gods; lifeless idols from which they sought guidance and favour. I mention this, not to compare ourselves with them, but to acknowledge we've all fallen short of God's glorious righteousness.[3]

Thank God for his unconditional, unfailing love for you and dwell with it for a moment.

Now consider the following prompts: which, if any, resonate?

- You've lapsed into an ungodly habit from the life you lived before knowing Jesus.
- You sense that your passion for God has faded over the years.
- You've lost your old desire to meet with God in his Word, prayer or in worshipping with his people.
- You lack God's promised peace, joy, reassurance or anointing.
- You're ignoring your conscience in regard to a behaviour trait that doesn't conform to God's loving, selfless, generous and holy ways.
- You're pursuing or allowing something that may risk your health, a relationship or your obedience to God.

Take time to be open with God, who urges you to turn back and draw close to him again.

Dwell with God's Word from Hosea through your day, spoken to you in love.

DAY 3

'Sow righteousness for yourselves' Hosea 10:12

The last time I perused the seed packets at our local garden centre I didn't spot any 'righteousness' seeds for sale. But righteousness isn't so much the 'seed' as what germinates from what we sow. And the seed we're being urged to sow and allow to grow in our lives is God's Word.

Hosea encourages us to pursue righteous living. God's righteous ways grow in us as we sow his Word in the soil of our hearts; as we dwell with and pray on it. But sowing God's Word isn't enough. Seed that remains in the ground without germinating rots and dies, failing to fulfil its potential. It's as we put into practice the seed of God's Word that it germinates into righteous living, righteous relating to others and of course, righteous devotion to God.

God says that his Word will not return to him without accomplishing what he desires; without fulfilling his purpose and promises.[4] But he also says that if we allow weeds of doubt, worry, greed, bitterness, ungodliness, etc., they choke his Word, limiting its effect.[5] Take time with God to confess and weed out whatever is choking the growth of his righteousness in your life.

If you've time, choose a familiar verse or passage and immerse yourself in it. Listen for how God wants to meet and inspire you through it.

Dwell with God's Word from Hosea through your day, spoken to you in love.

DAY 4

'Reap the fruit of unfailing love' Hosea 10:12

'Unfailing love' is translated from the Hebrew word, *hesed*. It's difficult to translate but sums up who God is; his steadfast love, mercy, goodness, compassion, tenderness, faithfulness . . . God never breaks his covenant *hesed* love to those who enter into relationship with him; it's we who break our commitment to it. And we who reap what we sow.

God's eternal law of reaping what we sow is established in creation and in our lives.[6] We can't reap a harvest of wheat from parsnip seeds. Nor do we reap the fullness of God's life in his Spirit when we keep doing our own thing. Of course, we can't 'earn' God's love, but as we intentionally seek to yield to his ways, we reap the abundant blessings of his life. In fact, when I sow individual pea seeds, each produces a plant and each plant an abundance of pods containing many peas. The harvest is disproportionate to the seed sown. That's the easiest way to explain the disproportionate blessing of God's 'unfailing love' when we live, imperfectly but sincerely, in pursuit of his righteousness.

Next time you're tempted to turn away from God's righteousness, be mindful that while you're free to choose what you do, you're not free to choose the consequences.[7] Be inspired to choose the disproportionate blessings of peace, joy, assurance and spiritual empowering as you seek to adopt God's character and ways.

Dwell with God's Word from Hosea through your day, spoken to you in love.

DAY 5

'Break up your unploughed ground' Hosea 10:12

The order of these instructions sounds confusing. We'd naturally assume we should first break up the unploughed ground *before* we sow then reap. The emphasis teaches us, however, that we may be tempted to start sowing *some* seeds of righteousness while ignoring other weedy parts of our lives; thistle and bramble that choke the growth of God's righteous life and its innate blessings.

'Unploughed' can also be translated as 'fallow' or 'uncultivated'. This suggests there may be areas of our life lacking fruitfulness or productivity for God. We may have resources, gifts and time which we've left untended and inactive; their God-given potential untapped.

I'm the first to admit I am happy to pursue certain godly habits while ignoring other ungodly ones. But to sow good seed in ground that remains untended will certainly limit the harvest. Talk with God now about bringing the whole of your heart, mind and will into the fullness of his ways. He loves you more than you can imagine and offers his very best life for you.

You can't do and be everything, nor did God create you with that capability. But in response to Hosea, ask God to help you discern if he's given you something to use to nurture fruit for his kingdom, which you've left uncultivated. How might you tend to its health and growth, that is, 'fan [it] into flame' (2 Tim. 1:6)?

Dwell with God's Word from Hosea through your day, spoken to you in love.

DAY 6

'For it is time to seek the LORD, until he comes and showers his righteousness on you.' Hosea 10:12

When I sow vegetable seed, I'm dependent on God to send life-giving rain. I then have to wait for God's season for harvest, as different seeds take different lengths of time to germinate, grow, then bear fruit. As seeds depend on water for life, we depend on God's Spirit to bring to harvest the effect of our 'sowing'. Our hope in God will never be disappointed. Our hope for what *we* want may not materialise, but he will fulfil all that *he* has promised as we seek to live in harmony with his ways and depend on his enabling.[8] With the goodness of his presence comes the abundant outflowing of his righteousness; his gracious, un-deserved mercy and spiritual blessings – in his time.

'Let us acknowledge the LORD', Hosea writes, 'let us press on to acknowledge him. As surely as the sun rises, he will appear; he will come to us like the winter rains, like the spring rains that water the earth' (Hos. 6:3).

God promises to draw close when you seek him 'with all your heart' (Jer. 29:13).[9] Be open in faith to the goodness of God's presence with you in this moment. Dismiss any doubts by proclaiming his promise to never leave you.[10] Talk with him about how you will seek to keep in close step with his ways.

Dwell with God's Word from Hosea through your day, spoken to you in love.

DAY 7

'Sow righteousness for yourselves, reap the fruit of unfailing love, and break up your unploughed ground; for it is time to seek the LORD, until he comes and showers his righteousness on you.'
Hosea 10:12

Hosea entreated Israel to repent, seek and return to God's ways before they reaped the consequences of their rebellion. Sadly, they didn't. I don't want to end my life with regret for having failed to fully commit all that I am to all God is and has promised. I don't want to regret having not loved, sought and depended on him with all my heart, soul, mind and will. I want to look back with gratitude for my abundant experience of his overflowing grace and blessings, and his enabling to help me glorify him through fulfilling my potential.

Be open with God about how you are feeling:

- Eager or reticent to 'seek' him in greater measure?
- Excited to seek him or tempted to put it off until . . . when and why?

Be embraced by his love. Remind yourself of your promised abundant life in Christ to inspire your soul to keep seeking him wholeheartedly, all the days of your life.

Join me in this prayer of commitment: Loving, faithful, merciful Father, I yield my life to you again. I say 'no' to [name what you've leaving behind] and 'yes' to your holy ways. Thank you for your presence and blessings. I wait in hope. I wait with you. I rest in all you've promised.

Dwell with God's Word from Hosea through your day, spoken to you in love.

DAY 1

'But blessed is the one who trusts in the LORD, whose confidence is in him. They will be like a tree planted by the water that sends out its roots by the stream. It does not fear when heat comes; its leaves are always green. It has no worries in a year of drought and never fails to bear fruit.' Jeremiah 17:7–8

Picture yourself in the desert scene that Jeremiah paints for us this week:[1]

A high walled canyon casts heavy shade over a fresh water oasis, offering some relief from the blazing heat. Just beyond you, the scorched, barren wasteland shimmers in the heat, mottled with occasional stunted bushes; their appearance stark for want of leaves and fruit. But here by the water you've found rest and rejuvenation from the desert's inhospitable environment. You lean back against a tree beside the water. Its leafy branches rustle overhead. Reaching up, you pluck one of its plump, refreshing fruits.

This picture explains why '*But*' introduces our place of dwelling this week. In the preceding two verses, Jeremiah describes those who rely on themselves, on people or other things, as stunted bushes, without prospect of creating leafy shade or edible fruit. *But* then he describes those who are rooted in God's life-giving presence and truth. They're like trees growing beside water, constantly flourishing, even within a hostile environment.

Dwell on this word-picture through your day. What might God be whispering to your heart?

DAY 2
'But blessed' Jeremiah 17:7

Blessed is rich with promise, describing something I'm sure we'd all like to experience in greater measure. *Blessed* implies abundant satisfaction, contentment, fulfilment and enrichment from experiencing God's life in yours. It's a depth of assurance, peace and inward strength. Even when tensions or difficulties surround you, you feel blessed with a sense of well-being, purpose, wisdom, resilience and enabling.

But perhaps you experience times when your thoughts and emotions waver between peace, purpose and assurance in God, to doubt, disillusionment, defeat or gloom. What causes these fluctuations? Too much on your to-do list, for example, a pressing deadline, convincing atheist arguments, overtiredness?

Perhaps distractions entice you away from this promise; confidence in financial investments, a comfortable home, material pleasures, affirmation, self-sufficiency in your skills and abilities, or reliance on a beloved partner or friend?

Have any significant problems undermined your peace in God? Financial pressure, health concerns, job loss, bereavement, prayers remaining unanswered in the way that you'd hoped, a long-term problem still unresolved, broken or unfulfilled dreams?

What about global issues: wars, natural disasters, pandemics, famine, downturns in economies, persecution of Christians, shortage in supplies?

So much of life has potential to undermine your peace and strength in God, but today you can choose to drink from God's life-giving water as you prayerfully respond to his presence and his Word.

Dwell with the beauty of Jeremiah's picture today. Let the promise of God's blessing inspire your devotion, fill you with peace, and shape your choices.

DAY 3

'But blessed is the one who trusts in the LORD,
whose confidence is in him' Jeremiah 17:7

Trust and *confidence* are mutually inclusive, and essential for you to experience more of what it means to be blessed. To *trust* someone or something you have to be *confident* in who they say they are and what they say they can be and do. It requires a firm belief in their ability and reliability. It's to refer to, defer to, depend on and yield to them at all times. To be *confident* in someone or something, you have to believe you can trust them. It's like handing over the steering wheel of your life as you move to the passenger seat. You have to believe in their driving skills, in their knowledge of the best directions and their choice of destination. Confidence in God enables you to be fruitful for his kingdom, no matter your situation or how inadequate *you* feel.

Who's in the driving seat of your life?

When the journey gets bumpy, are you content to stay in the passenger seat or do you shout directions, change gear, hit the brakes, or snatch back control of the wheel?

Consider what you struggle to trust about God's nature or Word. How does this hold back your confident response? If you could trust him more in that area, how might that change how you feel or what you do?

Be open and honest with God. Talk to him through the day as you dwell with his Word and let it dwell in you.

DAY 4

'But blessed is the one who trusts in the LORD, whose confidence is in him. They will be like a tree planted by the water'
Jeremiah 17:7–8

God, through his Spirit, provides an abundant and unfailing flow of life-giving assurance, counsel and equipping;[2] the glorious riches of our heavenly inheritance.[3] But we each have to choose to drink from his living water and resist the lure of the wastelands.

Some of us have found ourselves in 'parched places of the desert' (v. 6), when we've trusted in something other than God. A place which reminds us that no matter how hard we work or how popular, resourceful, talented or wealthy we are, we and all these things are finite and fallible. A place where security is insecure and promises are frequently broken. A place of fear, inadequacy, insecurity and anxiety. Where kindness can sour overnight. Friends abandon. Loved ones move on. Careers abruptly end.

If you find yourself in a wasteland today, identify its source; who or what are you depending on for purpose, value, guidance, security, joy, contentment, peace?

Talk to God about anything that draws you away from relying on him. Admit where you've abandoned him for temporary satisfaction or security. Then dwell with Jeremiah's beautiful image conveying God's promise. Let it inspire you to drink deep of his life-giving presence.

Be open and honest with God. Talk to him through the day as you dwell with his Word and let it dwell in you.

DAY 5

'But blessed is the one who trusts in the LORD, whose confidence
is in him. They will be like a tree planted by the water that sends
out its roots by the stream.'
Jeremiah 17:7–8

Picture a network of spreading roots, digging deep in search of water; roots that nourish the tree with nutrients, strengthen it in the heat, anchor it in a storm, and yet remain unseen.

There are various ways you can *send out your roots* into God's living water, but I'll name just a few. The Root of:

Prayer:	Prayer keeps you present to God's presence and how he may guide, shape or equip you.
God's Word:	Reading and engaging with *Dwell* will grow your roots in God's Word so, in turn, it strengthens and nourishes you.
Obedience:	To be transformed and equipped by prayerful reading of God's Word requires yielding and surrendering to its truth and commands.
Thanks and Praise:	Thanks for what you have and praise for who God is releases you from discouragement. It magnifies God above your problems. God's presence becomes your focus, your steadying hand, your guidance and reassurance.

How could you send your roots wider and deeper to encourage the flow of God's nourishing, transforming and empowering Spirit to flow freely and fully through your life?

Dwell with this image of roots spreading wide and deep to nourish and strengthen the tree. Be open and honest with God. Talk to him through the day as you dwell with his Word and let it dwell in you.

DAY 6

'But blessed is the one who trusts in the LORD, whose confidence is in him. They will be like a tree planted by the water that sends out its roots by the stream. It does not fear when heat comes; its leaves are always green. It has no worries in a year of drought and never fails to bear fruit.' Jeremiah 17:7–8

Heat and *drought* represent difficulties. They test the strength of your roots and the depth of your experience of God's life-giving water. Pain, problems and hardships may encourage you to run to God but can also distract from his presence and promises. They may cast doubt and disillusionment in who God says he is, turning your heart away from him in search of comfort and security elsewhere. Whether your problems are minimal or significant, however, God promises you his fullness of life to infuse your inner being, as you keep rooted in his living water.

Your *leaves* will remain *green*. Despite *the heat*, you will feel secure; an assurance that manifests itself in the beauty of your calm, non-anxious presence. And despite the *drought* of trouble and hardship, you will flourish with his life-transforming, life-giving fruit.

Dwell with this truth; this promise within your problems.

Talk with God about all that you're struggling with.

Open your heart to his life-giving presence and receive all that he wants to give you.

Dwell with this word-picture through your day. Listen to how God may continue to whisper to your heart.

DAY 7

'But blessed is the one who trusts in the LORD, whose confidence is in him. They will be like a tree planted by the water that sends out its roots by the stream. It does not fear when heat comes; its leaves are always green. It has no worries in a year of drought and never fails to bear fruit.' Jeremiah 17:7–8

Do you ever find yourself saying, *'I wish I had more faith'*? Me too! But faith isn't about *how much* we have, it's about *who* or what we put our faith in. And that's at the heart of Jeremiah's image this week, as I learned during a particularly pressured season:

> Worried, fretful, weak, uninspired, fruitless, stressed is Anne, when she trusts in herself and her own capabilities to enable her. But blessed – at peace, content, assured and enriched – is Anne, when she trusts God for equipping, and puts her confidence in His capability and anointing. The heat has come! A very intense schedule [I named each task], but Anne has nothing to fear if her roots are deep in God's life-giving water.[4]

Adapt Jeremiah's words into your own declaration of faith for whatever you're facing today, then join me in prayer: Thank you, Lord, that I can know absolute confidence in who you are. I choose to root myself ever deeper into the life-giving water of your Spirit.

Dwell on Jeremiah's word-picture for one last day as God continues to inspire your response.

DAY 1

'Do you not know? Have you not heard? The LORD is the everlasting God, the Creator of the ends of the earth. He will not grow tired or weary, and his understanding no one can fathom. He gives strength to the weary and increases the power of the weak. Even youths grow tired and weary, and young men stumble and fall; but those who hope in the LORD will renew their strength. They will soar on wings like eagles; they will run and not grow weary, they will walk and not be faint.' Isaiah 40:28–31

This week we're dwelling in a passage using Lectio Divina. The vital component of this practice is not so much for gaining information through Bible study, but to help you connect with God through his living words to your soul.

Lectio Divina encourages us to listen to the passage with the ear of our heart. This is a conversation between God and you, where God suggests what you might reflect on and talk through together in prayer.[1]

Open your heart to this conversation, one that will continue this week.

Prayerfully familiarise yourself with the passage, mindful of God's presence, wherever you are. God is tenderly speaking these words to *you*. Listen to him. How do his words inspire your imagination? How do they make you feel? What would you want to say in response?

Dwell with God's words through your day as they sink deep into your soul.

DAY 2

'Do you not know? Have you not heard? The LORD is the everlasting God, the Creator of the ends of the earth. He will not grow tired or weary, and his understanding no one can fathom. He gives strength to the weary and increases the power of the weak. Even youths grow tired and weary, and young men stumble and fall; but those who hope in the LORD will renew their strength. They will soar on wings like eagles; they will run and not grow weary, they will walk and not be faint.' Isaiah 40:28–31

Isaiah writes as if Israel's exile in Babylon is almost over.[2] He offers comfort, re-assurance and hope to God's people who feel he's lost sight of them; that they're no longer in his favour (v. 27).[3] They had stumbled and bruised themselves when they tried to live without him, but God, who remains faithful to his covenant promises, watches over them and picks them up (vv. 1–11).[4] God never loses sight of his loved ones. And God never loses sight of you.

Step One: Still your heart and mind to focus on God with you.

Step Two: Read the passage slowly, at least twice. Which words, phrases or images capture your attention? Which especially resonate with you personally, with a situation you face or for someone whom you care for?

Record your thoughts or feelings inspired by these words or phrases.

Dwell with God's presence through his Word through your day, mindful of how he's speaking into your life.

DAY 3

'Do you not know? Have you not heard? The LORD is the everlasting God, the Creator of the ends of the earth. He will not grow tired or weary, and his understanding no one can fathom. He gives strength to the weary and increases the power of the weak. Even youths grow tired and weary, and young men stumble and fall; but those who hope in the LORD will renew their strength. They will soar on wings like eagles; they will run and not grow weary, they will walk and not be faint.' Isaiah 40:28–31

'Do you not know? Have you not heard?' These are strong, faith-building words to speak to ourselves when we doubt God's forgiveness or love. When we fear what we've done has distanced us from him. When we feel hidden from his sight.

'Didn't you know, Anne? Hadn't you heard? Of course, you did and still do! You know who God is, you know his promises, why doubt his grace and redemption reaching out to your humbled heart?'

Step One: Still your heart and mind to focus on God with you.
Step Two: Read the passage, slowly.
Step Three: Linger over a word, phrase or image that especially resonates. Gently repeat it. Hold it in your heart and mind. Prayerfully reflect, meditate, contemplate and chew over it, attentive to what it's saying as it sinks deeper into your soul.

Record how God's Word is dovetailing with your life.

Dwell with how God is speaking to you through his Word, through your day.

DAY 4

'Do you not know? Have you not heard? The LORD is the everlasting God, the Creator of the ends of the earth. He will not grow tired or weary, and his understanding no one can fathom. He gives strength to the weary and increases the power of the weak. Even youths grow tired and weary, and young men stumble and fall; but those who hope in the LORD will renew their strength. They will soar on wings like eagles; they will run and not grow weary, they will walk and not be faint.' Isaiah 40:28–31

Everlasting: God's nature and promises are unchanging, enduring through all circumstances past, present and forever. In this you have unshakeable confidence.

Creator: 'Where can I go from your Spirit?' David asked (Ps. 139:7). Nowhere. All the world is his; he is present everywhere; there's no place that he's not with you.

Untiring: There's never a moment when God's presence and provision will dwindle and decline.

All-knowing: There's no deficiency in God's knowledge of you, of your circumstance, of the world at large.

Strength-giver: He who is who he is, shares his strength and understanding with you.

Once again, still your heart and mind to focus on God with you. Read the passage slowly.

Step Four: What response has your meditation on those words, phrases or images inspired? It may be confession, praise, repentance, thanksgiving, a new course of action or way of being or doing.

Dwell with how God is speaking to you through his Word, through your day.

DAY 5

'Do you not know? Have you not heard? The LORD is the everlasting God, the Creator of the ends of the earth. He will not grow tired or weary, and his understanding no one can fathom. He gives strength to the weary and increases the power of the weak. Even youths grow tired and weary, and young men stumble and fall; but those who hope in the LORD will renew their strength. They will soar on wings like eagles; they will run and not grow weary, they will walk and not be faint.' Isaiah 40:28–31

These words are more than descriptions of God, they're his nature for you to know and encounter, no matter your age or situation. As you *hope in the Lord* you can have absolute certainty that God is who he is. To *hope* is to know, believe and therefore receive what is true of God's presence and promises.

To *hope* can also mean to wait patiently, expectant for God's provision. It can mean rest; the calm, assured poise that comes from trusting God. It's a patient, non-anxious assurance in God to *renew your strength*, which literally means that your weakness will give way to his strength. Be assured, be expectant.

Once again, still your heart and mind to focus on God with you. Read the passage, slowly.

Step Five: Pray. And pray some more. Don't rush on from how God has been meeting with you through his Word. Receive his strength.

Dwell with how God is speaking to you through his Word, through your day.

DAY 6

'Do you not know? Have you not heard? The LORD is the everlasting God, the Creator of the ends of the earth. He will not grow tired or weary, and his understanding no one can fathom. He gives strength to the weary and increases the power of the weak. Even youths grow tired and weary, and young men stumble and fall; but those who hope in the LORD will renew their strength. They will soar on wings like eagles; they will run and not grow weary, they will walk and not be faint.' Isaiah 40:28–31

When eagles soar, they rely on rising air currents to gain altitude. There, they hold out their wings, rarely needing to flap, saving themselves considerable energy.[5] From this height they can glide over considerable lengths of ground before soaring again and repeating the process.

Soar, without flapping. Glide, without effort. Such is the strength and power of God's Spirit, raising you above the circumstance; to help you endure in *his* strength and keep moving forwards. Imagine yourself being lifted up, higher and higher, and the peace of gliding – dwelling – in his presence.

Once again, still your heart and mind to focus on God with you. Read the passage slowly.

Step Six: Be present to God's presence in a time of quiet rest. Receive the strength and reassurance that being with God infuses to your soul. Let your inner being soar with his Spirit; released from all that constrains.

Dwell with how God is speaking to you through his Word, through your day.

DAY 7

'Do you not know? Have you not heard? The LORD is the everlasting God, the Creator of the ends of the earth. He will not grow tired or weary, and his understanding no one can fathom. He gives strength to the weary and increases the power of the weak. Even youths grow tired and weary, and young men stumble and fall; but those who hope in the LORD will renew their strength. They will soar on wings like eagles; they will run and not grow weary, they will walk and not be faint.' Isaiah 40:28–31

There is a time to soar in God's strength; to delight and flourish, released from all that binds, constrains and undermines.

There's a time to run in God's strength; energising you to endure and respond to the exceptional demands of life.

There's a time to walk in God's strength; to be present to the everyday roles, relationships and responsibilities; the mundane and the inspiring, the rigour and the rest.

Reflect on what resonates for you today: soaring, running or walking in God's strength. Talk with God about it.

And now, let's pray together: God, my God, thank you for encouraging me this week. You never lose track of where I am, or stop caring what happens to me. When you came into my life, you came to stay. You are all things. You sustain all things. You know all things. I trust myself fully into the power of your presence with me.

Dwell with God's presence through his Word through your day.

DAY 1

'Jesus looked at him and loved him.' Mark 10:21a

What a reassuring and heart-warming verse this is to dwell with. But first, to understand its context, we'll use Ignatian contemplation to prayerfully enter the story to meet with God.

Ask God to help you feel and observe the things he wants you to. Read it twice, using all your senses to engage with the unfolding scene: What expressions do you see on their faces? Can you hear their tone of voice? What emotions stir within you?

Jesus is east of the river Jordan[1] when a wealthy young ruler[2] approaches him on the road:

> As Jesus started on his way, a man ran up to him and fell on his knees before him.
> 'Good teacher,' he asked, 'what must I do to inherit eternal life?'
> 'Why do you call me good?' Jesus answered. 'No one is good – except God alone. You know the commandments: "You shall not murder, you shall not commit adultery, you shall not steal, you shall not give false testimony, you shall not defraud, honour your father and mother."'
> 'Teacher,' he declared, 'all these I have kept since I was a boy.'
> Jesus looked at him and loved him. 'One thing you lack,' he said. 'Go, sell everything you have and give to the poor, and you will have treasure in heaven. Then come, follow me.'
> At this the man's face fell. He went away sad, because he had great wealth.
>
> *Mark 10:17–22*

Dwell with what's caught your attention as you continue with your day.

315

DAY 2

'Jesus looked at him and loved him.' Mark 10:21a

The ancient Greek word used for *looked* here means to look at *intently*. Prayerfully immerse yourself in the story again but not as an observer; today you take the place of the rich young man:

You're on your knees, staining your tunic and the hem of your cloak in the dust and muck of the road. People are watching you. The disciples have had to stop to wait for their Master.

Wherever your eyes are drawn, now look into Jesus' face.

He is focused on you. He's looking at you *intently*. And his look reveals his love.

For *you*.

Jesus sees and knows everything about you. And he still loves you.

Receive this truth.

Perhaps you know what the people are saying about you.

Receive Jesus' love.

Perhaps you feel guilty for holding up the disciples' journey.

Receive Jesus' love.

Jesus sees whatever is going on in your heart and mind, and he loves you.

Tears may come; of confession or relief.

Rest in whichever way you encounter God with you.

When I placed myself here, I didn't want to move. It was such a release to picture his all-knowing love. Continue with whatever feels right for you.

Dwell with this image through your day. Be mindful of how it may influence your thoughts, feelings and responses.

DAY 3

'Jesus looked at him and loved him.' Mark 10:21a

I'm deeply moved when I picture the finely dressed man running to Jesus; a rare sight in that culture. Evidently, he was desperate to speak with him before losing the opportunity. Jesus looked intently at him. He saw the man's earnest longing for eternal life. His outward compliance with God's law had left him with a felt need internally, though he misunderstood that it couldn't be earned.

Look again into Jesus' face. Steep yourself in his love as you reflect on what you earnestly long for. Who or what do you run to in the hope they can give it to you? Be honest with him in response.

When I wake early, it's tempting to stay snuggled in bed, waiting for the alarm. But picturing this man running to Jesus, eager for eternal life, is powerful. I feel my need of my true source of life, even before my set time of prayer, then the get up and go of the day. Sitting up to gaze and worship may not look like 'running', but expresses my desire.

What might 'running' to Jesus look like for you? Can you recall the last time you desperately 'ran' to him? Perhaps you do daily. If not, what urged you to on that occasion? Has something tempered your felt need of him? Who or what else do you run to for guidance, assurance – and 'life'?

Dwell with this image through your day. Be mindful of how it may influence your thoughts, feelings and responses.

DAY 4

'Jesus looked at him and loved him.' Mark 10:21a

The man ran to Jesus then 'fell on his knees before him'.

The man showed deep respect for Jesus' wealth of wisdom. Luke records his status as a ruler in Luke 18:18 (which may infer some kind of membership to an official court or council[3]), but he knew enough about Jesus to humble himself before him; a sign of respect, honour and submission.

Jesus wants you to enjoy intimate loving friendship with him in prayer. But there's also a place for humbling your heart, acknowledging that your Friend is still your Master. Kneeling connects our heart's desire to submit to and honour God with our mind and body. It's a tangible expression of our heartfelt reverence and respect. But even if you're physically unable to kneel, God sees the longing in your heart, a humbling of your attitude before him, a dependent waiting upon him, a desire to honour him.

Look up into Jesus' all-seeing, all-knowing, all-loving face. He loves you just as you are, but longs for you to encounter him in increasing measure as you submit to his authority and yield to his ways. Wait upon him now. Listen for what the Holy Spirit may be saying to your heart.

Prayerfully consider your response.

Dwell with this image through your day. Be mindful of how it may influence your thoughts, feelings and responses.

DAY 5

'Jesus looked at him and loved him.' Mark 10:21a

'Good teacher'. His words confirmed what Jesus had perceived; the man's limited understanding about who Jesus was. So, Jesus answered the man's first question in a way that might help him recognise his full nature and identity, and so increase his faith.

You're still on your knees before Jesus. Gaze into his face. Let his knowledge of you and love for you continue to reassure you.

What aspect of Jesus do you tend to focus on when you come to him? Are you attracted to certain characteristics more than others? How often do you see him as King and Lord outside of corporate praise at church, for example?

While dwelling with this verse, I found myself asking: *Do I take my Lord's holiness and power for granted? Do I approach him as a gift giver, problem solver, pain reliever, miracle worker, help desk . . . or God?*

Jesus wants to grow your faith as you encounter his full nature and purpose. His Sovereignty, magnificence and power.

See him not just as Lord, but as *your* Lord.
See him not just as King, but as *your* King.
See him not just as God, but as *your* God.
See how he looks at you with perfect love and understanding.
How does that prompt you to yield to him?
How does that fill you with reverence and awe?
How does that inspire your praise and worship?

Dwell with this image through your day. Be mindful of how it may influence your thoughts, feelings and responses.

DAY 6

'Jesus looked at him and loved him.' Mark 10:21a

'What must I do to inherit eternal life? . . . One thing you lack . . .'

The man's eagerness for eternal life promptly disappeared as Jesus called him on the spot to become his disciple; to give his wealth to those in need, then follow him. The man's god was exposed and his unwillingness to part with it. Sadly, he went away downcast. His temporary wealth was more important to him than experiencing God's life.

The riches of eternal life aren't just for our future in heaven; they're our spiritual inheritance in Christ which we receive, in part, now.[4] Jesus highlights the danger of wealth turning hearts away from God, but his command to sell everything wasn't aimed at everyone; in fact, both he and the foundling Church were supported not only by what they could offer but by wealthy believers.[5] But there may be other things we hold back, afraid to let go. Something, for example, that makes us feel good about life, about ourselves or secure.

You're on your knees before Jesus. You see the love in his face. But perhaps you've been asking Jesus for more of his Spirit, more of his enabling, more of his wisdom, more of his gifting . . . without receiving an answer. If so, ask him if there's something you 'lack'; anything that's holding you back from receiving a greater measure of blessings from his life in you.

Dwell with this image through your day. Be mindful of how it may influence your thoughts, feelings and responses.

DAY 7

'Jesus looked at him and loved him.' Mark 10:21a

This week, I've assumed that readers believe eternal life is God's gift.[6] There's nothing we can *do* to earn it. But if the man's question 'what can I *do*' nudges your heart, the Holy Spirit may be exposing a 'doing' mentality. Whatever you desperately long for from God, are you sensing you need to earn it somehow?

Jesus looks at you intently and with great love. He knows where you're driven to *do* rather than *be* or *receive*; where you still try to earn his approval, blessing or an answer to prayer, for example. Whether or not this resonates, return to the story one last time. Immerse yourself in the scene and delight in Jesus' gaze. Receive peace and assurance as you drink in his love for you, just as you are. Be inspired by his desire to help you experience his life in greater measure.

As the man turns his back on Jesus, I find myself recalling an occasion when Jesus posed a question to his disciples:

> 'You do not want to leave too, do you?' . . .
> Simon Peter answered him, 'Lord, to whom shall we go? You have the words of eternal life . . . you are the Holy One of God.'

> *John 6:67–69*

Let's pray: Lord, to whom would I go if not to you? You are my everything. Thank you for all you've reassured me with this week through your steadfast, eternal, love and life.

Dwell with all God has shown you through your day.

DAY 1

'You are my Lord; apart from you I have no good thing.' Psalm 16:2

The heat, humidity and pungent smell of 6 a.m. Bombay[1] accosted my awakening senses; a sour, spicy, earthy, fumy, sewer-and-sweat-type pungency. But the stifling air was alive with the sound of barking dogs, blaring horns and the shouts of street traders.

It was my niece's second birthday. For seven months I'd been travelling, first as a tourist then with YWAM New Zealand,[2] and my heart tugged for home. Sitting up, I turned to my bookmarked Bible page and began reading David's Psalm 16,[3] but stalled at verse 2.

'You are my Lord.' I wasn't perfect but yes, I could say that.

'Apart from you I have no good thing.' That was my sticking point. In that very moment my heart yearned for safe drinking water, bedbug-free sheets and the hugs of loved ones. But as I dwelt with this verse for the next three weeks:

> I wanted this prayer to be real for me too; that in comparison with everything and everyone else in my life, I could honestly say he was the only good thing; that despite the gift of many loving relationships and material blessings, Jesus would always have and be my first love.[4]

Dwell with David's prayer today. Let it infuse your heart, mind and soul.

DAY 2

'You are my Lord; apart from you I have no good thing.' Psalm 16:2

A number of key Scriptures have shaped and informed my life; words from God which I hold especially dear. But Psalm 16:2 has been a banner; a constant prompt to keep life in perspective of God's love, grace, righteousness and purposes, and of my eternal future in heaven. It wasn't just a verse to know or memorise. It was life-giving words to bed into the core of my being where it might form my priorities, values and sense of security.

I realise, however, that this prayer may sound confusing, for in Genesis, God said his created *world* was 'very good' (Gen. 1:31). God has blessed us with a beautiful, life-sustaining creation, plus relationships, possessions, homes, talents, roles, resources or work to fulfil us and enable us to serve and bless others. It's good to thank him for the many gifts of life, for they *are* good and God-given. But the heart of Psalm 16:2 says that 'compared' to these short-lived things, devotion and dependency on God far outweigh them all. God is the only good thing we can rely on forever.

I'm still a work in progress, but how did you feel when you began praying these words yesterday? Did David's passion for God resonate with yours? Be honest with God about things that tug at your heart more. But thank him too, for his many good gifts you enjoy in life and from his created world.

Dwell with David's prayer today. Let it infuse your heart, mind and soul.

DAY 3

'You are my Lord; apart from you I have no good thing.' Psalm 16:2

Like David, Paul's heart yearned for God too; a longing that sat in tension with his calling to remain in the world to encourage the Church.[5] 'I consider everything a loss', he wrote, 'because of the surpassing worth of knowing Christ Jesus my Lord, for whose sake I have lost all things. I consider them garbage, that I may gain Christ and be found in him . . . I want to know Christ' (Phil. 3:8–10a).

Like Paul:

> We need to 'find ourselves' in his love; revel in it, root and establish ourselves in it, and grow out from it so that we don't just know about it in our head, but experience it deep in our soul, that we 'may be filled to the measure of all the fullness of God' (Eph. 3:19).[6]

And a wonderful way to nurture this is praying Psalm 16:2, as it reminds us what life's all about and of the only thing we can depend on forever. It grows contentment in all circumstances, resets our priorities, helps us to cherish people and things in the light of eternity with God, and reassures us with the truth of who and whose we are.

Reflect on how life would be without God's love, care, provision, guidance, presence and assurance. Let that ache or longing in your soul inspire you to draw close.

Dwell with David's prayer today. Let it infuse your heart, mind and soul.

DAY 4

'You are my Lord; apart from you I have no good thing.' Psalm 16:2

Another way we can nurture devotion and dependency on God is through dwelling in and responding to Scripture. Unlike the passing of people, roles, jobs, health and possessions, God's Word 'endures for ever' (Isa. 40:8). It's our constant as we navigate life's changes. It's the source of our security. It informs our value and significance. It encourages and helps grow our faith and comforts us as we meet with God in his pages. But the subtle messages of social media, employer expectations, personal success, relationship breakdown, financial upheaval, etc. can distract us from these eternal truths that promise abundant well-being.

Apart from God's Word you have no better guidance, wisdom, comfort, reassurance or hope. Take a moment to highlight one or two verses in your Bible that encourage you to keep drawing closer to him. They may be words given to you prophetically, or descriptions of God's character. Alternatively, write them in a journal for quick reference in future.

Here are some examples that may inspire you with God's love and the deep longing that other souls have for him. Keep an eye out for more verses as you read:

Psalm 63:3–8; Psalm 73:25–28; Psalm 84:1–2,10; Psalm 86:5; Psalm 139:1–18; Jeremiah 31:3; Zephaniah 3:17
John 10:10; 15:15; 2 Corinthians 5:1–10; Ephesians 3:18; Philippians 1:21–24; 3:8–10; Hebrews 13:5–6; James 4:8

Dwell with David's prayer today. Let it infuse your heart, mind and soul.

DAY 5

'You are my Lord; apart from you I have no good thing.' Psalm 16:2

I sat in a hospital waiting room unable to get comfortable. The agonising light sensitivity in my swollen right eye was receding, but my back remained so painful and my mouth so full of ulcers, I was struggling to walk and speak. It would be another five years before the cause of these inflammatory symptoms was diagnosed, but I clearly recall the moment of sensing God's presence with me in that plastic seat, in a room crammed with people.

The fragility of my 40-something-year-old body threatened to alarm me, but the words of Psalm 131 settled my soul:

> My heart is not proud, LORD, my eyes are not haughty; I do not concern myself with great matters or things too wonderful for me. But I have calmed and quietened myself, I am like a weaned child with its mother; like a weaned child I am content. [Anne], put your hope in the LORD both now and for evermore.
>
> *Ps. 131:1–3*

I was that young child, fully present to God my Father with me, trusting him with whatever was happening to me physically. The stillness imparted from my only good and eternal source of reassurance was phenomenal, dispelling potential fear for the unknown.

Whatever is causing you fear or worry, draw close to your 'only good thing': God – with you – in this moment.

Dwell with David's prayer today. Let it infuse your heart, mind and soul.

DAY 6

'You are my Lord; apart from you I have no good thing.' Psalm 16:2

Psalm 16 is a prayer for safe-keeping; it's a psalm acknowledging trust in God. To truly believe and live in the truth that God is your only good thing is to reject all counterfeit gods. We may struggle to relate to the figurines or wooden poles that people used to worship gods in ancient times,[7] but modern gods still exist, i.e. things in which we place our security, other than God.

Take a moment to consider what or who you place your security in . . . Now check that alongside my list of ideas:

Investments. A pension. Savings. Regular income. Possessions. Homes. A particular relationship. Your online social media image. Your number of online 'friends'. The number of 'likes/shares' to a post. Success. Acclaim. Respect. A job. A role at church or in the community. What people think of you. Living in a safe neighbourhood. Settling your children in the best school. Keeping extra supplies for emergencies.

None of these are wrong in themselves; in fact, keeping a few emergency supplies can be wise. But if we lean on these things too heavily, they usurp the truth that nothing is forever. At some point your source of security will be threatened because nothing, other than God, is permanently secure.

Who or what might you need to loosen your hold on so you may grasp more tightly to God?

Dwell with David's prayer today. Let it infuse your heart, mind and soul.

DAY 7

'You are my Lord; apart from you I have no good thing.' Psalm 16:2

Praying Psalm 16:2 reminds us that God isn't merely here to fulfil all our 'wants'; but it helps us experience in deeper measure his promised 'life . . . to the full' (John 10:10). As St Augustine of Hippo said: 'Thou hast made us for thyself, O Lord, and our heart is restless until it finds its rest in thee.'[8] The assurance of God's love, the inspiration and shaping of his values, and the empowering of his Spirit, nurtures rich contentment, but also helps us reflect our true God to the world.

Read these alternative translations, slowly. Pray them from your heart. How else is the Holy Spirit speaking to you on this theme?

'I say to GOD, "Be my Lord!" Without you, nothing makes sense.' (MSG)
'I said to him, "You are my Lord; I have no other help but yours."' (TLB)
'Only you are my Lord! Every good thing I have is a gift from you.' (CEV)

Let's conclude our time of dwelling in Psalm 16:2 with another psalmist's prayer:

Whom have I in heaven but you? And earth has nothing I desire besides you. My flesh and my heart may fail, but God is the strength of my heart and my portion for ever . . . it is good to be near God. I have made the Sovereign LORD my refuge; I will tell of all your deeds.

Ps. 73:25–26,28

Dwell with David's prayer today. Let it infuse your heart, mind and soul.

DAY 1

'I do believe; help me overcome my unbelief!' Mark 9:24

When I was young, I wrote letters to Father Christmas, telling him what I'd like to find in my Christmas stocking – a shorn-off leg from an old pair of Mum's tights! Sometimes I was lucky enough to be given what I'd asked for. There were moments of disappointment, however, when I didn't receive what I'd been hoping for, suggesting to my young heart that I hadn't been good enough, or that Santa hadn't received my letter!

I wonder if, even subtly, we can feel that about unanswered prayer; that we've failed God somehow, that we're not good enough, that God doesn't listen . . . or that God doesn't exist after all. I sense this in the father who, in the absence of Jesus, asked the disciples to heal his son of a life-threatening demon. Disheartened by their failure, he saw Jesus arrive and approached him, wondering *if*, rather than confidently believing that he was able to help.[1]

Our faith isn't perfect; it can be undermined by unbelief for many reasons. So, this week we're going to dwell with the father's powerful prayer; his response to Jesus acknowledging his lack of belief, asking Jesus to meet him there and to help him grow. Jesus transforms struggling, deflated or undermined faith into an experience with the living God; just as he did for the father.

Dwell with this prayer through your day. Let it help you turn to God if you feel too discouraged or disillusioned to pray.

DAY 2

'I do believe; help me overcome my unbelief!' Mark 9:24

Jesus said, 'You may ask me for anything in my name, and I will do it' (John 14:14). It's an incredible promise, but perhaps not always your experience. You've prayed for healing, but you or your loved one remain unwell; for a partner, but you're still alone; for a job, but you're still out of work. And perhaps you wonder if God has broken his promise, or is simply ignoring you.

To ask for something in the 'name' of Jesus, however, isn't a magical incantation guaranteeing we'll get what we've asked for. Names in Bible times were more than personal identities; they represented someone's character, nature, ability or role. Praying in Jesus' name prompts us to pray with unconditional love, compassion, forgiveness, kindness and mercy. It's to pray prayers steeped in faith in God's incomparable power, wisdom and sovereignty. And it's to seek to pray God's will and purpose rather than our own.

Reflect on what you've been praying for. Does it dovetail with who Jesus is *and* his perspective and priorities? Are you taking time to ask and discern his leading for prayer?

Lord, I do believe you respond to prayer because you've promised to. Please help me overcome my doubts as you search my willing heart to discern where I'm not honouring your name in my prayer.

Dwell with this prayer through your day. There's no need to hunt for pride, sin, unforgiveness or 'me-centred' prayers. God will highlight them to an open heart *if* they are there.

DAY 3

'I do believe; help me overcome my unbelief!' Mark 9:24

Some of us live in a culture expecting instant results. We grumble about a long queue, a slow internet connection, or someone's delayed response to our text message. We're not used to waiting and we don't like it. And perhaps that subtly infiltrates our expectation of prayer.

But God's eternal being isn't bound by time as we are; there is no haste or delay in his response. So, let's not give up praying because he hasn't responded in the time we want or expect him to. God is patient, wanting *everyone* to come to faith;[2] your unanswered prayer may be allowing more time for your witness to someone. God's apparent delay may in fact reveal his power in ways we couldn't imagine, as when Jesus delayed attending to a poorly Lazarus, only to then raise him from the dead.[3]

Are you wearied by a long-standing prayer? Open your heart to how God may speak, and until he shows you otherwise, persevere in prayer.

Lord, I do believe you respond to prayer, but confess my impatience, my urge to control, even a hint of lack of trust in your greater understanding and perfect will. Please help me overcome my impatience. I wait for you, Lord, in eager, confident expectation and hope, strengthened in heart as I pray.[4]

Dwell with this prayer through your day, resting in the awareness of God's presence, infused with the assurance that God will respond in his perfect timing.

DAY 4

'I do believe; help me overcome my unbelief!' Mark 9:24

My father questioned the existence of God from a young age. Creation was his god and science his teacher. For many years I prayed for his salvation, but his choice to reject what he knew about God and what I'd shared about Jesus didn't suggest a lack of response from God to my prayer.

We were reminded yesterday of God's longing for everyone to be saved.[5] When I prayed for Dad's salvation, I was praying God's divine will. This inspired me to persevere in prayer for his ears to be open to truth, for protection from lying spirits, and for opportunities to share God's grace with him. Only God knew Dad's heart when he took his final breath.

If you're feeling discouraged about unanswered prayer for someone's salvation, remember God won't force their choice. But be encouraged knowing that God *is* working as you pray his will, even if you can't see what he's doing.[6]

Lord, I do believe you respond to prayer for unbelievers because you long for every soul to be saved, but I've grown worried and disheartened by [name]'s lack of response. Please help me overcome my discouragement. Thank you for the faith-building truth that you hear my prayers and are working in their lives, even if I can't see how.

Dwell with this prayer through your day, assured that God longs for the salvation of [name] even more than you, and offers them insights and opportunities to respond.

DAY 5

'I do believe; help me overcome my unbelief!' Mark 9:24

I don't know where you'd be on a scale of engagement with spiritual battle, but today we're reflecting on how it might interfere with an answer to prayer.

Daniel records God sending an angelic messenger with an answer to his prayer, who was delayed for three weeks by a fight in the spiritual realm.[7] You have the Holy Spirit to help you discern God's answers, but the activity in the demonic realm is still prevalent, with power to influence situations you may be praying for. Keep praying in the love, grace and purposes of God (see Day 2), and stand confident in your authority in Christ to impede demonic powers. You can also build up your faith by reading, reflecting on and responding to passages on the subject.[8]

Lord, I do believe you respond to prayer but I'm struggling with the pain of enemy onslaught through hostility, relentless problems, my lack of joy in the spirit [identify how you sense the enemy is oppressing you]. Thank you, that you have overcome the enemy; please help me discern the arrows launched against me, give me Spirit-inspired Scriptures to defeat their power, and help me stand firm in the truth of who I am in Christ.

Dwell with this prayer through your day, listening for God's insights to how the enemy is trying to intimidate you, so you may stand firm in heart, live close to God and pray powerfully in response.

DAY 6

'I do believe; help me overcome my unbelief!' Mark 9:24

Some Bibles say Jesus taught his disciples that fasting was necessary to empower their prayers to heal the boy (v. 29).[9] So, when you are believing in prayer for God's response but not seeing it, it's worth considering fasting.

Fasting isn't about 'earning' God's favour through self-deprivation. Fasting acknowledges our absolute need of him. We'd laugh at someone trying to use an electronic device without plugging into a power supply, but there may be times we pray or act in God's name without depending on his Spirit. We've no power in our natural selves to bear spiritual fruit from our work and service, not least take authority over demons. Fasting won't guarantee the answer we are hoping for; but it humbles our hearts in worship and dependency, it focuses our minds, and directs and empowers our prayers as God leads.

I've fasted sometimes for the wrong reasons. I've also tried fasting of things that in truth, I barely missed. So, I join with you today in opening my heart to hear from God as I continue to dwell with this prayer.

Lord, I do believe in your response to prayer but feel disheartened by your seeming lack of an answer. Please show me how fasting might clear my mind, focus my heart and enable me to keep in closer step with your Spirit.

Dwell with this prayer with an open heart to fasting, and discern how you feel led.

DAY 7

'I do believe; help me overcome my unbelief!' Mark 9:24

This week, we've been asking God to meet us where we're at in the places where faith for his response to prayer is faltering or failing, and to help us wait or persevere for his answer. But discouragement from unanswered prayer might also be relieved by simply coming back to God for himself. Of drawing close to talk, to listen, to be still and receive whatever it is of his Spirit that he wants to encourage and enrich us with.

On this, our last day with our dwelling place, just be with God in prayer for himself. Open your heart, mind and soul to his presence. Delight yourself in who he is. He knows what you need today. Let him reignite your joy in him and the vitality of his Spirit working in and through your life to bring truth, blessing and healing to others.

Lord, I do believe you respond to prayer, but sometimes I'm disheartened because I've stopped simply enjoying being with you in prayer, listening to you and delighting in your love. Please help me overcome all that distracts me from or intrudes upon times of prayerfully being in your presence, and of receiving the joy and vitality of your Spirit living in me.

Dwell with this prayer through the rest of your day. Be encouraged that God is meeting you just as you are and where you're at, with infinite love and understanding.

DAY 1

'Make it your ambition to lead a quiet life: you should mind your own business and work with your hands, just as we told you, so that your daily life may win the respect of outsiders and so that you will not be dependent on anybody.'
1 Thessalonians 4:11–12

I'd love to sell millions of books! But what's my motive? To earn substantial amounts of money, enhancing my present comfort and my sense of future security; to earn money to use in supporting others; or to help others find and grow a relationship with Jesus, from which their lives and work will draw others to him too? Which of these do I work my very hardest to achieve? What motivates me to persevere? My heart is deceptive[1] so I often ask God to help me know it as he does, something Paul prompts us with this week.

Paul addressed a particular concern in the Thessalonian church,[2] but all Scripture is useful to our situations too. His mention of 'ambition' is worth prayerful reflection in cultures that prize success, affluence, influence, growth and bigger and better things.

What are you ambitious for? What goals or desires are you passionate about and driven to achieve?

What drives, motivates and energises you?

Which goals are you convinced are God-given dreams? Which are you not sure about? Which might have arisen from your own ambitions?

Record your responses and talk with God about all the desires of you heart.

Dwell with God's Word through the day as it shapes your ongoing response.

DAY 2

'Make it your ambition to lead a quiet life: you should mind your own business and work with your hands, just as we told you, so that your daily life may win the respect of outsiders and so that you will not be dependent on anybody.'
1 Thessalonians 4:11–12

Paul clarifies godly ambition as eagerly seeking to live a life that *wins the respect* of others. It's to live a life that honours Jesus – his nature, values and truth – in our daily situations. A lifestyle that corrects other people's misunderstandings about Christianity, and hopefully arouses their interest to know more.

God gifts and equips us to play our part and make a difference in society. It's not wrong to set goals or for hard work to prove successful. Paul's context fiercely opposes idleness. But the foundation of godly ambition is to reflect Jesus by how we live and relate and through what we do. This is our greatest achievement of all.

Reflect on each of your ambitions. How do they resonate with the goal to honour Jesus? As you take steps to fulfil your ambitions, what opportunities do they offer to reveal Jesus' character, adopt his priorities, express his truth and wisdom? Is there room to enjoy being more dependent on his power and creativity? Talk with God about your responses. Are there any ambitions you need to abandon?

Dwell with God's Word through the day as it shapes your ongoing response.

DAY 3

'Make it your ambition to lead a quiet life: you should mind your
own business and work with your hands, just as we told you, so
that your daily life may win the respect of outsiders and so that
you will not be dependent on anybody.'
1 Thessalonians 4:11–12

The disciples argued over who was greatest among them. But Jesus taught that to be great was to serve.[3] He didn't value rank and status, and yet, a little later, James and John sidled up, asking if they could sit at Jesus' right and left hand in his kingdom; positions of power and prestige. Jesus patiently repeated his message: 'whoever wants to become great among you must be your servant' (Mark 10:43–44).

Jesus overturned the world's structure of values in how he served; even giving up his life for others.[4] Discipleship is stamped with this hallmark. Jesus didn't react to every need or demand pressed upon him, but was daily led by fulfilling his Father's will. That's what inspired his service and can inspire ours too.[5]

Do you ever see yourself in the disciples, craving the reputation or power of titles and prestigious roles? Jesus' ambition – his life's goal – was to fulfil his Father's will, to glorify him and make him known.[6] Ask him to envision you with this ambition too.

How do your goals and desires present opportunities to honour God and serve others? Being specific helps you to be mindful of this in future.

Dwell with God's Word through the day as it shapes your ongoing response.

DAY 4

'Make it your ambition to lead a quiet life: you should mind your own business and work with your hands, just as we told you, so that your daily life may win the respect of outsiders and so that you will not be dependent on anybody.'
1 Thessalonians 4:11–12

To aspire to a *quiet* life doesn't frown on being talkative or exuberant. Nor is it demoting a full and active life. Paul simply endorses Christ's calm, settled, undisturbed, unhurried way of life; a stillness of heart and soul from being at peace with oneself and with God. A life that has room to be present to others; faithfully serving, unassuming, working with diligence, loving unconditionally – where the beauty of Jesus commends him to others.

This godly ambition releases us to be who we are in the environment where we live, and to grow our giftings without comparing what we do or the nature of our achievements with others. It's a *quiet* life because we're content in who we are in God without needing to promote ourselves publicly. But let's not misunderstand 'quiet' and 'unhurried' for unproductive. Jesus led a calm, undistracted life, which still bears life-giving fruit today.

When you reflect on your life in this light, what most resonates or inspires you to adopt Jesus' assured, unhurried life for yourself? If this highlights things you need to let go of, talk with God to discern when and how that's appropriate.

Dwell with God's Word through the day as it shapes your ongoing response.

DAY 5

'Make it your ambition to lead a quiet life: you should mind your own business and work with your hands, just as we told you, so that your daily life may win the respect of outsiders and so that you will not be dependent on anybody.'
1 Thessalonians 4:11–12

There are many good reasons why some of us are unable to work for a living. Paul's warning to keep working at their occupation, however, at their daily roles and responsibilities, may have been because some despised manual work, or were idle (even busybodies!) as they waited for Christ's return. They'd become reliant on others when they were perfectly capable of providing for themselves.

Whatever the nature or existence of our 'work life', our godly ambition is be conscientious with what we *are* able to do.

Paul writes elsewhere, 'Whatever you do, work at it with all your heart, as working for the Lord, not for human masters' (Col. 3:23). Whether your responsibilities are inspiring or mundane, how would the approach of doing them for Jesus transform your attitude, motivation and perspective?

Your diligence with your role, your reflection of Jesus' nature and your openness to his creativity will help others develop their own understanding of him. Your friends and colleagues may never come to hear a church sermon, but your life is his message to them. Prayerfully reflect on this truth and let God inspire your response.

Dwell with God's Word through the day as it shapes your ongoing response.

DAY 6

'Make it your ambition to lead a quiet life: you should mind your own business and work with your hands, just as we told you, so that your daily life may win the respect of outsiders and so that you will not be dependent on anybody.'
1 Thessalonians 4:11–12

John the Baptist's disciples were worried about 'everyone' going over to Jesus (John 3:22–36). John gently challenged their distorted ambitions, reminding them that his role of preparing the way for Jesus[7] was reaching its conclusion. It was time for John to step back and let Jesus come to the fore. His words are challenging yet so inspiring, 'He must become greater; I must become less' (John 3:30).

Christ's longing for others to know him pulsates through our lives.[8] But John's words carry a beautiful resonance with our dwelling place. John wasn't to remain in competition with Jesus' presence. If we want to encounter more of Christ's life impacting our own, then: 'He must become greater; I must become less.'

'Our goal', Rick Warren writes, 'is to make God look good, not ourselves'.[9] There's a fine line between being kind, generous and helping others, with the subtle motive of attracting others to 'us', rather than Jesus. We're not seeking admiration for ourselves, but simply to love Jesus, thereby making space for his life to be lived through ours.

Reflect on John's words. What comes to mind? Adapt them into a personal prayer and listen for God's response.

Dwell with God's Word through the day as it shapes your ongoing response.

DAY 7

'Make it your ambition to lead a quiet life: you should mind your
own business and work with your hands, just as we told you, so
that your daily life may win the respect of outsiders and so that
you will not be dependent on anybody.'
1 Thessalonians 4:11–12

God uses the undistinguished ordinariness of life as much as the extraordinary.
Lives that faithfully reflect Christ's love and truth in raising family, being a
friend and working in so many 'ordinary' jobs are as powerful in making him
known as being famed for one's work, of achieving headline-worthy success or
even mega-sized ministries.

We can naturally be nice people; we can even fake it! But we can't fake conveying the tangible presence of Jesus; and most likely, we won't even know when we
do. Attracting the respect and desire of others for Christ grows from a lifelong
pursuit of deepening our relationship with him and allowing him to progres-
sively transform us into his likeness.

That's what underpins our reflections this week. God will raise some of you into
places and roles of worldly prestige, success and influence. But all of us, whether
upfront or behind the scenes, achieving breakthrough scientific research or remaining at home, have one ambition to pursue. To know, love and serve Jesus.

Let's pray: Beautiful Jesus, please continue to speak to my heart on this theme.
Help me discern your desired response and make yourself known through my life.

Dwell with God's Word through the day as it shapes your ongoing
response.

DAY 1

'Yes, my soul, find rest in God; my hope comes from him.
Truly he is my rock and my salvation; he is my fortress,
I shall not be shaken.
My salvation and my honour depend on God;
he is my mighty rock, my refuge.
Trust in him at all times, you people;
pour out your hearts to him, for God is our refuge.'
Psalm 62:5–8

Selah

What a wonderful Hebrew word this is, one I speak to my own soul at times; a word you may have seen when reading the Psalms. In my Bible, *selah* appears in Psalm 62 just before verse 5 and immediately after verse 8; our dwelling place. Its meaning is uncertain but possibly prompts a pause in the music, giving space for the worshipper to reflect on what's been sung.

This, of course, is the very nature of *Dwell*, but this week, we'll adopt the practice of Lectio Divina. It gives space for you to dwell with this short passage sitting snugly between its '*selahs*', to give you sufficient time for deep, prayerful reflection and response. I will sit on the side-lines, softening my voice to a few whispered thoughts on the context and meaning of the passage, alongside some guidelines for each *Lectio* step, trusting you will hear from God without further prompts from me.

For today, focus your mind and your whole being on God with you. Read this passage slowly, more than once if you're able, mindful of God's love, power and protection.

Dwell with the affirmation of God's presence through your day.

DAY 2

'Yes, my soul, find rest in God; my hope comes from him.
Truly he is my rock and my salvation; he is my fortress,
I shall not be shaken.
My salvation and my honour depend on God;
he is my mighty rock, my refuge.
Trust in him at all times, you people;
pour out your hearts to him, for God is our refuge.'
Psalm 62:5–8

One of my favourite descriptions of Lectio Divina says:

> *Lectio divina*, Latin for 'sacred reading', is a contemplative practice designed to open us to the presence of God through Scripture. Since it is meditative in nature, it can serve as a natural complement to the intellectual, historical-critical method of Bible study traditionally practiced . . . *Lectio divina* is a simple method that invites us to approach Scripture the way we might open a love letter from our beloved.[1]

How precious. This isn't just another practice of engaging with Scripture, it invites you to 'open a love letter' from God. Do keep that in mind as you follow through the *Lectio* steps this week.

Step One: Still your heart and mind and turn your attention onto God.
Step Two: Read the passage slowly, at least twice. Which words, phrases or images capture your attention? Which especially resonate with you as a person, with a situation you face, or which raise questions for further research or prayer?

Dwell with how God is ministering to you through his Word through your day. And if you're able, read the passage again before going to sleep.

DAY 3

'Yes, my soul, find rest in God; my hope comes from him.
Truly he is my rock and my salvation; he is my fortress,
I shall not be shaken.
My salvation and my honour depend on God;
he is my mighty rock, my refuge.
Trust in him at all times, you people;
pour out your hearts to him, for God is our refuge.'
Psalm 62:5–8

David wrote this psalm from a place of felt weakness, as assaults and conspiracies threatened his throne (vv. 3–4).[2] But verses 5–6 echo his faith pronounced in the opening lines (vv. 1–2), as David commits himself to God's care in a phenomenal expression of trust and hope. Hope in God isn't wishful thinking; it's a firm conviction for God to remain faithful to his goodness and promises in everything we face.

Whatever assaults or conspires against you – health issues, demanding deadlines, unrealistic expectations, financial challenges or indeed, like David, individuals maliciously set against you – remember to dwell with these words as an expression of God's love and faithfulness to you.

Repeat steps One and Two if that's helpful.

Step Three: Gently repeat one of the words, phrases or images that especially resonates, then hold it quietly in prayerful awareness of God with you. Reflect, meditate, ponder and chew over it, being attentive to what it's saying to you as you let it sink ever deeper into your heart, mind and soul. Record how God is revealing the ways it dovetails with your life.

Dwell with these insights through your day.

DAY 4

'Yes, my soul, find rest in God; my hope comes from him.
Truly he is my rock and my salvation; he is my fortress,
I shall not be shaken.
My salvation and my honour depend on God;
he is my mighty rock, my refuge.
Trust in him at all times, you people;
pour out your hearts to him, for God is our refuge.'
Psalm 62:5–8

Reflect on these descriptions of God: *Rock. Salvation. Unshakeable Fortress. Refuge.*

What images or ideas come to mind? Trust that God is these things to you. And as you do so, you will experience deep joy from reassured hope.

Once again, still your heart and mind and turn your attention onto God.

Step Four: What response has your meditation inspired from the words, phrases or images from yesterday or today? Perhaps it's confession, praise, repentance, thanksgiving, a new course of action or way of being or doing, or else something you want to ask. Consider any practicalities you need to put in place, then move on to the next step.

Step Five: Pray. 'Pour out your hearts' (v. 8). Hold back from rushing on from how God has been meeting with you. Be honest with him and give space to listen for and discern any response.

Dwell with how God is ministering to you through his Word through your day.

DAY 5

'Yes, my soul, find rest in God; my hope comes from him.
Truly he is my rock and my salvation; he is my fortress,
I shall not be shaken.
My salvation and my honour depend on God;
he is my mighty rock, my refuge.
Trust in him at all times, you people;
pour out your hearts to him, for God is our refuge.'
Psalm 62:5–8

When David speaks to his soul, he's talking to his whole being. His mind, body, heart and spirit are to *find rest* in his knowledge of who God is, what he has said and what he can do. The Hebrew for this expression literally means 'be silent; cease; quiet; wait'. So, an alternative translation of verse 5 which I particularly appreciate is 'Let all that I am wait quietly before God, for my hope is in him' (Ps. 62:5, NLT).

David speaks to his soul to silence and still its fretful thoughts, emotions and reactions, because God, as described, is his greatest reassurance. Perhaps you'll agree that the rich tranquillity of quiet rest born of trust and hope in God is immensely appealing.

Once again, still your heart and mind and turn your attention onto God. Read the passage slowly, at least twice.

Step Six: Be present to God's presence in a time of quiet rest. Give space for his Word to nourish your relationship. Receive strength and reassurance from simply being with God, and let it infuse your soul.

Dwell with how God is ministering to you through his Word through your day.

DAY 6

'Yes, my soul, find rest in God; my hope comes from him.
Truly he is my rock and my salvation; he is my fortress,
I shall not be shaken.
My salvation and my honour depend on God;
he is my mighty rock, my refuge.
Trust in him at all times, you people;
pour out your hearts to him, for God is our refuge.'
Psalm 62:5–8

Eugene Peterson's paraphrased translation of our passage reads:

God, the one and only – I'll wait as long as he says.
Everything I hope for comes from him, so why not?
He's solid rock under my feet, breathing room for my soul,
An impregnable castle: I'm set for life.
My help and glory are in God – granite-strength and safe-harbor-God –
So trust him absolutely, people; lay your lives on the line for him.
God is a safe place to be.

Ps. 62:5–8, MSG

How does this add further clarity to your understanding of the words and phrases? Do they suggest any further response?

'God is a safe place to be.' What a beautiful, alluring truth; the very nature of a refuge. If the demands or circumstances of your life feel risky, threatening, precarious, then dwell with God as your safe place today. His presence is your haven, hideaway and retreat for storm-tossed thoughts and emotions. Find rest – stillness of being – as you hope in him and wait for his direction, provision or deliverance.

Dwell with how God is ministering to you through his Word through your day.

DAY 7

'Yes, my soul, find rest in God; my hope comes from him.
Truly he is my rock and my salvation; he is my fortress,
I shall not be shaken.
My salvation and my honour depend on God;
he is my mighty rock, my refuge.
Trust in him at all times, you people;
pour out your hearts to him, for God is our refuge.'
Psalm 62:5–8

Whatever issue has been on your heart this week, *truly* (v. 6) it rests with God alone. He may have prompted prayers of confession, acts of reconciliation, or guidelines for facing the pressures you face, but as you commit to following through on these things, know that *truly* – God alone – is your *rock*. Your *honour* is in his hands. You may feel weak, but as you trust God to be faithful to all he is and says, let *hope* – absolute expectation – arise.

David spoke of his adversaries in verses 3–4 but he didn't brood on their activities. He filled his thoughts with truth about God. Likewise, today and in future, be intentional in focusing on how God has reassured you, rather than on what assaults you.

But now, still your heart and mind with God. Read the passage slowly. Thank God for how it speaks into your life.

Let's pray: God, my rock, life and unshakeable fortress – my safe refuge – I trust who you are and what you have said, and now rest, in quiet assurance.

Dwell with how God is ministering to you through his Word, through your day.

DAY 1

'Whoever watches the wind will not plant;
whoever looks at the clouds will not reap.' Ecclesiastes 11:4

I've been reading through some old journals, and oh, deary me! I'm ashamed to admit there are spiritual prompts still waiting my response from one, three or even eight years ago; convictions of bad habits that still fester, or ideas to act upon which as yet, I haven't. The question I must ask is, 'Why?' A question God will gently probe our hearts with this week.

If you read Ecclesiastes from chapter 11 verse 1, you'd be forgiven for thinking it was offering a handful of trade, business and farming tips.[1] But the writer had just taken ten chapters to describe and commend a life of faith in contrast to one of indifference or unbelief. Now, he asks us to stop procrastinating; to make up our mind which life we will choose. He then appeals for wholehearted commitment (chapter 12), even when we face obstacles, as each day leads us closer to meeting God face-to-face.[2]

'Tomorrow never comes', the old maxim suggests. So, today is the day to know and live well for God. Today and every day holds opportunities to seek him, honour him and join in with his story. Enthusiasm can wane for many reasons, some of which we'll consider this week. But for now, prayerfully reflect on this verse. How is God leading your thoughts?

Continue to dwell with this verse through your day, open to the Holy Spirit's stirrings.

DAY 2

'Whoever watches the wind will not plant;
whoever looks at the clouds will not reap.' Ecclesiastes 11:4

Has God been prompting you to respond to a conviction or to take some kind of action, which as yet, you haven't? If so, ask yourself, 'Why?' God wants to meet with you in this verse to encourage your life of faith, not condemn it, and to help you reap an abundant harvest. But perhaps, like the image of the farmer, we're waiting for the right conditions before we respond to a command, promise or godly characteristic that God has prompted to our heart.

Perhaps you fear conditions aren't good enough: that you're not good enough, worthy enough, able enough, young enough, old enough. Perhaps you believe you cannot *plant* then hope to *reap* godly things, while you're dealing with certain problems, roles or responsibilities. Perhaps you find yourself preferring the lie that your guilty pleasure satisfies you more than yielding to God's righteous life with its promised blessings, intimacy and empowering. Or perhaps you're put off by the need to learn new things, the financial commitment or the volume of work required in an already busy life, to fulfil what God's asked you to do.

There are many reasons we procrastinate, so just be open to God to hear his specific word to *you*. Then pray about it. Confess any persistent ungodly habits, and/or commit to taking any action needed in response.

Dwell with this verse and its prompts through your day, being mindful of God with you.

DAY 3

'Whoever watches the wind will not plant;
whoever looks at the clouds will not reap.' Ecclesiastes 11:4

'Bloom where you're planted.'[3]

I love this idiom for its uplifting inspiration at times when we might believe life's problems prevent us from living meaningfully for God. It assures us we can still be fruitful even when life throws its worst at us. We can still do what's right when it's hard to. In fact, problems may nurture sweeter fruit, if we meet with God in the pain and let his love do its work in and through us.

If we wait for perfect conditions before planting or reaping, says Ecclesiastes, we'll be waiting forever. There are no perfect conditions in agriculture, nor in living a life of faith. But there's always an opportunity in every circumstance to do and say and be the right thing; the thing that reflects God's character and truth. God is with us in the best as well as the worst of times. As we acknowledge his presence, we'll see opportunities to bring light into darkness as we yield to his ways and his Word.

Consider your present situation. Remind yourself that God is living life with you. He will inspire, comfort and guide. Whether you find yourself in a place of ease or difficulty, what opportunities arise for you to live life well for him, in a way that reflects his love and truth?

Dwell with this verse and its prompts through your day, being mindful of God with you.

DAY 4

'Whoever watches the wind will not plant;
whoever looks at the clouds will not reap.' Ecclesiastes 11:4

Opportunity or obligation?

Whether we're in a season of relentless busyness or one of mundane routine, we can wake up feeling blue. If it weren't for dependants needing our care, pets needing the loo, or bills demanding we get to work, we could be tempted to remain beneath our snug duvet. But we don't have to drag ourselves out of bed. Rather, on waking, we can choose to thank God for his presence that will walk with us through our day, and for the opportunities it presents to live well and reflect his presence. It puts a lightness in our step and a smile on our heart; I know, because I often have to do it. And perhaps it puts a smile on God's face too!

Adopting a mindset of opportunity rather than obligation is an invigorating wake-up call to God's presence and purpose. Today is an opportunity to be loved by God and to share his love with others. Today is an opportunity to plant seeds for God's kingdom, in prayer and in action. Today is ripe for reaping the fruit of his Spirit at work through your life.

God has equipped you with specific gifts, resources and a personality to convey his presence in whatever you do or face. Reflect on this in prayer, your heart open to all that God may encourage you with.

Dwell with this verse and its prompts through your day, being mindful of God with you.

DAY 5

'Whoever watches the wind will not plant;
whoever looks at the clouds will not reap.' Ecclesiastes 11:4

Would you consider yourself 'risk averse', i.e. disinclined or reluctant to take risks? I am. I'd rather keep what little savings we have in a guaranteed but low-interest bank account than risk losing them in an investment that could flourish or fail, depending on market fluctuations.

But being risk-averse isn't just about finances. Ecclesiastes 11:1 resonates with the principle of verse 4; of waiting for conditions which might be better than today's.[4] But its sea trade analogy speaks of faith as an adventure where we take calculated risks. The future is unknown so we take the long-term view, enthusiastically investing our time, talents and resources in a variety of ways, believing that at least some will be spiritually fruitful (see also vv. 2,6[5]).

Living a life of faith involves trust and commitment rather than playing it safe[6] or being confined by pursuing only immediate success. The writer isn't encouraging us to act recklessly but to prayerfully discern God's leading and act prudently in response.

Trust. Commitment. Enthusiasm. Reflect on these words and how alive they are in your life of faith. Has God promised you something which you've side-lined in preference for other activities? Talk with him about how you'll recommit to praying for and pursuing it.

How else can you invest your life for God's kingdom purposes?

Dwell with this verse and its prompts through your day, being mindful of God with you.

DAY 6

'Whoever watches the wind will not plant;
whoever looks at the clouds will not reap.' Ecclesiastes 11:4

The long hedge running down our vegetable garden needs regular pruning; hard work but an opportunity for gaining fuel for the fire. To make the most of this opportunity, my husband uses an axe, but it needs to be sharp. He's learned that time spent sharpening the axe is time well spent. The job would take much longer and prove far harder if he didn't take regular breaks to sharpen the blade with a whetstone.

Ecclesiastes links this analogy with our life of faith.[7] An enthusiastic response to God includes a willingness to yield to his will and his ways. We may relish getting stuck into God's work but our 'cutting edge' is the anointing of his Spirit. Our work will be sheer slog and potentially fruitless without keeping ourselves spiritually sharp. Without his wisdom, anointing and empowering we can do nothing of meaningful consequence for God's kingdom.[8]

God's Word is your 'whetstone'. But it takes more than knowing it; it's your response to it that 'thoroughly equips' you – and keeps you sharp – for living the life of faith and making the most of opportunities it presents (2 Tim. 3:16–17).

What has especially resonated from your reading of *Dwell*? Pray once again on how you've felt prompted to respond, and how you may continue to nurture a fruitful life of faith.

DAY 7

'Whoever watches the wind will not plant;
whoever looks at the clouds will not reap.' Ecclesiastes 11:4

What if I get it wrong? What if I didn't hear God as I thought I did? What if . . . ?

We can ruminate on the 'what ifs' for as long as it takes for that legendary perfect weather to appear for planting and reaping. If we do walk up a wrong road, we can always turn around. But if all we do is 'ask' without 'knocking' on doors (Matt. 7:7–8), they may remain shut.

Paul was adventurous in faith and lived enthusiastically for God in fluctuating circumstances, because he *knew* God's perfect nature, and aspired to his divine purpose. He was twice blocked from entering countries he thought he should take the gospel to, but as he kept moving in faith, God opened the right door.[9] Making the most of opportunities doesn't guarantee success. But inspired by our relationship with God, we can give ourself wholeheartedly to our current responsibilities and to however God leads.

'Remember your Creator', Ecclesiastes concludes.[10] Take time today to dwell on who God is and what he has done. It's knowing God and being thankful that inspires you to pursue opportunities that life lived with him presents.

Let's pray: Loving God, help me to grasp the joy of living life with and for you, and to reach out for its opportunities.

Continue to dwell with this verse for one more day.

DAY 1

'KING OF KINGS AND LORD OF LORDS' Revelation 19:16

I shuffled forward on the pew at my first senior school carol service, my heart pounding as the choir sang their annual rendition of Handel's 'Hallelujah Chorus'.[1] 'KING OF KINGS' their layered harmonies powered Scripture through the old church. My eyes misted with tears. 'LORD OF LORDS' their triumphant declaration of Jesus reverberated through the rafters – and through my soul. Enraptured, I longed for the day I'd be old enough to take part, and belt out my own 'Hallelujah' to this King of kings. It would be some years, however, before I opened my heart to him too.

As we explore our King and his kingdom this week, I'm praying it will revitalise adoration and devotion. Today, picture Jesus as revealed in the Gospels; his character and personality, his priorities and perspective, and how he related to others.

Ask the Holy Spirit to help you discern what he wants you to pause with and ponder; the beautiful nature and awesome power of your King.

And then, quiet your heart and mind. Prayerfully declare this verse one phrase, one word at a time, and respond as you feel prompted: in prayer, praise, adoration or confession, in bowing your head or falling to your knees.

King of kings and Lord of Lords
King of kings and Lord
King of kings
King
Jesus. Is. King.

Dwell with an awareness of King Jesus with you through your day; let his presence rule in your heart, mind and soul.

DAY 2

'KING OF KINGS AND LORD OF LORDS' Revelation 19:16

God is love so the essence of his kingdom is love, as is the nature of its King. It's because God loves [you] that Jesus is [your] King. And King Jesus loves [you].[2]

Many kings of the earth rule with force; reigning over subjects who tremble in abject fear of the consequences should they cause offence, while others work relentlessly to earn their favour. But Jesus rules with love. Love is the nature of God and the nature of his kingdom. Your King loves you unashamedly, unceasingly and unconditionally. King Jesus isn't aloof on a high and heavenly throne; he dwells within you. You may feel unlovable for many reasons, but King Jesus loves you. You may feel rejected, but King Jesus accepts and embraces you. You may feel overlooked, but King Jesus sees and cares for you. But if your head belief isn't rooted deep into your being, you may find yourself trying to *earn* his love.

Reread the first paragraph, inserting your name into the square brackets. Have an open heart to God's love, poured out to you through the death, resurrection and exaltation of his Son, Jesus. Rest in his love for as long as it takes to extinguish doubts, cast out fear and dismiss the impossible task of trying to earn his free gift. Let love fill your heart, mind and soul.

Dwell with an awareness of King Jesus with you through your day; let his love rule in your heart, mind and soul.

DAY 3

'KING OF KINGS AND LORD OF LORDS' Revelation 19:16

Double titles in the Bible are used to emphasise God's supremacy, and here, as Christ's absolute Sovereignty. But when we're battling excruciating pain from life's problems, it may be hard to sense our King's ruling power. In our struggle with the fallout of personal and global storms and wars, we may even begin to question why he doesn't intervene.

Jesus knew we would suffer anguish, affliction, distress and trouble in this world. Yet, he urged us to take heart; to be comforted and courageous in his victory over death because our lives are 'in him'.[3] We have a dual existence. We live physically in the dominion of God's enemy but we live spiritually in Christ. And despite the hostile pressure the world exerts, a gift of our union with King Jesus is peace.[4] This is your King's power to intervene in your trouble and pain today; peace of heart and mind. As you choose to trust him, you'll know the unshakeable assurance of his presence in your problems.

Still your mind and heart before him. If it helps, open your palms to symbolise your desire to experience his gift of peace through the ministry of his Spirit within you. You may not receive any answers or resolutions to your problems but, as a child of our King, engage with his peace to strengthen and enable you to endure.

Dwell with an awareness of King Jesus with you through your day; let his peace rule in your heart, mind and soul.

DAY 4

'My kingdom is not of this world', Jesus said (John 18:36); it isn't built, expanded or maintained through military force. It's a heavenly kingdom, present in the world through the person of its King.[5]

If King Jesus and his kingdom feel aloof or disconnected to your daily reality, Paul offers help through Colossians 3:1–3 to re-engage with it:

> Since, then, you have been raised with Christ, set your hearts on things above, where Christ is, seated at the right hand of God. Set your minds on things above, not on earthly things. For you died, and your life is now hidden with Christ in God.

- You are already raised with King Jesus and are 'seated . . . with him' in his heavenly kingdom (Eph. 2:6). Dwell with this awesome truth.
- To 'set your heart and mind' is literally to actively seek to follow the life of King Jesus, in thought and action. How does that speak into your relationship with and response to God's transforming work in your life, to your relationship with others, and to your roles and responsibilities?
- 'Things above' are the characteristics of God's kingdom; for example, self-giving love and a holy life. Is your heart set on these or on other things?

Dwell with an awareness of King Jesus with you through your day; let his presence inspire your heart, mind and soul.

DAY 5

'KING OF KINGS AND LORD OF LORDS' Revelation 19:16

When I was old enough to join the senior choir (see Day 1), I *loved* singing 'Hallelujah' to the King of kings. But I was merely paying him lip service; I sang with gusto to a King on a music score who wasn't yet King of my life. The magnificent music stirred my heart, but my insincere praise didn't affect how I lived.

Forty-plus years later, I'm humbled to admit I can be roused on Sunday singing songs to my King, but by Monday fail to live out my praise in yielded, devoted response. My head belief hasn't always matched the allegiance of my heart. Consequently, I've often lacked his kingdom character or priorities infusing my daily reality. And there've been times when attempting to use his gifts, I've lacked his anointing power. Perhaps I'm not alone.

To call Jesus King from the depth of our heart affirms his sovereignty, inspiring reverence, worship and awe. And the more we yield to his life, the greater our experience of his glorious, loving, guiding, providing, affirming presence and power; and the more we are transformed by his beautiful character.

Prayerfully reflect on each of these descriptions of allegiance:

Wholehearted devotion. Commitment. Loyalty. Conformity.

This isn't an exercise to demoralise or condemn, it's to inspire and revitalise your devoted loving response to Jesus.

Dwell with an awareness of King Jesus with you through your day; know his loving delight in your commitment.

DAY 6

'KING OF KINGS AND LORD OF LORDS' Revelation 19:16

God's promises are ours through King Jesus;[6] but we may often have to live by faith rather than felt experience, and that can be challenging. Our ultimate hope is for the completion of God's kingdom; an eternity of peace, joy and perfection. But that hope can fade from the forefront of our minds when today is hard-going. So, when we're struggling to bridge the gap between faith in his kingdom for today and hope for its fullness in the future, it helps to remind ourselves that this life is short.

Our true, forever-after life is not in this world, but in the presence of our glorious King Jesus. Our primary purpose now is to be loved by God, which inspires our response of love for him, and which, in turn, overflows to loving others. But this life isn't our destination, it's the journey to the full experience of living with him face-to-face.

Talk openly with God about your loved ones, your dreams, your longing for resolution to your problems and pain. He cares for all these things.

Also ask him to envision your heart with his glory – his radiant love, power and majesty – and your forever-after life filled with the fullness of his presence, without tears, pain or heartache.

Let the awe of his Kingly presence and promise fuel joy-filled hope for that day.

Dwell with an awareness of King Jesus with you through your day; let your hope in his return inspire your heart, mind and soul.

DAY 7

'KING OF KINGS AND LORD OF LORDS' Revelation 19:16

We've looked at different ways to engage with Jesus as King this week, but here are a few more ideas to further encourage your focus and faith response on this final day of our dwelling place. If you're able, do them all; if not, choose the one that most inspires you and return to the others later.

Read through Revelation 19:5–16, or if you've time, Revelation chapters 19 – 22. Pause every so often to let the beauty, power and exaltation of Christ fill your heart. Pause to pray the verses of praise, or to worship the beauty of who he is. Meet with your King through this vision of hope for your future.

Take a walk where you can enjoy God's creation, even if it's a small park in your town or city. This too shall be perfected when Jesus returns to establish his kingdom.[7] Focus on a particular aspect of it, even the ever-changing clouds in the vast expanse of the sky. Meet with Jesus as King over all creation and let that inspire your heart's hope, your prayerful response and your worship.

Worship Jesus as King in song. There are some suggestions in the endnotes if one hasn't come to mind.[8]

Let's pray: King Jesus. King of kings. Be King of my heart's desires, King of my thoughts, King of my life. I trust and love you forever.

Continue to dwell with an awareness of King Jesus through your day.

DAY 1

'Write down the revelation and make it plain on tablets so that a herald may run with it.' Habakkuk 2:2

'Write down the revelation', you begin reading.

'What revelation?' you may ask. 'What vision [as the word can be translated] has God given me?'

Or perhaps you've been actively seeking but are still waiting for God to reveal his will for a changing season of life, or for the coming year. Let's start by giving our dwelling place some context.

Perplexed that God seemed to permit festering sin to permeate his holy people without taking measures to curb it, Habakkuk, the prophet, asked him why. In response, God explained he would use Babylon to discipline his people on his behalf.[1] Shocked that he would use such a ruthless people against his own, Habakkuk again asks why. Although the precise nature of the revelation isn't known, God assures Habakkuk that discipline is for a season; Babylon would itself be conquered and God would restore his people to himself and to their home in Israel.[2] But it was imperative that Habakkuk should write down God's revealed will in such a way that it could be clearly read, recalled and conveyed. And that's the key principle we're going to dwell with this week.

Prayerfully familiarise yourself with this verse and ask God to reveal his will, his vision, his revelation to your heart in the coming week.

Continue to dwell with God's Word through Habakkuk through the rest of your day.

DAY 2

'Write down the revelation and make it plain on tablets so that a herald may run with it.' Habakkuk 2:2

In my own changing seasons of life, I've asked God to help me discern his ongoing will. I must admit, however, that sometimes I've asked with ears only listening for the answer *I* want to hear, rather than what God may want to say. I regret, too, that on one occasion I discerned his revelation, but with time, muddied his vision with my own aspirations, pursuing more than he'd actually asked me to.

God knows how easily our hearts can deceive us,[3] even when we've the best intentions of hearing from him. Habakkuk, however, determined to wait to hear from God.[4] The *revelation* or *vision* was prophetic. It wasn't Habakkuk's idea, his ideal, or his expressed goal or dream. The message was from God.

> Come . . .
> Listen, listen to me . . .
> Give ear and come to me; listen, that you may live.

> *Isa. 55:1–3*

Still your thoughts. Silence your own desires or agenda. And come to God. Listen to discern the fullness of life that he longs to lead you in. This may take time. It may take days or weeks, and longer still for it to be fulfilled.[5] And perhaps in some ways, a lifetime. But you can believe God's promise to answer when you ask for his wisdom,[6] and trust patiently as you wait.

Dwell with God's Word through Habakkuk through the rest of your day.

DAY 3

'Write down the revelation and make it plain on tablets so that a herald may run with it.' Habakkuk 2:2

In the shadow of Babylon's imminent oppression, God's revelation to Habakkuk reassured and revived the downhearted. It gave them hope through subsequent years of exile. It reminded them they were still God's chosen and beloved people, despite their failures or hardships. It affirmed their ongoing purpose and identity to inspire them to live up to their calling, even in captivity.

Scripture clearly reveals God's nature and promises which instil hope, reassurance and meaning to life, whatever situations we face. It affirms his unconditional, unfailing love, no matter our failings. It teaches us and, through Jesus, shows us how to live. This is our vision. This is God's revelation for you and for me today, whatever our background, circumstances, roles or responsibilities. Even if you've been seeking God's revelation for a specific matter, be mindful how God's revealed will in his Word and how it's lived out in Jesus speaks into it.

Ask God to remind you of Scriptures about himself, for promises that he has in mind for you and/or images and teachings of Jesus – stories that show you how he lived and related to others. Reflect on how they envision, inspire, guide or reassure you in your current season of life. How might God be revealing his will for the future? Pray these things through with an open heart.

Dwell with God's Word through Habakkuk through the rest of your day.

366

DAY 4

'Write down the revelation and make it plain on tablets so that a herald may run with it.' Habakkuk 2:2

I can hear an inspiring or challenging preach on Sunday and have forgotten most of it by Monday. Life is busy. Distractions distract. So, I've learned to take notes as I listen. Sometimes, my scribbles end up in recycling. But so often, the nuggets God wants me to chew on are recorded for ongoing prayer and response.

Habakkuk was told to *write down the revelation* and *make it plain*. Writing out a prophetic message signifies its importance. God knows how quickly our memories fade, or how feelings can override fact; how despondency, for example, can obscure the truth that God is with us and for us.

Habakkuk's written revelation also ensured it could be read and reread in future. He was to write it down clearly (legibly and without rambling) so it was easy to read and understand. And it was inscribed on wooden tablets covered with wax for durability. The message needed to endure and not fade from the forefront of their minds as months turned into years.

Whatever God has revealed to you, or reveals in future, write – it – down. If it touches on more than one area of life (work, family, lifestyle, etc.), rewrite the points on different pages. Keep the revelation in a place where you can refer to it easily. And do so – often. Memories fade, but not the things we write down.

Dwell with God's Word through Habakkuk through the rest of your day.

DAY 5

'Write down the revelation and make it plain on tablets so that a
herald may run with it.' Habakkuk 2:2

The interpretation of the latter part of this verse is uncertain. It could mean that
passers-by should be able to read the revelation quickly and without difficulty
in the hurry and haste of the day and, in turn, convey it to others. It could
also speak of an individual whose role it was to spread the message through the
land. But one thing is for certain, the easily readable message was one of hope,
intended to energise and inspire a response.

Having written down the revelation, we're to live it out. It inspires us to examine
and realign our lives as needed; to recalibrate our values, goals and priorities ac-
cordingly. Without responding to God's revelation, we're likely to drift through
life without purpose, or to stray from the path of God's blessing, for the word is
the same as that used in Proverbs 29:18: 'Where there is no revelation, people
cast off restraint; but blessed is the one who heeds wisdom's instruction.' We
stumble, fall, and even abandon God's ways, when we forget or ignore God's
revealed way of life in his Word and in Christ.

'Father, where have I yet to yield to your revealed nature and will? Forgive me,
for [name it].' Continue to pray as you feel led in committing to God's revelation, encouraged and inspired for his promised blessing as you do.

Dwell with God's Word through Habakkuk through the rest of your day.

368

DAY 6

'Write down the revelation and make it plain on tablets so that a herald may run with it.' Habakkuk 2:2

God's ultimate revelation is for life restored in his presence in the new heaven and earth.[7] That's the destination of God's story of which we are now a part. Our lives are no longer of this world – we're already living out our eternal life in Christ.[8] This is what we *lean into*; his love, grace, provision, guidance, anointing and so much more. It's our life in Christ we *live out of*, living the rest of our days on earth reflecting his ways. It's God's eternal kingdom that we *live for*; it's our source of true life now and forever, inspiring us to discard whatever holds us back from his purpose.

Therefore:

> Do not store up for yourselves treasures on earth, where moths and vermin destroy, and where thieves break in and steal. But store up for yourselves treasures in heaven . . .

> *Matt. 6:19–20a*

If you feel envious or inadequate when you compare your earthly treasure and success with others, be honest with God about it. Ask him to fill you with the glorious revelation of the perfect life you're living *for* in the imperfect life of this world. Your most valuable treasure is knowing God, yielding to his life and trusting for the eternal effect it may have on others. Talk with God about all these things, with faith and thanksgiving.

Dwell with God's Word through Habakkuk through the rest of your day.

DAY 7

'Write down the revelation and make it plain on tablets so that a herald may run with it.' Habakkuk 2:2

God raised Jesus from the dead. That's what undergirds the validity of the life we live in Christ, now and forever.[9]

> Therefore . . . let us throw off everything that hinders and the sin that so easily entangles. And let us run with perseverance the race marked out for us . . .
>
> *Heb. 12:1*

Reflect on God's revelation to you this week. What might you need to 'throw off' that is holding you back from living an abundant life in Christ? Talk with God about how you intend to follow through, and ask for his help as needed.

If you've yet to discern God's revelation, you may like to repeat the reflective exercise and prompts from Day 2 and 3, and/or prayerfully immerse yourself in one or more scenes of how Jesus lived and related to others; see the endnotes for suggestions.[10] How is God envisioning, inspiring, guiding, energising or reassuring you for your current season? Talk to him about it now.

Let's pray: Thank you, Lord, for already giving me your revealed will in your Word and for showing me through Jesus how to live it out; Jesus, my ultimate vision for life. Please continue to help me discern what is pertinent to my life today and show me where I still have scope to yield to your ways. Thank you for your peace and reassurance.

Dwell with God's Word through Habakkuk through the rest of your day.

AFTERWORD

My heart for writing *Dwell* is that you won't stop here. We've dwelt with fifty-two verses or short passages of Scripture, but there are thousands more. If you continue to make your home in God's Word, you will delight in how he continues to nurture his home in you, and transform you increasingly into your Father's likeness, revealed in Jesus. What a precious gift God's Word is. What a privilege to own a copy of it, to hold it in our hands and saturate our souls with its living truth.

As I leave you to continue your life's journey, may our God of wisdom and understanding meet with you through his Word and open the eyes of your heart to see, know and be transformed by his love and truth within it. And so, 'I pray that out of his glorious riches he may strengthen you with power through his Spirit in your inner being, so that Christ may dwell in your hearts through faith' (Eph. 3:16–17a).

ACKNOWLEDGEMENTS

No book is written in isolation. I feel part of an invaluable family who've prayed, supported and journeyed with me through the first ideas to placing this book in your hands. Thank you to *everyone* who has taken an interest and encouraged me along the way . . . there are too many of you to name here.

I must, however, thank my husband, Neil, to whom this book is dedicated. I could never have written it without your loving and practical support, your wise insights – and your wonderful library of commentaries! You are ever-patient when I'm in book mode, you ensure I come up for breath, and are a daily inspiration through your own response to God's Word.

My deep gratitude, also, to my inner prayer circle: Ali, Amy and Julie. Empowered by God as intercessors, these humble women give of their time and endure in prayer for others. Thank you for faithfully upholding me in prayer. And an additional thank you to Amy, who helped tweak my initial book proposal with her gifted eye and long years of experience. You will find more details of one of her wonderful books in the Bibliography: *7 Ways to Pray: Time-tested Practices for Encountering God* (Amy Boucher Pye).

Special, heartfelt thanks to 'The 3G's' – to my outer prayer circle: Anne, Gene and Marian, for praying for the writing of *Dwell*, long before I even knew, and for your longstanding, loving support. An additional thank you to Anne, too, whose prophetic word given while praying for the book, encouraged me (and brought tears of relief) on a bitterly painful day.

I am also beyond words grateful for some very dear friends, who walked and talked with me, listened to and counselled me, during a difficult chapter of life while I was writing *Dwell*. Thank you for your care, wisdom and understanding.

And of course, immense thanks to Donna and Rachael at Authentic; for your passion for the idea and saying *yes* to publishing *Dwell*. For your inspired modifications to some of my original proposals. For your patience, compassion and understanding when I asked to delay the deadline. To Claire and Sheila, for your highly skilled editing that polished the manuscript to a shine, and to the creative gifts of the wider Authentic team in their design, format and promotion of the final manuscript.

KEEP IN TOUCH

You can link in with Anne on her Facebook author page, on Instagram or Twitter, but if you'd like to connect with her personally you can sign up to receive her regular 'Word for the Month' email for further inspiration on how to engage with God's Word. The sign up link can be found on her website www.anneletissier.com and her social media bios.

INDEX OF WEEKLY SCRIPTURES

BIBLIOGRAPHY

Allcock, Linda. *Deeper Still: Finding Clear Minds and Full Hearts Through Biblical Meditation* (Surrey: The Good Book Company, 2020), Kindle Edition.

Anderson, Clive. *Opening Up 2 Peter, Opening Up Commentary* (Leominster: Day One Publications, 2007).

Barclay, William. *The Daily Study Bible, The Gospel of Matthew, Volume 2* (Edinburgh: The Saint Andrew Press, 1975).

Barclay, William. *The Daily Study Bible: The Gospel of Luke* (Edinburgh: The Saint Andrew Press, 1975).

Barclay, William. *The Daily Study Bible: The Gospel of John, Volume 1 Chapters 1–7* (Edinburgh: The Saint Andrew Press, 1975).

Barker, Kenneth L. ed., commentary in *The Compact NIV Study Bible*. As. eds. Donald W. Burdick, John H. Stek, Walter W. Wessel, Ronald Youngblood (London: Hodder & Stoughton, 1987).

Blythe, Teresa. *Praying with Scripture.* https://www.patheos.com/resources/additional-resources/2000/01/praying-with-scripture-06172009 (accessed 3 May 2023).

Boucher Pye, Amy. *7 Ways to Pray: Time-tested Practices for Encountering God* (London: SPCK Form, 2021).

Brother Andrew. *One Week Walking With Your Persecuted Brothers and Sisters* (Oxon: Open Doors Booklet, 2013).

Brother Lawrence. *The Practice of the Presence of God* (London: Hodder & Stoughton, 1981).

Centering Prayer, *About Lectio Divina.* http://www.centeringprayer.com/lectio_divina.html (accessed 8 May 2023).

Comer, John Mark. *The Ruthless Elimination of Hurry* (London: Hodder & Stoughton Ltd., 2019), Kindle Edition.

Cordeiro, Wayne. *The Divine Mentor: Growing Your Faith as You Sit at the Feet of the Savior* (Grand Rapids, MI: Bethany House Publishers, 2007).

Eaton, M.A. *Tyndale Old Testament Commentaries, Ecclesiastes* (Leicester: IVP, 1983).

France, R.T. *Tyndale New Testament Commentaries, Matthew* (Leicester: IVP, 1985).

Green, Michael. *Tyndale New Testament Commentaries, 2 Peter and Jude* (Leicester: IVP, 1987).

Greig, Pete. *How to Pray: A Simple Guide for Normal People* (London: Hodder & Stoughton Ltd., 2019).

Hudson, Trevor. *Seeking God: Finding Another Kind of Life with St. Ignatius and Dallas Willard* (Colorado Springs, CO: NavPress, 2022), Advanced Reader Copy.

Ignatian Spirituality, *How Can I Pray?* https://www.ignatianspirituality.com/ignatian-prayer/the-examen/how-can-i-pray/ (accessed 4 May 2023).

Kendall, R.T. *The Sensitivity of the Spirit* (London: Hodder & Stoughton Ltd., 2000).

Kidner, Derek. *Tyndale Old Testament Commentaries, Psalms 1–72* (Leicester: IVP, 1973).

Kidner, Derek. *Tyndale Old Testament Commentaries, Psalms 73–150* (Leicester: IVP, 1975).

Leonhardt, Douglas J. *Praying with Scripture.* https://www.ignatianspirituality.com/ignatian-prayer/the-what-how-why-of-prayer/praying-with-scripture/ (accessed 21 February 2023).

Le Tissier, Anne. *Restoring the Balance* (Surrey: CWR/Waverley Abbey, 2019).

Le Tissier, Anne. *The Mirror That Speaks Back* (Abingdon: The Bible Reading Fellowship, 2018).

Martin, Ralph P. *Tyndale New Testament Commentaries, Philippians* (Leicester: IVP, 1959).

Misseo Dei: Falcon, *How to Pray a Prayer of Lament.* https://missiodeifalcon.org/how-to-pray-a-prayer-of-lament/ (accessed 6 May 2023).

Moo, Douglas J. *Tyndale New Testament Commentaries, James* (Leicester: IVP, 1985).

Morris, Leon. *Tyndale New Testament Commentaries, 1 and 2 Thessalonians* (Leicester: IVP, 1984).

Motyer, Alec. *Tyndale Old Testament Commentaries, Isaiah* (Leicester: IVP, 1999).

Ortberg, John. *The Me I Want to Be* (Grand Rapids, MI: Zondervan, 2010).

Spangler, Ann., and Lois Tverberg. *Sitting at the Feet of Rabbi Jesus: How the Jewishness of Jesus Can Transform your Faith* (Grand Rapids, MI: Zondervan, 2009, 2018), Kindle Edition.

Tasker, R.V.G. *Tyndale New Testament Commentaries, John* (Leicester: IVP, 1960).

The Northumbrian Community Trust. *Celtic Daily Prayer, Book One: The Journey Begins* (London: William Collins, an imprint of HarperCollins Publishers © 2000, 2005, 2015).

Warren, Rick. *The Purpose Driven Life* (Grand Rapids, MI: Zondervan, 2002).

Wiersbe, Warren W. *The Bible Exposition Commentary, Volume 1* (Wheaton, IL: Victor Books, 1996).

Wilkerson, David. *Hallowed Be Thy Names: The Revelation of God Through His Names* (Buckingham: Rickfords Hill Publishing Ltd, 2012).

Williams, Rowan. *God With Us: The Meaning of the Cross and Resurrection – Then and Now* (London: SPCK, 2017).

Xavier University's Center for Mission and Identity. *The Examen: A Daily Prayer.* https://www.xavier.edu/jesuitresource/jesuit-a-z/terms-e/daily-examen (accessed 4 May 2023).

Zschech, Darlene. *You Are Great.* https://www.newreleasetoday.com/article.php?article_id=2216 (accessed 14 March 2023).

NOTES

Introduction
[1] I completed my DTS with *YWAM* in New Zealand, at the Pahi base in North Island.
[2] Colossians 3:16.

Week 1
[1] To read the context of this week's verse, see Gen. 19:1–29.
[2] Eccl. 3:4.
[3] Phil. 4:11–13.
[4] A gratitude journal is used to name three, five, ten or more things you can be grateful for, each day. It keeps your focus on the present goodness of God with you to protect you from feeling discontent over things you no longer have.
[5] Exod. 1:1 – 2:4.
[6] By letting go of her baby, God placed him in a place where he'd learn to be one of Israel's greatest leaders, who would bring his people out of Egyptian slavery.

Week 2
[1] To read the context of this week's verse, see Matt. 6:5–15.
[2] Jas 1:5–7.
[3] Exod. 16:1–20.
[4] Matt. 6:25–34.
[5] Ps. 66:18.
[6] Matt. 18:35; Mark 11:25.
[7] Ann Spangler and Lois Tverberg, *Sitting at the Feet of Rabbi Jesus: How the Jewishness of Jesus Can Transform your Faith* (Grand Rapids, MI: Zondervan, 2009, 2018), Kindle Edition p. 91.
[8] Jas 1:13.
[9] R.T. France, *Tyndale New Testament Commentaries, Matthew* (Leicester: IVP, 1985), p.136–137.

Week 3
[1] Matt. 6:25–33.
[2] To read the context of this week's verse, see Ps. 20:1–9.
[3] Ps. 31:15–24.
[4] 1 Sam. 17.
[5] Matt. 28:20; Heb. 13:5.
[6] 2 Cor. 5:7.
[7] Ps. 20:1–5.

Week 4

[1] Thanks to Dave Charlton, who kindly gave his permission to share this story which he related while hosting a church service one Sunday.

[2] To read the context of this week's verse, see Luke 18:9–14.

[3] The tense of 'beat' in Luke 18:13 indicates that it's a continuous action.

[4] 1 John 1:9.

[5] Prayer based on Ps. 23:3.

Week 5

[1] To read the context of this week's verse, see Mark 4:35–41.

[2] God's promise of peace: John 14:27; 20:19,21.

[3] God's promise to provide, for example Matt. 6:25–34.

[4] God's promise when you feel overwhelmed, for example Matt. 11:28–30.

[5] God's promised presence, for example see Matt. 28:20.

Week 6

[1] To read the context of this week's verse, see Ps. 19:1–14.

[2] Lectio Divina is an ancient practice of prayerfully reading Scripture not for study and knowledge, but to open ourselves to what God wants to say to us and in turn, pray and respond.

[3] Mark 7:14–23.

[4] Matt. 12:34–35.

[5] Douglas J. Moo, *Tyndale New Testament Commentaries, James* (Leicester: IVP, 1985), p. 129.

[6] Prov. 27:2.

Week 7

[1] Prayer based on 1 John 3:1.

[2] John 13:34–35; 1 John 3:16; 4:7.

[3] Protecting someone's reputation assumes no one is at risk of physical harm or mental abuse, where love must first protect the vulnerable.

Week 8

[1] 2 Cor. 3:18; Heb. 1:3; 12:10.

[2] Heb. 2:11.

[3] Phil. 1:6; 2:12.

[4] 2 Cor. 7:1; Eph. 1:4–6.

[5] Examples of songs to help us worship God's holiness:

'When I Look Into Your Holiness', https://www.youtube.com/watch?v=o2ab-1Pixcg or 'Holy, Holy, Holy! Lord God Almighty', https://www.youtube.com/watch?v=JwuDSw-9cUQ (both accessed 18 April 2023).

[6] Lev. 20:7–8.

[7] John 15:1–14; Rom. 8:13; 1 Cor. 3:1; Gal. 5:16,25; 1 John 3:24.

[8] For an excellent and inspiring explanation of the difference between doves and pigeons and how that relates to our living with the anointing of the Holy Spirit, I highly recommend a book by R.T. Kendall, *The Sensitivity of the Spirit*. See Bibliography for details.

[9] Acts 5:1–11 relates one of Scripture's examples where the nature of God's Holy Spirit isn't respected.

Week 9

[1] For example, if you need work, God promises to provide your daily needs as you invest your life in his righteous presence and purposes (Matt. 6:25–33). If you're reeling from rejection, God hasn't stopped loving and caring for you; his presence is with you every moment of your day and your purposes are still his to help you fulfil (1 Pet. 5:7; Heb. 13:5b–6; Ps. 31:15; Jer. 29:11).

[2] Pss 27:13–14; 130:5.

[3] Luke 5:16. Mark 1:21 is also an example of Jesus attending synagogue worship on the Sabbath, which of course involved praying with others.

[4] Eph. 6:18.

[5] Matt. 6:5–13.

[6] To read the context of this verse, see Rom. 11:33 – 12:13.

Week 10

[1] This personal story first appeared in my book *The Mirror That Speaks Back* (Abingdon: The Bible Reading Fellowship, 2018), pp. 100–101.

[2] Commentary to Deuteronomy 30:20 in *The Compact NIV Study Bible* (London: Hodder & Stoughton, 1987), p. 277.

[3] Josh. 24:12–13; Eph. 2:8–10.

[4] To read the context of our verse, see Deut. 30:11–20.

[5] For example, Gideons International: https://gideonsinternational.org.uk/, the Bible Society: https://www.Biblesociety.org.uk/ or Wycliffe Bible Translators: https://wycliffe.org.uk/ (all accessed 22 September 2023).

[6] Ps. 16:2.

[7] Deut. 30:1–10.

Week 11

[1] To read the context of this week's verse, see Ps. 27:1–14.

[2] Ps. 23:1.

[3] Ps. 16:2.

[4] Ps. 36:8–9.

[5] Pss 27:5; 62:8.

[6] Ps. 16:11.

[7] 1 Sam. 16:13.

[8] Eph. 1:13–14.

[9] See for example, Rom. 12:1–2.

Week 12

[1] John 20:14–15.

[2] Luke 24:13–35.

[3] John 21:4.

[4] Noel Richards, 'To Be in Your Presence', https://www.youtube.com/watch?v=typ7cueKdT4 (accessed 22 September 2023).

Week 13

[1] Matt. 22:15–22.

[2] Pss. 7:8; 25:21; 41:12.

[3] Dan. 1:1–7.

[4] https://totallyhistory.com/daniel-timeline/ and https://Biblehub.com/timeline/daniel/1.htm (both accessed 19 December 2022).

[5] Babylonians enjoyed eating pig and horse which Mosaic Law prohibited.

[6] Dan. 6:10.

[7] Ezra 3:1–4:24; https://Biblehub.com/timeline/ezra/1.htm (accessed 19th December 2022); https://scholar.valpo.edu/cgi/viewcontent.cgi?article=1271&context=jvbl and https://www.theology ofwork.org/old-testament/ezra-nehemiah-esther/ezra/restoration-of-the-temple-ezra-11-622/ (accessed 26 September 2023).

[8] Hag. 1:1–11

[9] Wayne Cordeiro, *The Divine Mentor: Growing Your Faith as You Sit at the Feet of the Savior* (Grand Rapids, MI: Bethany House Publishers, 2007), p. 129.

[10] First part of prayer adapted from 2 Pet. 1:3–4.

Week 14

[1] To read the context of this week's verse, see 1 John 3:11–18.

[2] Name has been changed.

[3] Matt. 22:37–40.

[4] For more information about becoming a prison pen pal and other ways to support prisoners, visit https://prisonfellowship.org.uk/ (accessed 22 September 2023).

[5] Luke 10:25–37.

[6] Phil. 2:3–4.

[7] Exod. 23:11; Lev. 19:10; Isa. 58:7; Luke 3:11; Acts 2:45; 4:32.

[8] 2 Cor. 8:1–3.

Week 15

[1] 'Saint Ignatius Loyola invited a person when an individual made a retreat in the pattern of his Spiritual Exercises to pray to come to know Christ so that one may love him in a more real way and following from this knowledge and love become a more faithful disciple.

'In order to grow in this faith knowledge, Ignatius invited the retreatant to engage in a prayer method called contemplation. This is not some kind of mystical prayer but a prayer form in which one uses his or her senses in an imaginative way to reflect on a Gospel passage. One uses the senses, seeing, hearing, tasting, touching, and smelling to make the Gospel scene real and alive.' 'Praying with Scripture' by Douglas J. Leonhardt, S.J., from *Finding God in All Things*. A Marquette Prayer Book. Marquette University, Milwaukee, WI. ©2009. Used by permission.

Week 16

[1] To read the context of this week's verse, see Ps. 27:1–14.

[2] Ps. 23:6.

[3] Luke 18:1–8.

[4] Heb. 13:5.

[5] Pss 16:2; 73:25.

[6] Ps. 5:3.

[7] Ps. 38:15.

[8] Ps. 40:1.

[9] Isa. 40:29–31.

Week 17

[1] To read the context of this week's verse, see 1 Cor. 6:12–20.

[2] Exod. 15:13–17.

[3] Exod. 30:34–36.

[4] 2 Cor. 2:14–16.

[5] Heb. 7:27.

[6] Gen. 22:1–19.

[7] Exod. 28:40.

[8] 2 Chr. 23:19.

[9] 1 Tim. 4:2.

[10] John 14:23.

[11] 2 Cor. 3:18.

Week 18

[1] To read the context of this week's verse, see Neh. 7:73 – 8:12.

[2] A 'Daniel Fast' includes omitting meat, dairy, wheat, yeast and sugar from the diet . . . and anything but water to drink. For example, see https://ultimatedanielfast.com/ (accessed 9 October 2023).

[3] I appreciate how difficult, if not impossible, it is for some readers to take time out to be with God (for example, if you care for young children). So if that's you, ask God to prompt you with unexpected moments to pause, and know him with you; to love and worship, and receive whatever he has for you. But if that's not you, how can you choose to make regular time each day or week to nurture your joy in your relationship with God?

[4] Rom. 8:25–27.

[5] Isa. 41:10; Rom. 8:31.

[6] Derek Kidner, *Tyndale Old Testament Commentaries, Psalms 73–150* (Leicester: IVP, 1975), p. 305. Commentary on Ps. 84:6.

[7] Based on Ps. 84:6.

[8] Jas 1:4.

[9] Ps. 94:19.

[10] See an example of this in Ps. 107.

[11] Ps. 100:4; Phil. 4:6.

[12] Matt. 7:18–21.

[13] Matt. 13:44.

[14] Adapted from Rom. 15:13.

Week 19

[1] See other promises pertaining to coming close to God and remaining there; Jas 4:8; John 15:1–5.

[2] Matt. 23:4; Luke 11:46.

[3] Here's an example of how we can overcomplicate something God's asked us to do which ends up feeling more burdensome than it ought: God's Word calls us to provide hospitality (see 1 Pet. 4:9); but if we feel we need to first clean the house or offer more than a simple meal, it can feel onerous. Consequently, we may resent the time and effort needed to do it. We might get so focused on the

meal that we barely connect with our guests. Or else, we decide we haven't the time or money. But none of these scenarios reflect what Jesus has called us to be and do.

[4] Warren W. Wiersbe, *The Bible Exposition Commentary, Volume 1* (Wheaton, IL: Victor Books, 1996), p. 41.

[5] Commentary in *The Compact NIV Study Bible*, p. 1467.

[6] France, *Tyndale New Testament Commentaries, Matthew*, p. 201.

[7] William Barclay, *The Daily Study Bible, The Gospel of Matthew, Volume 2* (Edinburgh: The Saint Andrew Press, 1975), p. 17, and Wiersbe, *The Bible Exposition Commentary, Volume 1*, p. 41.

[8] John Mark Comer explains the helpful understanding of disciples as 'apprentices' in his book, *The Ruthless Elimination of Hurry* (London: Hodder & Stoughton, 2019) Kindle Edition, p. 77–78.

Week 20

[1] I am aware that many of us will be taken in an instant or else in great pain, and will be unable to think or do anything about the themes discussed, in the way that I've oversimplified matters this week. But I'm using this phrase to shift our attention away from the here and now. It reminds us that we *will* have a last day, encouraging us to live well, with and for God, as we approach it, and with the perspective of eternal life with him thereafter. Dwelling on the prospect of living with God in heaven will shape our priorities today.

[2] To read the context of this week's verse, see Ps. 103:1–22.

[3] Forgiving others is essential to enjoy close relationship with God: Matt. 6:12; 18:35; Mark 11:25.

[4] 2 Tim. 1:6.

[5] Phil. 2:13.

[6] Eph. 2:10.

[7] H.F. Lyte (1793–1847), 'Praise, My Soul, the King of Heaven', https://www.youtube.com/watch?v=BAn66HtnuCw (accessed 22 September 2023).

[8] Housefires, 'Build My Life', https://www.youtube.com/watch?v=xLSDBG1OcGE (accessed 22 September 2023).

[9] Oct. 28, 1984: 'A man who is not courageous enough to take risks will never accomplish anything in life,' Muhammad Ali said at a news conference on Oct. 28, 1984 in Houston. 'Don't count the days. Make the days count,' he said, according to ESPN. https://time.com/4357493/muhammad-ali-dead-best-quotes/ (accessed 22 September 2023). See also https://www.goodreads.com/quotes/200873-don-t-count-the-days-make-the-days-count (accessed 9 October 2023).

[10] Pss 31:15; 139:16.

Week 21

[1] Eph. 2:2; 6:12; Col. 1:13; 1 John 5:19.

[2] 2 Cor. 5:20.

[3] See also John 15:19.

[4] 2 Cor. 3:3.

[5] Based on Eph. 1:12,14.

Week 22

[1] To read the context of this week's verse, see 1 Sam. 23:1–18.

[2] Matt. 6:25–33.

[3] Heb. 10:19–25.

[4] 1 Sam. 23:19–24.

[5] Ps. 119:105.

[6] Ps. 32:8–10; Prov. 3:5–6.

[7] Jas 1:5–8.

Week 23

[1] I've heard this expressed in a number of ways over the years, one quote being attributed to F.F. Bosworth, 'Believe your beliefs and doubt your doubts', https://quotefancy.com/quote/1595039/F-F-Bosworth-Believe-your-beliefs-and-doubt-your-doubts (accessed 13 May 2023).

[2] For the context of this week's verse, see Luke 1:26–45.

[3] The news was a blessing, to be so highly favoured by God to give birth to his Son. But it was also a potential burden; as an unmarried but engaged virgin, Mary would expect to be ostracised from her community, rejected by her fiancé, and potentially condemned by Mosaic Law to death by stoning for perceived infidelity.

[4] God promises that his word will be fulfilled – for example, see Isa. 55:11; Jer. 1:12.

[5] Jer. 31:3; Lam. 3:22–23.

[6] Heb. 13:5.

[7] 1 John 1:9.

[8] Jas 1:5.

[9] John 14:27.

[10] 1 Cor. 12:11.

[11] Youth With a Mission (Pahi, New Zealand, 1992).

[12] Name has been changed.

[13] For example, Pss 27:14; 38:15.

[14] Josh. 1:7–9.

Week 24

[1] To read the context of this week's verse, see Isa. 41:8–14.

[2] There are promises that are pertinent to us all (for example, Matt. 28:20; Heb. 13:5–6). There are promises that have a context (as in v. 33 of Matt. 6:25–33). And there are promises for specific situations (for example, Luke 12:11–12) or received prophetically through words inspired by God's Holy Spirit.

[3] See Matt. 6:19–21; Col. 3:1–3.

[4] Taken from *The Me I Want to Be: Becoming God's Best Version of You* by John Ortberg Copyright © 2010 (Grand Rapids, MI, USA: Zondervan) p. 116. Used by permission of HarperCollins Christian Publishing. www.harpercollinschristian.com.

[5] Taken from *The Me I Want to Be: Becoming God's Best Version of You* by John Ortberg Copyright © 2010 (Grand Rapids, MI, USA: Zondervan) p. 115. Used by permission of HarperCollins Christian Publishing. www.harpercollinschristian.com.

Week 25

[1] Inspired by the Spanish priest, Ignatius of Loyola (1491–1556).

[2] To read the context of this week's verse, see Ps. 139:1–24.

[3] Ideas inspired from https://www.ignatianspirituality.com/ignatian-prayer/the-examen/how-can-i-pray/ (accessed 4 May 2023).

[4] With thanks for the helpful teaching and inspiration from https://www.ignatianspirituality.com/ignatian-prayer/the-examen/how-can-i-pray/ (accessed 4 May 2023) and Amy Boucher Pye, *7 Ways to Pray: Time-tested practices for encountering God* (London: SPCK Form, 2021), pp. 142–144.

[5] Ideas inspired and adapted from https://www.ignatianspirituality.com/ignatian-prayer/the-examen/how-can-i-pray/ (accessed 4 May 2023).

[6] We must first forgive that we may know God's forgiveness: Matt. 5:23–24; 6:12.

[7] https://www.ignatianspirituality.com/ignatian-prayer/the-examen/how-can-i-pray/ (accessed 4 May 2023).

[8] John 15:15.

Week 26

[1] John 10:10.

[2] To read the context of this week's verse, see Phil. 4:4–9.

[3] Ralph P. Martin, *Tyndale New Testament Commentaries, Philippians* (Leicester: IVP, 1959), p. 171.

[4] Col. 3:2.

[5] We should uphold a holy silence rather than criticise and malign, but I appreciate there's a place when we have to speak out if someone's behaviour is putting another person's life at risk or falsely undermining someone else's good reputation.

Week 27

[1] This week we are using the practice of 'Ignatian contemplation' to help us immerse ourselves in the story. For explanations of this practice see, for example, Week 15.

[2] Rowan Williams, *God With Us: The Meaning of the Cross and Resurrection – Then and Now* (London: SPCK, 2017), p. 87. Reproduced with permission of the Licensor through PLSclear.

[3] Matt. 28:7; Mark 14:28.

Week 28

[1] Conflicts over nuclear programmes https://conflicts2022.crisisgroup.org/ (accessed 7 March 2023).

[2] Statistics on Global Warming from https://www.lshtm.ac.uk/newsevents/news/2022/expert-comment-over-40-worlds-population-are-highly-vulnerable-climate (accessed 7 March 2023).

[3] Rev. 21:1–4.

[4] See also Isa. 2:4.

[5] Commentary on Ps. 46:4 in *The Compact NIV Study Bible*, p. 815.

[6] https://bpc.org/shorter-catechism (accessed 27 September 2023).

Week 29

[1] Aidan was an Irish monk who'd been living in a monastery on the western island of Iona, but when his heart was warmed to the so-called 'hard-hearted' Northumbrians, he travelled east to share the good news of Jesus among them.

[2] For sources on Aidan's life and ministry, see The Northumbrian Community Trust, *Celtic Daily Prayer, Book One: The Journey Begins* (London: William Collins, an imprint of HarperCollins Publishers, © 2000, 2005, 2015), pp. 57, 282; https://www.lindisfarne.org.uk/general/aidan.htm (accessed 22 September 2023); https://www.britannica.com/biography/Saint-Aidan (accessed 9 October 2023).

[3] To read the context of this week's verse, see Ezra 7:1–10.

[4] For examples of Ezra's effective ministry, see Neh. 8 – 10.

[5] God loves you. Meditate on his love to inspire your response: For example, Ps. 63:3; 86:15; Isa. 54:10; Zeph. 3:17; John 15:9; Rom. 5:8; 8:37–39; Eph. 2:4–5; 3:17–19; 1 John 3:1; 4:16.

[6] Luke 24:45; John 14:16,26; 2 Tim. 2:7.

[7] Anne Le Tissier, *Restoring the Balance* (Surrey: CWR/Waverley Abbey, 2019), p. 40.

[8] Brother Andrew, *One Week Walking With Your Persecuted Brothers and Sisters* (Oxon: Open Doors Booklet, 2013), Day 7. Used with permission of Open Doors UK&I.

[9] Jesus concluded his teaching on how to live his life by telling his listeners to put into practice what they'd learned: Matt. 7:24.

[10] Luke 6:46.

[11] Jas 2:14–24.

[12] Luke 6:47–49.

[13] Phil. 4:8–9; Jas 1:22–25.

[14] For example, Mal. 3:10; Heb. 11:7–12.

[15] The Levites helped Ezra with this role, see Neh. 8:7–8.

[16] Matt. 28:19–20.

Week 30

[1] To read the context of this week's verse, see 1 Cor. 15:50–58.

[2] With thanks to William Barclay for helping me unpack this paragraph from his commentary on John: *The Daily Study Bible, The Gospel of John, Volume 1 Chapters 1–7* (The Saint Andrew Press: Edinburgh, 1975), p. 214.

[3] John 10:10; 17:6; 1 John 5:11–12.

[4] Jonah 1 – 3.

[5] See footnote to NIV 2011 UK version which notes this alternative translation: 'With your help I can advance against a troop'.

[6] https://www.brainyquote.com/quotes/saint_augustine_165165 (accessed 19 October 2023).

Week 31

[1] To read the context of this week's verse, see Isa. 9:1–7.

[2] 'You Are Great', https://www.youtube.com/watch?v=dY8jyVtOi_M.

[3] https://www.newreleasetoday.com/article.php?article_id=2216 (accessed 14 March 2023).

[4] David Wilkerson, *Hallowed Be Thy Names: The Revelation of God Through His Names* (Buckingham: Rickfords Hill Publishing Ltd, 2012), p. v.

[5] Isa. 8:12–14,17; 9:1–5.

[6] Eph. 6:17–18.

[7] John 10:30; 14:9.

[8] Heb. 12:10–11.

[9] Matt. 6:8.

[10] Wilkerson, *Hallowed Be Thy Names*, p. 87.

[11] Isa. 48:18.

[12] George Frideric Handel (1685–1759). To worship Jesus using Handel's *Messiah*, Number 12, 'For Unto Us a Child Is Born', you could prayerfully listen to or sing along to one of the following: https://www.youtube.com/watch?v=MS3vpAWW2Zc. Or https://www.youtube.com/

watch?v=FJ9wS2J0GOs (both accessed 22 September 2023). Or else use a modern version – there's plenty to choose from!

Week 32

[1] To read the context of this week's verse, see Luke 11:1–8.

[2] Leeland, 'Way Maker', https://www.youtube.com/watch?v=29IxnsqOkmQ (accessed 22 September 2023).

[3] The verse was Isa. 40:11.

[4] Jas 4:8.

[5] The name has been changed.

Week 33

[1] Matt. 14:13–21.

[2] Rom. 8:28.

[3] Praying Matt. 6:25–33 may also prompt you to consider what 'seeking' his kingdom and righteousness might look like in your life.

[4] Jesus reminds us that God already knows what we need when we pray in Matt. 6:7–8.

[5] Jas 1:5 teaches: 'If any of you lacks wisdom, you should ask God, who gives generously to all without finding fault, and it will be given to you.'

[6] 1 Thess. 5:18.

Week 34

[1] Matt. 22:36–38. To read the context of this week's verse, see Deut. 6:1–9.

[2] Matt. 6:24.

[3] Rev. 3:16.

[4] Rom. 8:31.

[5] Heb. 13:5.

[6] Acts 13:22.

[7] Matt. 6:6–7.

[8] Luke 10:38–42.

[9] Matt. 22:36–40.

[10] 1 John 4:12.

Week 35

[1] To read the context of this week's verse, see Luke 2:41–52.

[2] 'Though the Eternal Word united with a human soul from his conception, yet the divinity that dwelt in him manifested itself to his humanity by degrees *ad modum recipientis—in proportion to*

his capacity; as the faculties of his human soul grew more and more capable, the gifts it received from the divine nature were more and more communicated', Matthew Henry, *Matthew Henry's Commentary on the Whole Bible: Complete and Unabridged in One Volume* (Peabody, MA: Hendrickson, 1994), p. 1832.

[3] This quote is attributed to British journalist Miles Kington, https://www.independent .co.uk/news/uk/this-britain/fond-farewell-to-the-genius-of-miles-kington-781024.html (accessed 11 August 2023).

[4] Inspired by Prov. 9:10 which teaches that wisdom is birthed from our fear of the Lord.

[5] Prov. 3:3–4.

[6] 'The verb "grow" is a present imperative, which could be rendered, "be continually growing."' Clive Anderson, *Opening Up 2 Peter, Opening Up Commentary* (Leominster: Day One Publications, 2007), p. 114.

[7] Michael Green, *Tyndale New Testament Commentaries, 2 Peter and Jude* (Leicester: IVP, 1987), p. 163.

[8] 2 Pet. 1:5–8.

[9] https://quotepark.com/quotes/1008976-john-newton-i-am-not-what-i-ought-to-be-ah-how-imperfect-an/ (accessed 22 September 2023). As quoted in *The Christian Pioneer* (1856) edited by Joseph Foulkes Winks, p. 84. Also in *The Christian Spectator*, Volume 3 (1821), p. 186, https:// books.google.co.uk/books?id=mv4oAAAAYAAJ&pg=PA186#v=onepage&q&f=false. Often paraphrased as, 'I am not the man I ought to be, I am not the man I wish to be, and I am not the man I hope to be, but by the grace of God, I am not the man I used to be.'

Week 36

[1] Matt. 5:21–22.

[2] To read the context of this week's verse, see Matt. 6:25–34.

[3] Matt. 6:7–8.

[4] Practising the Presence of God, a mindful awareness and response to God's constant presence, is a spiritual discipline now widely taught, but originally inspired by a book collating letters, to and from Brother Lawrence, a seventeenth-century lay brother in a Carmelite monastery, entitled *The Practice of the Presence of God* (London: Hodder & Stoughton, 1981).

[5] Taken from *The Me I Want to Be: Becoming God's Best Version of You* by John Ortberg Copyright © 2010 (Grand Rapids, MI, USA: Zondervan), p. 115. Used by permission of HarperCollins Christian Publishing. www.harpercollinschristian.com.

Week 37

[1] For the context of this passage, see Lam. 3:1–66.

[2] The song I used to express my lament on the piano after my brother died was 'Blessed Be Your Name' by Matt and Beth Redman, https://www.youtube.com/watch?v=tTpTQ4kBLxA (accessed 22 September 2023).

[3] I am grateful for a number of resources that have taught me how to lament, but I recommend the following: https://missiodeifalcon.org/how-to-pray-a-prayer-of-lament/ (accessed 22 September 2023), Chapter 5 on the prayer of lament in the book, by Boucher Pye: *7 Ways to Pray*, and Chapter 7 on 'Unanswered Prayer' in Pete Greig's book *How to Pray: A Simple Guide for Normal People* (London: Hodder & Stoughton Ltd., 2019).

[4] Rom. 8:28.

Week 38

[1] Linda Allcock, *Deeper Still: Finding Clear Minds and Full Hearts Through Biblical Meditation* (www.thegoodbook.co.uk: The Good Book Company, 2020), Kindle Edition. Loc. 438. Used with permission.

[2] Allcock, *Deeper Still*, Kindle Edition. Chapter 4, beginning at Loc. 461.

[3] Allcock, *Deeper Still*, Kindle Edition. Chapter 5, beginning at Loc. 598.

[4] Allcock, *Deeper Still*, Kindle Edition. Adapted from Loc. 621–674.

[5] Allcock, *Deeper Still*, Kindle Edition. Loc. 674.

[6] Allcock, *Deeper Still*, Kindle Edition. Chapter 6, beginning at Loc. 735.

[7] Allcock, *Deeper Still*, Kindle Edition. Loc. 814.

[8] Allcock, *Deeper Still*, Kindle Edition. Chapter 7, beginning at Loc. 917.

[9] Allcock, *Deeper Still*, Kindle Edition. Section 3, beginning at Loc. 1074.

[10] Putting God's Word into practice: Prov. 2:1; Matt. 7:24–27; Phil. 4:9; Jas 1:22.

Week 39

[1] Jer. 31:33; Ezek. 36:24–28.

[2] Jude 1:20.

[3] Mal. 2:7; Neh. 8:8.

Week 40

[1] R.V.G. Tasker, *Tyndale New Testament Commentaries, John* (Leicester: IVP, 1960), p. 45.

[2] For example, the King James version.

[3] I've listed the other 'fruit of the Spirit' here from Galatians 5:22–23, but it's a representative description of Christ's life, not an exhaustive list.

[4] For example, see Titus 1:8.

[5] Heb. 4:12.

[6] 1 Thess. 5:17.

[7] Heb. 13:15.

[8] Heb. 10:25.

[9] Heb. 13:16.

Week 41

[1] To read the context of this week's verse, see John 14:15–31.

[2] Matt. 26:36–39; Luke 22:42–44.

[3] Matt. 14:23–33; Mark 4:35–39; John 8:1–11.

[4] John 20:19.

[5] Phil. 4:7.

[6] Prov. 12:20.

[7] Eph. 2:14–18; Col. 1:20.

Week 42

[1] To read the context of this week's verse, see Hos. 10:1–15.

[2] Rom. 8:37–39.

[3] Rom. 3:23.

[4] Isa. 55:10–11.

[5] Mark 4:18–19.

[6] Gal. 6:7–8.

[7] Inspired by reading some thoughts from Dallas Willard, quoted by Trevor Hudson in *Seeking God, Finding Another Kind of Life with St. Ignatius and Dallas Willard* (Colorado Springs, CO: NavPress, 2022), p. 86. Advanced Reader Copy.

[8] John 15:1–10.

[9] See also Jas 4:8.

[10] Heb. 13:5.

Week 43

[1] To read the context of this week's verse, see Jer. 17:5–8.

[2] Isa 55:1; John 4:10–14; Rev. 21:6.

[3] Eph. 3:16.

[4] Quoted from my book, *Restoring the Balance* (Surrey: CWR/Waverley Abbey, 2019), p. 146.

Week 44

[1] http://www.centeringprayer.com/lectio_divina.html (accessed 12th April 2023).

[2] Commentary in *The Compact NIV Study Bible*, p. 1053.

[3] To read the context of this week's verse, see Isa. 40:1–31.

[4] Alec Motyer, *Tyndale Old Testament Commentaries, Isaiah* (Leicester: IVP, 1999), pp. 243, 250.

[5] https://americanornithology.org/fly-like-an-eagle/ (accessed 12 April 2023).

Week 45

[1] Mark 10:1.

[2] Matthew's Gospel records that the man was young (19:20); Luke's, that he was some kind of official or ruler (18:18).

[3] The commentary on Mark 10:17 in *The Compact NIV Study Bible*, p. 1483, explains the nature of a 'ruler' as this man is described in Luke 18:18.

[4] Rom. 8:32; Eph. 1:18–19.

[5] For example, Luke 8:2–3.

[6] Eph. 2:8.

Week 46

[1] Bombay in India has since been renamed, Mumbai.

[2] The YWAM discipleship-training course included a two-month mission to India.

[3] To read the context of this week's verse, see Ps. 16:1–11.

[4] A fuller account of this story is recorded in my book, *The Mirror that Speaks Back*, pp. 28–30.

[5] Phil. 1:21–26.

[6] Le Tissier, *The Mirror that Speaks Back*, p. 31.

[7] David refers to these other gods in Psalm 16:4.

[8] St Augustine of Hippo, *Confessions*, https://www.goodreads.com/quotes/42572-thou-hast-made-us-for-thyself-o-lord-and-our (accessed 9 October 2023).

Week 47

[1] To read the context of this week's verse, see Mark 9:14–29.

[2] 2 Pet. 3:8–9.

[3] Jesus could have discreetly healed Lazarus in his home, but many came to faith when Jesus raised him in public view from the dead; revealing God's presence and power at work in his life. John 11:1–45.

[4] Adapted from Ps. 27:14.

[5] See also 1 Tim. 2:4.

[6] Examples of God already working and responding even when we aren't aware of it: Exod. 3:7–9; Isa. 65:24; John 5:17.

[7] Dan. 10:1–14.

[8] For example: Matt. 4:1–11; 6:13; Luke 10:18–20; John 16:33; 2 Cor. 10:1–5; Eph. 6:10–18.

[9] It's quite possible Jesus said this because fasting is mentioned elsewhere in Scripture as an aid to prayer (1 Cor. 7:5). Although he condemned self-glorifying outward shows of fasting without any

inward, spiritual reality (Matt. 6:16), he did expect his disciples to adopt this spiritual self-discipline (Matt. 6:17–18).

Week 48

[1] Jer. 17:9.

[2] To read the context of this week's verse, see 1 Thess. 4:9–12. Some Thessalonians were taking undue interest in other people's business. Furthermore, as Greeks with a tendency to look down on manual labour and anticipating the imminent return of Christ, they'd become idle, consequently relying on others to support them.

[3] Mark 9:33–35.

[4] Isa. 53; Mark 10:45.

[5] John 13:1–17; Phil. 2:5–8.

[6] John 6:38; 17:4,26.

[7] Luke 1:17.

[8] Matt. 28:19–20; John 17:18; 2 Cor. 5:20.

[9] Taken from *The Purpose Driven Life* by Rick Warren Copyright © 2002 (Grand Rapids, MI, USA: Zondervan), p. 268. Used by permission of HarperCollins Christian Publishing. www.harpercollinschristian.com.

Week 49

[1] *Praying with Scripture*, Teresa Blythe, 2009. https://www.patheos.com/resources/additional-resources/2000/01/praying-with-scripture-06172009 (accessed 3 May 2023).

[2] To read the context of this week's verse, see Ps. 62:1–12.

Week 50

[1] For the context of this passage see Eccl. 11:1–6.

[2] Michael A. Eaton, *Tyndale Old Testament Commentaries, Ecclesiastes* (Leicester: IVP, 1983), p. 139.

[3] St Francis de Sales (1567–1622).

[4] Eccl. 11:1, 'Ship your grain across the sea; after many days you may receive a return.'

[5] Eccl. 11:2,6, 'But divide your investments among many places, for you do not know what risks might lie ahead … Plant your seed in the morning and keep busy all afternoon, for you don't know if profit will come from one activity or another – or maybe both' (NLT).

[6] Inspired by Eaton, *Tyndale Old Testament Commentaries, Ecclesiastes*, p. 140.

[7] Eccl. 10:10.

[8] See John 15:1–10.

[9] Acts 16:6–10.

[10] Eccl. 12:1.

Week 51

[1] Handel's 'Hallelujah Chorus' from his oratorio, *Messiah*. Handel wrote the music but the lyrics were written by Charles Jennens (1700–73).

[2] 1 John 4:8; John 3:16; John 15:9.

[3] For example, see Acts 17:28; 1 Cor. 1:5; 2 Cor. 5:21; Eph. 1:7; Col. 2:10–11.

[4] John 14:27.

[5] Luke 17:21.

[6] 2 Cor. 1:20.

[7] Rev. 21:1.

[8] Worship King Jesus in song with one of the following:

'King of Kings', Hillsong, https://www.youtube.com/watch?v=Of5IcFWiEpg

'King of Kings', Jarrod Cooper, https://www.youtube.com/watch?v=1QXgWQbFNBM

'Praise Him You Heavens', Russell Fragar, https://www.youtube.com/watch?v=zdB65diCzEM (all accessed 22 September 2023).

Week 52

[1] See Hab. 1.

[2] See Hab. 2.

[3] Jer. 17:9.

[4] Hab. 2:1.

[5] Hab. 2:3.

[6] Jas 1:5–7.

[7] Read Rev. 21.

[8] Rom. 8:17; 2 Cor. 5:17; Gal. 2:20; Eph. 3:12; Col. 1:13–14.

[9] 1 Cor. 15:17,19.

[10] Jesus' intentional response to pursue God's will despite other people's expectations (Matt. 16:23); his devotion to being with God in prayer (Mark 1:35–39); his love expressed in caring for the poor, the sick, the ostracised (there are many Gospel stories with Jesus reaching out to them, but his teaching is summed up in Matt. 25:31–45) and in forgiving the sinner (John 8:2–11), his resistance to temptation (Matt. 4:1–10), or any other story that comes to mind.

Be – Godly Wisdom to Live By

365 devotions for women

Fiona Castle and friends

Jesus gave us the greatest love of all. We are called not just to keep it to ourselves, but to overflow with that love to others. But how can we really do that in the busyness of our lives?

In these daily devotions, women from many walks of life share insights on Scripture and practical life lessons to gently encourage you to live for Jesus, and to be more like him in your thoughts, character, and actions.

Discover godly wisdom that will help you navigate the world as a Christian woman and live out God's unique purpose for your life.

978-1-78893-239-4

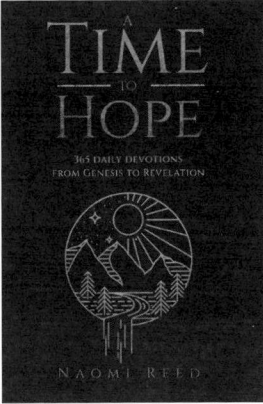

A Time to Hope

365 Daily devotions from
Genesis to Revelation

Naomi Reed

Many of us have favourite Bible verses that we draw comfort from, but we don't always know their context or understand how they fit into the main story arc of the Bible.

Tracing the big picture of God's story through the key themes and events from Genesis to Revelation allows us to see the abundant riches in God's Word. As you read the unfolding story day by day, you can encounter God in all his glorious holiness and faithfulness.

If you have ever struggled to read the Bible from cover to cover, then this devotional will help you find a way in to God's big story and help you fall in love with Jesus all over again.

978-1-78893-144-1

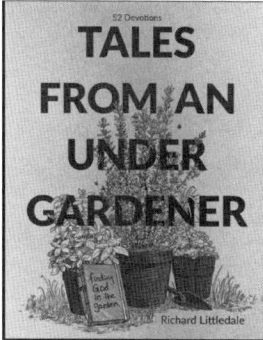

Tales From an Under-gardener

Finding God in the garden

Richard Littledale

Richard Littledale invites you to push open the garden gate and join him as he discovers the joy of gardening.

A reluctant gardener, Richard took up 'project garden' to help combat the loneliness of bereavement, only to find that the physical transformation of his garden mirrored a real change in himself too. Follow Richard's journey through 52 tales and uncover what gardening can teach us about patience, humility, hope, fruitfulness and the abiding goodness of God. Beautifully illustrated throughout, each tale includes a gardening story, a biblical reflection and a prayer.

Whether you are an enthusiastic beginner or naturally green-fingered, this gentle and encouraging book reveals inspirational thoughts about life and God from the perspective of the gardener.

978-1-78893-220-2

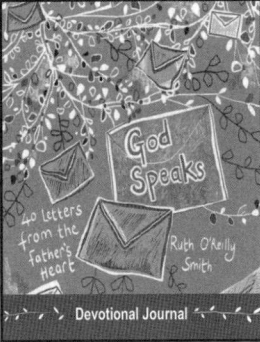

God Speaks

40 letters from the Father's heart

Ruth O'Reilly-Smith

Ruth O'Reilly helps us to slow down, listen to God and respond to him in this beautiful devotional journal.

God speaks. If we take the time to quiet our racing thoughts and be still for a moment, we can hear him. He is speaking all the time.

Draw closer to God as you listen to 40 messages of love straight from the Father's heart, reflect on Bible verses and learn to talk to God with guided questions and prayers. As you write your thoughts in the journaling space provided, you will create a precious record of how God speaks to you that you can always treasure.

Deepen your walk with God as you listen and respond to him speaking to you in this beautiful devotional journal.

978-1-78893-222-6

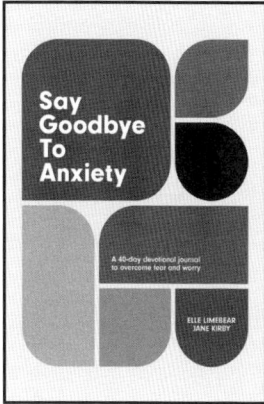

Say Goodbye to Anxiety

*A 40-day devotional journal to
overcome fear and worry*

Elle Limebear and Jane Kirby

Anxiety has been calling the shots for too long. Enough is enough, it's time to say goodbye.

Elle and Jane get it. Having both suffered with anxiety, they understand how it can impact our daily lives. They also know the difference Jesus can make.

As they honestly share their story, Elle and Jane support and cheer us on as they offer God-given practical tools and strategies to overcome anxiety.

Be encouraged, through these 40 devotional thoughts and journaling reflections, to take daily steps with God's help to move past anxiety and live life to the full.

978-1-78893-312-4

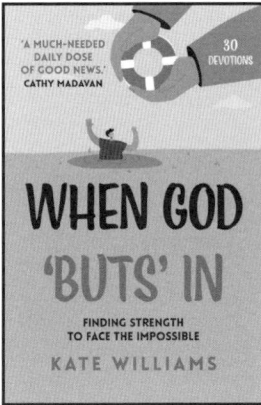

When God 'Buts' In

*Finding strength to face
the impossible*

Kate Williams

Are you facing a situation that looks impossible?

Many biblical characters faced huge obstacles too, until God brought a 'but' into the situation that changed their circumstances in a powerful way.

When God 'buts' in he isn't meddling or interfering, he is divinely intervening in the situation. Whether that results in a miraculous turnaround in circumstances or grace to sustain you through a trial, God wants to 'but' in and be actively involved in your life.

Kate Williams interweaves her personal experience of challenge with biblical truth to help stir your faith and trust in God.

978-1-78893-308-7

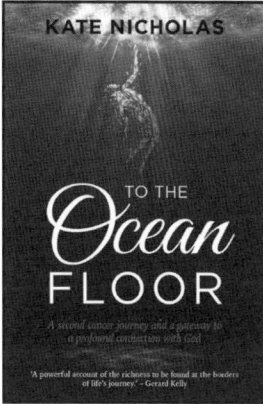

To the Ocean Floor

*A second cancer journey and a gateway
to a profound connection with God*

Kate Nicholas

Seven years after surviving advanced breast cancer, Kate is diagnosed with cancer again.

Desperately ill, she sinks beneath the waves of consciousness where she experiences a profound encounter with God. As she seeks to understand and recapture that experience, she discovers a contemplative practice that offers her a deeper way into the presence of God.

Follow Kate's inspirational story and experience a profound and deep connection with God.

978-1-78893-300-1

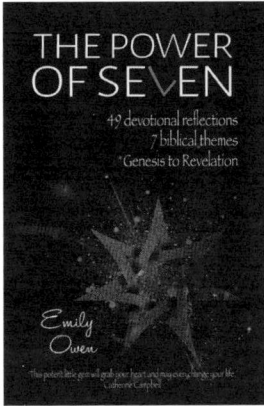

The Power of Seven

49 devotional reflections
7 biblical themes
Genesis to Revelation

Emily Owen

Written in Emily Owen's unique, poetic style, this series of forty-nine devotions on seven biblical themes will inspire and gently steer you into a closer walk with Jesus.

Emily seamlessly weaves together reflections, prayers, personal stories and the encouraging 'voice' of God. Enjoy the world he gave you and stand together with him, with these seven themes as your guide: Creation, God Is, The Lord is My Shepherd, I AM, Echoes from the Cross, Add to Faith and Revelation Churches.

Be refreshed as you allow these powerful, thoughtful and imaginative reflections to point you to Jesus.

978-1-78078-990-3

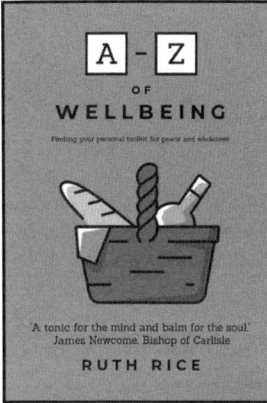

A-Z of Wellbeing

Finding your personal toolkit
for peace and wholeness

Ruth Rice

A-Z of Wellbeing is an accessible introduction to help you attend to your own wellbeing and live out your own alphabet of peace. It presents twenty-six words of wellness to help you discover new practices, connect with God, and share wellbeing with others.

Each topic guides the reader to:
· Connect the word to a biblical theme
· Learn a new habit to practise
· Get active sharing the habit with others
· Take notice of a personal story
· Give back with questions and further resources

By sharing the words that were helpful in her own journey of recovery from breakdown, Ruth Rice gently encourages us to find our own toolkit of words and habits that will help us maintain our own wellbeing.

978-1-78893-237-0

Authentic

We trust you enjoyed reading this book from Authentic. If you want to be informed of any new titles from this author and other releases you can sign up to the Authentic newsletter by scanning below:

Online:
authenticmedia.co.uk

Follow us: